Imperialisms

Pierre Bourdieu

Imperialisms

The International Circulation of Ideas and the Struggle for the Universal

Edited by Jérôme Bourdieu, Franck Poupeau and Gisèle Sapiro, with commentary by Franck Poupeau and Gisèle Sapiro

With translations by Peter Collier, Loïc Wacquant, Richard Shusterman and Priscilla Parkhurst Ferguson

polity

Originally published in French as *Impérialismes. Circulation internationale des idées et luttes pour l'universel*. Copyright © Éditions Raisons d'agir, 2023. Rights arranged through Editions du Seuil.

This English edition first published by Polity Press in 2025.

Except for the translations by Loïc Wacquant, Richard Shusterman and Priscilla Parkhurst Ferguson, this translation © Polity Press, 2025.

Excerpt from *On Television* copyright © 1998 by Pierre Bourdieu.
Excerpt from *Firing Back* copyright © 2003 by Pierre Bourdieu.
Both reprinted by permission of The New Press. www.thenewpress.com

Polity Press
65 Bridge Street
Cambridge CB2 1UR, UK

Polity Press
111 River Street
Hoboken, NJ 07030, USA

All rights reserved. Except for the quotation of short passages for the purpose of criticism and review, no part of this publication may be reproduced, stored in a retrieval system or transmitted, in any form or by any means, electronic, mechanical, photocopying, recording or otherwise, without the prior permission of the publisher.

ISBN-13: 978-1-5095-6232-9 – hardback
ISBN-13: 978-1-5095-6233-6 – paperback

A catalogue record for this book is available from the British Library.

Typeset in 10.5 on 12 pt Times NR MT Pro
by Cheshire Typesetting Ltd, Cuddington, Cheshire
Printed and bound in Great Britain by Ashford Colour Ltd

The publisher has used its best endeavours to ensure that the URLs for external websites referred to in this book are correct and active at the time of going to press. However, the publisher has no responsibility for the websites and can make no guarantee that a site will remain live or that the content is or will remain appropriate.

Every effort has been made to trace all copyright holders, but if any have been overlooked the publisher will be pleased to include any necessary credits in any subsequent reprint or edition.

For further information on Polity, visit our website:
politybooks.com

Contents

Editors' Note	vii
Publisher's Note	x

Introduction	**1**
From Structural Comparatism to the Sociology of International Fields	3

1 Universalism and Domination	**25**
1.1 Two Imperialisms of the Universal: On the Strategies of Unification of the Cultural Field	27
1.2 The Cunning of Imperialist Reason (with Loïc Wacquant)	33

2 Texts without Contexts	**47**
2.1 The International Circulation of Ideas	49
2.2 Programme for a Sociology of the International Circulation of Cultural Works	61
Final Discussion	72
2.3 Does Belgian Literature Exist? The Limits of a Field and Political Frontiers	76

3 A Relational Comparatism	**79**
3.1 Passport to Duke	81
3.2 Social Structures and Structures of Perception of the Social World	87

vi Contents

3.3 The Specifics of National Histories: Towards a Comparative History of the Relevant Differences between Nations 93

Final Discussion 109

Annex: Preparatory Notes 114

3.4 The Scholarly Unconscious 123

4 Sketch of Analyses of International Fields **131**

4.1 The Olympics: An Agenda for Analysis 133

4.2 The Global Legal Field 136

4.3 The Internationalization of the Economic Field 139

Guide **149**

To a Flourishing Research Programme

Notes 153

Index 184

Editors' Note

This book is a collection of texts, some unpublished or not easily accessible, in which Pierre Bourdieu questions the international or transnational dimension of the workings of the social world. This dimension was not part of the original project of *Microcosmes*, his book devoted to the theory of the field, published in the series bearing the same title. At first glance, Bourdieu's main works deal with topics situated within national borders, whether the research concerns Algeria, the educational system or the artistic world. Although there is no doubt that the analytic framework advanced in each case aims to solicit a more general perspective, it is above all as a source of tentative suggestions to be tested in other contexts, and not because it contains any explicit analysis of the supranational dimension of the phenomena studied. It is no doubt for this reason that Bourdieu's work has not been thought of as belonging to the global visions of Braudel (the 'world economy'), Wallerstein (the 'world system') or Harvey (the 'space of capital').

This work proceeds, then, from an editorial project whose logic needs all the more explication since the texts collected here are of varied status and format: short analytic articles, lectures, contributions to collective works, often the result of colloquia, transcriptions of research seminars, or collaboration with French, Brazilian, Greek or Hungarian colleagues, among others. Its objective is to use texts written by Bourdieu in different contexts to show that his work does in fact comprise both a theoretical and an empirical project for the analysis of the logics of internationalization. What is more, the principle of construction that Bourdieu promotes, true to his habitual approach to research, remains reflexive: it is based on the conclusion that it is not sufficient to announce the international character of social phenomena, for we also need to take into account the manner in which the scientific categories of perception of these phenomena are constructed,

viii *Editors' Note*

categories which are themselves the product of national traditions embroiled in the specific logics of their international struggles.

Two sets of social mechanisms hold a central place in the analysis of the international dimension of social phenomena which Bourdieu proposes and which is highlighted in the texts that compose this volume. The first deals with a method of structural comparatism rooted in the idea of a social invariant in (national) relational spaces that may be at once distinct and connected. The second entails the international circulation of ideas and frames of perception of the social world. In both cases the idea of the field forms the common foundation needed to underpin these constructions. One difficulty specific to the social sciences, then, is that the categories which scholars use in order to construct the social are products of their national context, and the effects generated by the relations between these specific national contexts remain largely ignored by those who use them.

The aim of this volume is thus to collect in a freestanding work the original constructions of the international proposed by Bourdieu, sometimes without saying so, not in terms of an isolated issue, concerning only specific topics and resulting from a de facto separation of things national from things international, but rather in terms of a set of phenomena and mechanisms present in the national logics or situations that on the face of it seemed strictly local.

For this reason, our volume brings together in the first instance a set of texts concerning the relations of domination between nations and struggles over the universal that form the network of rival imperialisms at an international level. The analysis of 'imperialist reason' is nonetheless inscribed in broader processes of the import and export of symbolic goods between countries, whose mechanisms are the object of a vast programme of research, and whose principles are revealed in the second part of this work. The international circulation of ideas appears in fact as an objective phenomenon which must be taken into account in any analysis of the social world, even the most local, because the categories of analysis which it mobilizes are its own product. There is then a structural exercise – which is, it should be said, fairly innovative – in the comparatist approach, exposed in the third part, which is needed to understand the variations produced by these phenomena of international circulation, which constantly re-fertilize the different national categories of thought in the 'educational unconscious'. The notion of the international field, whose analysis is sketched out in the fourth and last section, is then introduced as a conceptual necessity for understanding phenomena that emerge outside the unifying State categories.

Editors' Note

The introduction by Franck Poupeau and Gisèle Sapiro provides a context for the texts by Bourdieu. They discuss all these perspectives of research in greater detail, and stress the coherence of the different approaches combined in this volume but also in Bourdieu's works elsewhere, whether in analysing struggles for the universal, drafting programmes of research into the international circulation of ideas, or sketching an analysis of the internationalization of fields. They also point up the link between his critique of the phenomena of 'globalization' and his reflections on the international, which feed into each other, thus enabling us to see in a different light the way in which Bourdieu, throughout his career, attempted to construct collective and international networks: to understand even the most strictly national or local social problems, we need to bear in mind, on the one hand, that these are international problems which have not been recognized as such, and on the other hand, that they can only be tackled at the expense of a break with the national categories germane to each national tradition, which perceives itself as universal (in particular in the case of the American or French perspectives). Finally, the 'guide' that figures at the end of the volume shows that, although the articulations between these axes are only episodically made explicit by Bourdieu, many later works were inspired by the programme for research that he outlined.

Publisher's Note

Translations of all texts are by Peter Collier unless otherwise indicated.
Chapter 2.1 was translated by Richard Shusterman.
Chapter 4.1 was translated by Priscilla Parkhurst Ferguson.
Chapters 1.2, 3.1 and 4.3 were translated by Loïc Wacquant.

Introduction

From Structural Comparatism to the Sociology of International Fields

Franck Poupeau and Gisèle Sapiro

It was initially comparatism and the methodological problems it raises that led Bourdieu to rethink the national analytical framework. But other problematics arose as his work progressed: studying the social conditions of the international circulation of ideas and symbolic goods; accounting for the forms that imperialism assumes (political, economic, legal or cultural), which led him to examine the issue of the struggles among nations for universalism; analysing the international or transnational dimension of fields. Although the articulations between these axes which inform this volume were only occasionally made explicit by Bourdieu, they have been developed in later studies inspired by the research programme that he mapped out (see the 'Guide' at the end of the volume). Just as the theory of fields is presented as an 'exploratory model' and a 'tool for construction' of scientific objects of study,[1] so the analyses dealing with international problematics open up areas of research that the social sciences continue to explore.

Comparatism against ethnocentrism and evolutionism

Because of his philosophical training, Bourdieu's universe of intellectual references was international from the start. We can mention, among others, the cultural anthropology from the United States used in *Sociologie de l'Algérie* (1958), Edmund Husserl's phenomenology in the analysis of the sub-proletariat's relation to time in *Travail et travailleurs en Algérie* (1963), Erwin Panofsky's iconographic approach in the formulation of the notion of habitus (postface to *Architecture gothique et pensée scolastique*, 1967), or Ernst Cassirer's philosophy of symbolic forms in elaborating the notion of symbolic power, and, of course, the sociology of Max Weber, which Bourdieu discovered at

4   *Introduction*

the end of the 1950s.[2] These references helped him to position himself against the American sociology that became dominant in Europe after the war.

Beyond these references, Bourdieu's experience of Algeria played a fundamental part in the construction of his sociology. Many of the concepts that he went on to develop later took shape in the empirical enquiries that he undertook in Kabylia. In *Esquisse d'une théorie de la pratique* (1972; translated as *Outline of a Theory of Practice*), he relates how this unfamiliar experience enabled him to look with alien eyes on a very familiar terrain, the Béarn of his childhood, where, despite the differences, he discovered comparable structural traits, which reflect the position of these 'traditional societies' (that he later called 'precapitalist') in relation to a rampant capitalism. The mental experience of comparing the Algerian and Béarnais terrains was a means of defusing the ethnography implicated in adopting the exotic gaze of the 'other', and of overcoming ethnology, torn at the time between its original vocation as a 'colonial science'[3] and its withdrawal into the study of rural society in a conjuncture of decolonization.[4] This experience calls into question the territorial and methodological division between ethnology and sociology (he combined qualitative and quantitative approaches in both studies), while at the same time unlocking the objects of study that sociology had constituted as distinct specialisms: the rural world, the worlds of labour, the sociology of organizations, etc. And finally, in the line of Durkheim, Mauss and Lévi-Strauss, it breaks with the more or less explicit evolutionism of the social sciences of the period, which tended to assign the precapitalist societies to an earlier phase of the process of modernization. However, this approach must also take into account the differences between the cases compared and their specific characteristics, especially in the colonial dimension: the imposition of capitalism by force in Algeria had particular effects, following the displacement of the population into camps, and involving the relations between colonists and colonized, which are connected with the imperialist power relations between societies (see *infra*).[5]

Inspired by his readings of Durkheim and Weber, for whom comparison is the primordial tool of sociology, Bourdieu's comparatist method is thus rooted in this twofold founding experience. In *Le Métier de sociologue* (1968; translated as *The Craft of Sociology*), he and his co-authors underline the fact that sociology has the specific property 'that it can only constitute its object by the *comparative approach*'.[6] It is analogical reasoning that enables Bourdieu to 'escape from ideographic consideration of cases that do not contain their own reason', by restoring them to a family of possible cases and a set of relations.[7]

Introduction

It also leads to denaturalizing the obviousness of the social world and desubstantializing its cultural signification, without lapsing into a homeostatic functionalism such as that promoted at the time by the proponents of Talcott Parsons's structural-functionalism.

While in the years 1960–70 the sociological enquiries led by Bourdieu were focused on French society, the structural approach he elaborated aimed to make diachronic comparison between different states of the social structure and the fields, as well as a synchronic comparison between societies, possible. From this period, with Jean-Claude Passeron, he looked at educational systems to investigate the 'conditions of comparability' and the pertinence of the indicators used without preliminary consideration about the comparability of social institutions.[8] This reflection, like that on the publics of European museums,[9] takes its place in the framework of the European enquiries that involved the Centre for European Sociology (CSE) at the time, with Bourdieu as general secretary in 1962 and deputy director in 1964.[10] At the seminar in 2000 during which he discussed the conditions of comparatism (Chapter 3.3), he explains that this enquiry 'enabled us to learn a lot about the comparability and incompatibility of statistical information' (p. 94 of this volume).

In 1971, with a team from the Centre for the Sociology of Education and Culture (CSEC), which he had founded in 1968 after leaving the CSE, Bourdieu participated in the congress at Varna of the International Association of Sociology, whose 'Sociology of Education' section he founded. He very soon shed this responsibility. He spent the following year at the Institute for Advanced Study at Princeton. These international experiences strengthened his critique of the domination exerted by American sociology, which, he explained, 'through the Capitoline triad of Parsons, Merton and Lazarsfeld, subjected social science to a whole series of reductions and impoverishments, from which, it seemed [to him], it had to be freed, in particular by a return to the texts of Durkheim and Max Weber, both of whom had been annexed and distorted by Parsons'.[11] Along with Victor Karady's publication of the works of Durkheim and Mauss, Bourdieu's importing of symbolic interactionism[12] – with translations of the works of Erving Goffman in the series 'Le sens commun', which he edited at Minuit – played a part in the combat against what he qualified as 'orthodoxy on a planetary scale'. In 1975 he published a critique of the ethnocentrism of sociology in the United States and of the 'evolutionist model, which encourages us to see different societies as so many stages on the path leading to American society' (p. 87). This short article, reproduced as Chapter 3.2 of the present volume, appeared in the second issue of the review

6 *Introduction*

Actes de la recherche en sciences sociales (*ARSS*), which he had just launched. Articles by Michael Pollak on the role of US philanthropic foundations in the 'planning of the social sciences' in Europe after the war, and on the role of Lazarsfeld as 'founder of a scientific multinational', continued this reflection on the forms and modalities adopted by American domination over the social sciences.[13]

Beyond his methodological reflection, Bourdieu also wanted to construct a transnational space of research in the social sciences outside of the hegemony of the United States (while still maintaining increasingly intense exchanges with American researchers, as we can see from his correspondence).[14] The aim was twofold: on the one hand, to articulate empirical research with a theoretical reflection, nourished by international collaboration; on the other hand, to set up programmes of international research into modes of domination. Bourdieu later described this enterprise in these terms:

> I wanted to launch an enterprise of 'scientific liberation' . . . first we had to destroy the opposition between theory and practice, we had to do theory empirically. Then we had to export it, not in a logic of imperialism, but a logic of composing a geopolitical force of resistance. To Hungary . . . to Algeria and North America, to Brazil and Latin America. It was a 'war of intellectual liberation'. The whole publishing enterprise contributed to this: making the texts accessible, providing the means, helping people to publish.[15]

This 'war of intellectual liberation' was put into practice through the construction of networks linking the sociologists of the CSE, and then the CSEC, with international researchers and research teams. Situated in Europe and around the Mediterranean for the first part of the 1960s, these networks were not restricted to the regions dominant in the academic space (Western Europe and the United States) but reached out to the 'periphery' (Eastern Europe, North Africa, Latin America, and then Asia) of a global field of social science whose centre had moved to the United States. The internationalization of Bourdieu's sociology thus involved the circulation of researchers, passing through academic selection circuits sponsored by institutional funding and exchange programmes. It was presented partly as a collective enterprise, articulated around editorial and institutional channels for research and publication. An international scientific network grew up around the many scholarly collectives directed or inspired by Bourdieu (research centres, publishers' series, the review *Actes*). From the outset, *Actes* published researchers of different nationalities

Introduction 7

and disciplines, such as Gregory Bateson, Norbert Elias, Jack Goody, E. P. Thompson, Raymond Williams, Paul Willis, Moshe Lewin, Iván Szelényi, Carlo Ginzburg, Eric Hobsbawm, Francis Klingender, Michael Baxandall, Albert Boime, etc. The permanent dialogue with foreign authors was backed up by a policy of translating works in the series 'Le sens commun' (Erving Goffman, Richard Hoggart, Basil Bernstein, William Labov, Ernst Cassirer, Erwin Panofsky, etc.).[16] Alongside participation in international conferences like that at Varna, the transnational networks were constructed through visits of foreign researchers or doctoral students. Thus, in the 1970s, while Bourdieu's articles and books started to appear in German, Italian, Spanish, Portuguese, English, Romanian and Hungarian,[17] foreign researchers and students like Sergio Miceli, writing a thesis on intellectuals in Brazil under the supervision of Bourdieu, helped to feed this comparative reflection.[18] In 1975, Bourdieu himself published a study of Heidegger and the conservative revolution in Germany between the wars.[19] Among the members of the CSE and then the CSEC, Abdelmalek Sayad, who had worked with Bourdieu on Algeria, undertook a study of Algerian immigration into France;[20] Francine Muel-Dreyfus, in collaboration with Arakcy Martins Rodrigues, mounted an enquiry into a sect in Brazil;[21] and, after his work on the history of French sociology, Victor Karady engaged in the 1980s in research on the Jews of Eastern Europe, and on Hungary.[22]

For a structural comparison

It remains the case that, apart from the work on Algeria and the conservative revolution in Germany, Bourdieu's sociology was principally constructed on the basis of empirical enquiries into French society, in conformity with the 'methodological nationalism'[23] that was then prevalent in the discipline. It was, on the one hand, the theoretical dimension of Bourdieu's sociology (in particular the concepts of cultural capital, habitus and field), and on the other hand its appropriation as research programme, that enabled its international reception. However, the question of what was specifically French very soon arose. More even than the indicators of cultural capital, discussed in the sociology of education, the cultural practices described by Bourdieu were questioned in the framework of the reception of the translations of *La Distinction* into German (in 1982) and English (in 1984).[24] In the United States as in Germany, some researchers contested the possibility of generalizing a theory based essentially on what they considered

8   *Introduction*

to be national particularities.[25] This rejection derived to a large extent from the positivist appropriation of the theory, which attempted to simply transpose the model rather than adapt it.

Increasingly translated and invited abroad, Bourdieu broached a reflection on the cultural specifics that necessitate an adjustment to theory. This concern surfaces in the preface to the English edition of *Homo Academicus*, published in 1988 by Polity Press. In it he describes two types of possible reading for someone alien to the culture being studied: either highlighting the differences from their own system (a reading in bad faith), or concentrating on the invariants of *homo academicus*. In order to encourage this second type of reading, Bourdieu argues (pp. xv–xvi) that we need to propose a series of transformative laws through which the passage from one system to the other would operate. This reflection was stimulated by exchanges with foreign researchers, in particular during his stays in the United States between 1986 and 1989, as we see in *Invitation to a Reflexive Sociology*, which he published with Loïc Wacquant in 1991.[26] The year 1989 was a turning point: during the lectures he gave in Japan and East Berlin in October, Bourdieu questioned the conditions of the transposition of his theory to the societies accepting it. Thus these lectures were, as their subtitles indicate, introductions to a Japanese or German reading of *La Distinction* and, for Japan, of *La Noblesse d'État*.[27]

Introducing his first lecture at the University of Tokyo in Japan by mentioning the irritation you may feel when you hear researchers from other countries explaining to you what your culture is, Bourdieu reassures his audience: he will not speak to them of Japan but of the society that he knows best and that he has most studied, France. Nonetheless, he continues, the model of social and symbolic space that he has constructed for the French case is in no way specific to France, and so speaking of France is also speaking of Japan, or elsewhere of Germany or the United States. He therefore begs his audience to go beyond the localized reading of his work, seemingly invited by the fact that it is rooted in empirical studies and not presented in the garb of a 'grand theory', and attempt to transpose the framework of analysis to their own culture, in a comparative approach that sees empirical reality historically situated and dated as 'a special case of what is possible', according to Gaston Bachelard's expression.[28] This framework does in fact lay claim to a 'universal validity' in order to 'register the real differences that separate both structures and dispositions (habitus), the principle of which must be sought . . . in the particularities of different *collective histories*'.[29] The transposability across time and space of the model developed in *Distinction* depends on its relational character:

Introduction 9

the position of a cultural practice in social space does not result from properties that are inherent to it, but from its usage by social groups as a manner of distinguishing themselves or differentiating themselves from other practices. Thus the fact that in France tennis or golf are no longer exclusively associated with dominant positions does not invalidate the model of analysis but bears witness to the change of position of a practice whose use has become banal and which for this reason has become less distinctive. This is why, Bourdieu stresses, 'comparison is possible only *from system to system*'.[30] He therefore invites his Japanese audience and readers to make 'a relational but also a *generative* reading', to 'apply the model in this other "particular case of the possible", that is, Japanese society'.[31]

The second lecture delivered in Japan proposed a reading of *La Noblesse d'État* centred on the mechanisms of social reproduction and more particularly on family educational strategies. Comparing the action of the educational system to Maxwell's demon, Bourdieu shows the work of formation of a *'hereditary scholastic nobility . . . of* leaders of industry, senior medics, higher civil servants and even political leaders',[32] a model that applies to Japan as well as France. And he suggests a comparison with the process

> that led the samurai, one segment of whom had already in the course of the seventeenth century been transformed into a literate bureaucracy, to promote, in the second half of the nineteenth century, a modern state based on a body in whom noble origin and a strong scholastic culture were combined, a body anxious to affirm its independence in and through a cult of the national State and characterized by an aristocratic sense of superiority relative to industrialists and merchants, let alone politicians.[33]

But above all, replying to those who reproached his theory with not taking social change into account, Bourdieu calls for a comparative analysis of the impact on social transformation of the contradictions specific to the educational system, as analysed in the chapter of *La Distinction* (1979) entitled 'Classes and Classification', and of the impact on political mobilization, as illustrated by the study of the case of May 1968 at the end of *Homo Academicus* (1984). Other comparative approaches are suggested, like 'the link between the new school delinquency, which is more widespread in Japan than in France, and the logic of furious competition which dominates the school institution, especially the *effect of a final verdict or destiny* that the educational system exerts over teenagers',[34] the hierarchization of the system

10 *Introduction*

that relegates technical education to the bottom of the scale, or, again, the tensions between the major and the minor State nobility, pregnant with future conflict:

> Everything points to the supposition that, facing an ever more tenacious monopoly of all the highest positions of power – in banking, industry, politics – on the part of the old boys of the Grandes Écoles in France, or the great public universities in Japan, the holders of second-class titles, the lesser samurai of culture, will be led, in their struggle for an enlargement of the circles of power, to invoke new universalist justifications, much as the minor provincial nobles did in France from the sixteenth century to the beginnings of the French Revolution, or as did the excluded lesser samurai who, in the name of 'liberty and civil rights', led the revolt against the nineteenth-century Meiji reform.[35]

Similarly, in his lecture in East Berlin, Bourdieu starts out from the question of the validity of his analytical model beyond the special case of France, and its possible applications to the country that at the time was still the German Democratic Republic (GDR). In order to break with all substantialist temptation, he proposes to construct the social space as a 'structure of differentiated positions, defined in each case by the place they occupy in the distribution of a particular kind of capital'. Which supposes bringing to light the principles of differentiation specific to the GDR – the main difference from the French case being the exclusion from consideration, at least officially, of economic capital defined as private ownership of the means of production, which has the effect of increasing the relative importance of cultural capital, highly esteemed in the German tradition as in the Japanese. But this principle does not suffice to explain the 'opportunities for private appropriation of public goods and services' in the communist regimes (which he prefers to call 'Soviet'), nor in the Scandinavian countries where a social-democrat elite, installed in power over several generations, has appropriated the collective resources. Bourdieu proposes therefore to introduce another species of capital, which he calls 'political capital', to explain this. This type of capital, 'which is acquired in the apparatuses of the trade unions and the Labour Party, is transmitted through networks of family relations, leading to the constitution of true political dynasties',[36] such as the *Nomenklatura* in the USSR. Bourdieu undertakes to construct the pertinent indicators to apprehend this political capital in the case of the USSR, in particular the position in the hierarchy of apparatuses, starting with the Communist Party, and the

Introduction 11

seniority of each agent and his line of descent in the political dynasties. We should also take into account, especially for Germany, the effects of the emigration that decimated the categories capable of providing alternative cultural models. In contrast to these holders of political capital, commanding the dominant positions, there are the holders of cultural capital, whether technocrats, researchers or intellectuals, who partly share the same origins, but who tend to resent the privileges that the holders of political capital have appropriated. While he does see in them the origins of the revolution that is already under way in the communist countries, at the end of his lecture Bourdieu questions the capacity of the intellectuals attached to 'true socialism' to enter into alliance with the dominated, the manual labourers in particular, and the lesser employees of the State bureaucracies, who cannot fail to be seduced by the mirages of the liberal economy. A prediction which, we might notice in passing, has since been confirmed, with the very active attraction of the intellectuals in many countries, like Romania, to a newly won liberalism.

Thus it is certainly a programme of comparative research that Bourdieu has to offer his Japanese and German colleagues, through this rereading of his own works. He continued to pursue this methodological reflection on the conditions of comparatism on the occasion of two surveys conducted between 1998 and 2001 in the framework of European contracts with the CSE.[37] One, coordinated by Franz Schultheis, dealt with the insecurity of young people in Europe, the other, directed by René Lenoir, with European social and penal policies.[38] One of the aims was to establish indicators to measure the 'social pathologies' linked to neoliberal policies. While these large-scale comparative surveys were made possible through funding by the European Commission, the seminar of 2000 published in this volume reflects the difficulties encountered by the comparative approach of the second project, pointing out the differences which depend not only on the legislative framework but also on the histories of these societies, and their historical unconscious (or national habitus):

> In the first confrontations that we had with researchers from Greece, the Netherlands, Belgium and Germany, we noticed that a certain number of differences in practices which we observed, in forms of delinquency for example, could be linked to profound historical differences. On the one hand there were differences in legislation relatively easy to grasp since we were dealing with things that were declared, patent, codified and recorded in law. And on the other hand there were differences much more difficult to grasp,

12   *Introduction*

and which are linked for example to religious traditions, or the 'aftermath' of some historical trauma, transposed into dispositions. These might be the government of the colonels in Greece, or perhaps the Occupation and Resistance in France, long-lasting after-images of historical events or actions that we are obliged to consider still operative in order to understand certain differences. There is a third, even more unconscious level, the profound differences in 'mentality' (a very dubious concept), in the historical unconscious or the historical transcendental, in short, the habitus. How do we handle all this? The majority of the research financed by Europe is not concerned with these problems, and nobody is asking us to take them on. But if we don't, our comparatism will be amateur, and we will be in danger of finding false differences and false similarities, of being dazzled by *curiosa* devoid of interest. (p. 94)

In order to 'map the deep, hidden structural principles of differentiation' (p. 95), Bourdieu proposes a critical recourse to the national statistical indicators (indicators of integration or *anomie*, of rates of unemployment, etc.). This 'programme of structural description of the space of national and regional unconscious minds' should produce 'a research programme into the specifics of national history capable of explaining these differences' (p. 95). Such a history should be written abandoning the 'national point of view', in order 'to prevent the comparative analysis becoming trapped in a national ethnocentrism with its correlative censorship' (pp. 95–6). It should also overcome the mechanical comparisons of national indicators, which are themselves the product of national categories: 'looking for the system of pertinent differences means that we need to construct the space of the nations and the space of the differences that differentiate them' (p. 96). Such operations intend to 'defamiliarize' these categories by redrafting the script of their own historical narrative, 'unless you want to go in for a UNESCO-type sociology, based on mistranslation and misunderstanding' (p. 97). Bourdieu also mentions problems of translation ('middle class' must be translated as *bourgeoisie* and not *classe moyenne*), reminding us that 'the sociologist is not looking for equivalences' but has comprehension as his aim, beyond the false familiarities that interfere with comprehension. To manage to 'understand that we don't understand', he points out, 'we need to make our own practices feel foreign to us by using our knowledge of foreign practices' (p. 99). This precaution is valid not only for international comparatism, but also for the 'disciplinary historical unconscious', calling for 'a double

Introduction 13

historicization, both of the knowing subject and of the object known'. Warning about what he calls the *lexical fallacy*, the sociologist sees the *Begriffsgeschichte* (conceptual history) as a safety net, giving as a model Émile Benveniste's *Dictionary of Indo-European Concepts and Society* (1969). In a second phase, he needs to take into account the fact that national identities are constructed by marking out their distance from one another: 'It is important to realize that comparison lies in the object, because we are going to compare people who are comparing one another and whose makeup is partly the product of these comparisons' (p. 104). Here he cites Linda Colley's *Britons*,[39] which shows how the English have constructed themselves in contrast to the French, and also the analysis by Norbert Elias of the opposition between culture and civilization in Germany.[40] 'In the real life of Germany and England a host of things . . . have been introduced by the concern to be different from France, and vice versa', he argues (p. 104). Nevertheless, Bourdieu reminds us that such a construction should not disguise the internal divisions among the inhabitants of these nations in their relation to France. To illustrate his argument, he continues with a discussion of E. P. Thompson's article, 'The Peculiarities of the English',[41] which criticizes the attempt by Perry Anderson and Tom Nairn to answer the question 'Why was there not a revolution in England?' He ends up with *The Germans* (1989) by Norbert Elias, which had just been translated into English, and which Bourdieu considered to be an exemplary attempt to grasp national specifics.[42] In conclusion, he also refers to Durkheim's *L'Évolution pédagogique en France*.

The reference to Durkheim echoes the reflections that he expressed in his article on 'The Scholarly Unconscious'[43] (reproduced here as Chapter 3.4), which dates from the same period and displays a similar preoccupation. This scholarly unconscious designates 'the whole set of cognitive structures, in this historical transcendental, that are imputable to specifically scholarly experiences, and which are therefore largely common to all the pupils produced by the same – national – school system or, in a specified form, to all the members of the same discipline' (p. 123). To objectify the subject of the objectification,[44] Bourdieu suggests studying institutions such as the dialogue, the *disputatio*, the disputes of the Jesuit colleges, the *ex cathedra* lecture, the inaugural lecture, the seminar, the oral examination (including the viva of the doctoral thesis, he specifies), and the video conference, showing how they determine our cognitive structures. This programme, which echoes his first lectures at the Collège de France on classification,[45] aims to 'historicize our modes of thinking, not in order to relativize them, but, paradoxically, to tear them away from history' (p. 127).

14 *Introduction*

The international circulation of ideas and cultural works

In parallel with his work on comparatism, in 1989 Bourdieu started to reflect on the international circulation of ideas and symbolic goods. In the context of globalization and the construction of the European Union, which encouraged the intensification of international exchanges, this reflection found a practical application in the launch that year of the review *Liber*, at first subtitled *Revue européenne des livres*, then, from 1994, *Revue internationale des livres*. Drawing on a worldwide network of researchers, it was published in several languages, as a supplement to five major European newspapers (*Le Monde*, *L'Indice*, *El Pays*, the *Frankfurter Allgemeine Zeitung* and the *Times Literary Supplement*).[46] If some of them, starting with *Le Monde*, soon abandoned an enterprise judged too uneconomical or directed at too narrow an audience, translations continued to appear – from time to time – in German, Bulgarian, Hungarian, Swedish, Italian, Czech, Romanian, Greek, Turkish, Norwegian and Spanish.

Reproduced as Chapter 2.1 in this volume, Bourdieu's reflection on 'The social conditions of the international circulation of ideas' was presented as a lecture under this title at the Frankreich-Zentrum of the University of Freiburg in Germany.[47] In it Bourdieu insists on the structuring role of the power relations between national fields, and the import/export mechanisms that these unequal relations imply, generating a certain number of 'misunderstandings'. The fact that texts circulate without their context has the consequence that scientists' national categories of perception have a palpable impact on the way the works imported will be perceived in the host culture. For in fact the transfer from one national field to another is mediated through a series of social selection operations which concern not only what is being translated, but more fundamentally the characteristics of those selecting and transmitting between the national fields (acting as gatekeepers). The operations of social marking or labelling implied by importing an author engage the publishing house, the series, the translator and the prefacer (who in presenting the work being translated appropriates it and annexes it to his own vision, or, in any case, to a problematic inscribed in the field of reception).[48] This marking procures benefits of ownership all the more effective in a national field since they are bathed in an aura of internationalization. The power relations between countries explain the fact that the international struggles for domination in cultural matters and for the imposition of 'a particular definition of the legitimate exercise of intellectual activity, for example, Germany's valorization of ideas of *Kultur*, depth, philosophical content, etc., over

Introduction 15

what they saw as the French stress on *Civilisation*, clarity, literature, etc.' (p. 59), are rooted in the struggles at the heart of each national field.

This article, which became a reference text, laid the basis for a programme of research into intellectual exchanges between countries, which Bourdieu established with Joseph Jurt during a colloquium organized in February 1991 at the Hugot Foundation of the Collège de France, under the auspices of the Frankreich-Zentrum. The lecture that Bourdieu gave here, entitled 'Programme for a Sociology of the International Circulation of Cultural Works', is published for the first time in the present volume (Chapter 2.2). Starting out from the observation that there has not been much reflection on 'international problems', it focuses mainly on the method that would allow circulation and comparison to intersect in order to apprehend 'the field of international cultural relations' (p. 62). The programme includes a section on the social issues at stake in translation.[49] On a first level, Bourdieu suggests analysing the flows of works per country and per category (literature, social science). On a second level, he is interested in understanding the mechanisms that would explain these flows, and in 'proceeding to compare non-national pantheons of authors', for instance 'the German authors most translated in Italy, or France, etc.' Among the 'other indicators', he mentions the translators, their status, the conditions of exercise of their activity, then the critics of foreign works.

Bourdieu proposes to plot these mechanisms along four axes: the relations between national and international fields; the accumulated national symbolic capital; the agents importing and exporting; the strategies in the international field. He then asks under what conditions we may speak of 'international fields', which can only be grasped through the effects that they produce, and in particular their symbolic power relations (he attempts to do this on the subject of the Olympic Games, the law and the economy, as we see in the articles collected in the last section of this volume). He compares the high degree of internationalization of mathematics as opposed to law, situating sociology between the two. He also questions the relation between national and international fields, and the degree and type of autonomy of the first as compared with the second, distinguishing three factors: protectionist policies, inertia of the educational system, and linguistic isolationism. According to him, the linguistic areas furnish an experimental situation where we can see whether the effects of the State can 'counteract' the effects of the field. He gives the examples of Switzerland and Belgium (on which he wrote an article that we have placed here as Chapter 2.3). These are States divided linguistically and culturally, just like Quebec,

16   *Introduction*

which is 'subject to an effect of *double domination*, with the United States on one side and France on the other, and able (or obliged) to use one domination to counteract the other' (p. 64). The Spanish language area constitutes a supplementary case.

Varying according to its fields (literature, science, human science), the *national symbolic capital* must be subjected to objectification in terms of its volume and structure, using indicators such as Nobel Prizes, numbers of translations, etc. (he gives the example of those constructed for the survey of European museums[50]). Bourdieu suggests drawing up 'a map of the main cultural pathways, for example the great traditional highroads of literature and sociology', such as that travelled by Auguste Comte, and then by Fernand Braudel, Lévi-Strauss and René Bastide (pp. 64–5). And, making it clear that 'these well-trodden routes are often the lasting result of linguistic and cultural colonization', we should look into what it is that perpetuates them.

The third axis, the agents of import/export, must be the object of a specific study, distinguishing between these two circuits with a view to determining 'who has an *interest in the foreign*, and in importing from abroad, who has an *interest in the international*, (p. 67, Bourdieu's emphasis): publishers, booksellers, series editors, critics, professors, but also philanthropic foundations, as well as the representatives in charge of the State's export policies. The sociologist calls for a study of their social recruitment, their training and their social properties (cosmopolitan, immigrant), but also their categories of perception, which would enquire about the 'national stereotypes' liable to guide people's choices in literature (p. 66). During these transfers, the perception of the authors may evolve, for instance, from the regional to the universal. Bourdieu suggests that 'we should therefore submit this notion of universal literature to scrutiny. If what the Germans like most in France is what appears most exotic to them, and vice versa, then a universal literature could be a meeting point for exotic extremes.' He does qualify this, however: 'But things are doubtless more complicated' (p. 67).

The fourth axis concerns the 'strategies in the international field' deployed by the intermediaries, the publishers and authors (Bourdieu went on to put this programme into practice in his empirical enquiry into French publishers).[51] He suggests distinguishing between strategies imitating the dominant model, strategies of resistance and strategies that 'practise a selective, liberating borrowing, either from the dominant or from other dominated agents (like the African writers who claim allegiance to the South American model)' (p. 68). Among the mechanisms that favour 'the reproduction of the international

Introduction 17

field', he mentions the role of the University and the teaching of foreign languages, which enables the acquisition of a linguistic capital and forms an 'attachment' to the culture being studied. The study of 'transnational migrations of an academic nature' seems to him to be a fertile trail, as does that of both 'voluntary' and 'forced émigrés' (p. 69).

Finally, considering that 'one of the functions of research is also to direct action', Bourdieu intends to draw on this analysis of the operation of the international fields to lay the foundations of a 'methodological internationalism'. In which case, an analysis of the 'obstacles' to circulation seems necessary to him, with a view to establishing a 'genuine cultural cosmopolitanism'. Among these obstacles, he mentions the cult of a national literature, which contributes to the formation of the 'national cultural unconscious' (p. 57). In this light we need to analyse the differential usages of the foreign, whether as principle of legitimization, instrument of criticism, challenge, or source of profits. He points out that the review *Liber* was intended to overcome the twofold slippage, both temporal and cultural, involved in the international circulation of ideas, which he returns to here.

It is again with this twofold slippage that Bourdieu opens the lecture delivered at Duke in 1995,[52] reproduced here as Chapter 3.1. When authors are translated, he explains, they are detached from the system of objective relations that surrounds them, as illustrated by the figures of 'French Theory' (Foucault, Derrida, Lyotard). The transfer authorizes the imposition on them of grids of reading that stem from the local field of reception, such as the opposition between modernism and postmodernism. Bourdieu also explains that a personal appearance provides the opportunity to rectify some of the misunderstandings by reformulating the issues that provided the original context of their writing. But he reminds us that this is not sufficient. Indeed, he expresses his surprise at seeing himself labelled as a postmodernist, given everything that separates him from the thinkers who are usually classified in this category, not least his choice of leaving philosophy for sociology, a discipline that was something of a 'pariah' at the time (p. 83), and to invest in topic areas as ill-favoured as labour or education. This did not prevent him, he points out, from finding himself placed in the same political camp as a Derrida or a Foucault, sharing 'subversive or anti-institutional dispositions' with them (p. 84). Finally, underlining the heuristic benefits of the concept of field for his audience of researchers in the humanities, Bourdieu makes a strong case for 'methodical comparatism'.

While the research programme elaborated by Bourdieu to study the international circulation of ideas is largely based on methodological

18   *Introduction*

nationalism, the latter is not a necessary framing. What is more, unlike many of the analysts of international cultural exchanges at the time, Bourdieu considers that we cannot ignore the economic, political and cultural power relations (we might add the military ones, too), nor the symbolic hierarchies between countries. Finally, in an article on the Belgian literary field (published here as Chapter 2.3), he had already questioned the national frontiers of fields. In fact, the French-language Belgian writers often take up positions in relation to the French literary field, where they aspire to be recognized, the alternative being a 'strategy of retreating into the national market', which 'becomes the more imperative, the more the chances of success in the first diminish' (p. 76). Being the fruit of institutions created within the framework of a policy of construction of national identity, the Belgian literary field is characterized by its heteronomy, given the absence of specific institutions of consecration. Its dependence on the French literary field derives from relations of hegemony that Bourdieu will continue to explore in the 1990s in the light of domination by the United States.

From imperialist reason to the international fields

In 'La cause de la science' (an article published in 1995 in the review *Actes*, of which a first version had been presented at the Chicago colloquium on 'Social Theory and Emerging Issues in a Changing Society'),[53] Bourdieu observes that 'the field of the social sciences has always been international, but rarely for the better, and mostly for the worse' (RR 85), since it fosters relations of domination and scientific imperialism. Bourdieu reminds us how, in the 1950s, the socially dominant sociologists comprised 'an invisible international, based on affinities owing more to social than to intellectual motivation' (RR 86), and how challenges to their authority at the end of the 1960s incited them to transform their 'previously informal connections . . . into networks organized around foundations, journals and associations', so that 'the well-bred conservatism of the guardians of orthodoxy gave way to the explicit professions of faith and the extremist manifestos of a genuinely reactionary international' (RR 86).

In this light, we can measure the role of the national, regional or international professional organizations in the social sciences, and their contribution to the structuring of disciplines, as they take carefully defined sub-specialisms and bring the experts on specific questions together to attend congresses where both the form of their contributions and the problems they address are formatted. This internationali-

Introduction 19

zation of professionalization can only disseminate 'spurious antitheses' (RR 87) on an international scale, and proves to be 'profoundly fatal for the progress of science: between quantitative and qualitative methods, between the macro and the micro, between structural and historical approaches, between hermeneutic or internalist visions (the "text") and externalist visions (the "context"), between the objectivist vision, often associated with the use of statistics, and the subjectivist, interactionist or ethnomethodological vision' (RR 87).

However, it is nonetheless in the internationalization of the social sciences that Bourdieu sees a way of reinforcing their autonomy, by drawing on scientific strategies liable to make progress towards the universal. This internationalization of sociology is not to be restricted to a circulation between intellectual spaces, disciplinary traditions or national authors: it amounts to elaborating what we might call a veritable 'scientific international'[54] which would take note of the structures of the national academic and cultural unconscious. It should lead to 'transforming the social organization of scientific production and communication, and in particular, the forms of exchange that channel the exercise of logical control' (RR 92), and should lead more precisely to a scientific policy which would aim to unify the sociological field, particularly at an international level, by favouring scientific circulation, 'to loosen the grip of national or nationalistic traditions, most often translated into divisions between theoretical or methodological specialisms and disciplines' (RR 92). The search for a *'Realpolitik* of reason' (RR 92) designed to encourage the emergence of the universal in the intellectual fields should thus be based on an analysis of the social structures of the scientific field and its modes of operation, and more precisely on an account of the mental structures engaged in each national intellectual field, which circumscribe the space of its thinking (RR 93).

In parallel with this effort towards scientific reflexivity, Bourdieu set up a network of intellectuals, the International Parliament of Writers, for the defence of universal causes,[55] designed to support public position-taking on political questions such as the fall of the Berlin Wall and the war in Yugoslavia.[56] At the same time, he was also an active member of the International Committee of Support for Algerian Intellectuals (CISIA), created in 1993. This 'corporatism of the universal' was part of a drive to internationalize the struggles for the defence of the intellectual field. The increasing visibility of Bourdieu's political commitment against neoliberalism after 1993 (with the wide reception of *The Weight of the World*), and above all after 1995 (with his support for the strikes against the reform of the pension system[57]), led to a

20 *Introduction*

second phase of the internationalization of his reflection. While his most visible political interventions until then, with a few exceptions,[58] were principally focused on French issues such as the treatment of immigrants, or social policies, he gradually broadened the scope of his analysis, henceforth convinced that one has to place oneself at a global level in order to understand contemporary social transformations. In an intervention organized by the International Parliament of Writers in 1995, for example, he mentioned the challenge by certain Islamic countries to the 'false universalism of the West' that amounts to an 'imperialism of the universal'.[59] He returns to the analyses in progress since the beginning of the 1990s, which open this volume, studying this form of imperialism 'that operates above all on the political terrain, but which is also effective in the area of lifestyle and everyday life, enjoying a legitimacy which it derives from its more or less widely recognized claim to universality' (p. 27). The struggles between nations for the monopoly of the universal tend to oppose two imperialisms, one waxing, that of the United States, the other waning, that of France, even if the latter maintains the advantage of incarnating the universal model of all revolutions: 'the French Revolution figures as the legitimizing myth founding France's claim to universality, and thereby to the right to universalize its national culture' (p. 28).

This claim to universality, or what Bourdieu qualifies as 'an extraordinary self-confidence, based on the certainty *of having the particularity of universality*', is to be found in what has been presented as the 'civilizing and liberating mission' of French colonization. Whereas his conversion to sociology occurred during his study of the destructuring effects of French colonization on the traditional societies of Algeria in the 1950s, it was on the cultural dimension of imperialism that his studies concentrated in the 1990s: 'cultural imperialism relies on the power to universalize the particularisms linked to a singular historical tradition by making them unrecognizable as such', he writes in the article written with Loïc Wacquant on 'The Cunning of Imperialist Reason' (reproduced as Chapter 1.2 of this volume). It is the conditions of the (international) circulation of texts which largely help to explain the 'neutralization of the historical context' of their production and which thus allow certain national problematics (in particular those produced in the United States) to impose themselves internationally. The theme of 'multiculturalism' is one of the 'commonplaces' of the 'new global vulgate' (p. 34), in a context where 'globalization' appears as a universalization of American problematics. Bourdieu uses very different terms when he envisages the invention of a universal culture respectful of cultural identities:

Introduction 21

This calls for the invention of a universal culture that is not the simple product of the universal imposition of an individual culture (a culture that would not be any more universal than what they promise when they tell us that the United States is the 'world's policeman'). In fact, we can only expect to make any progress towards a really universal culture, *that is, a culture composed of multiple cultural traditions unified by mutually shared recognition*, through struggles between imperialisms of the universal. These imperialisms, through the more or less hypocritical homage that they must pay to the universal to impose themselves, tend to make it progress, and at the very least to establish the universal as a potential recourse to be invoked against even those imperialisms that claim allegiance to it. (pp. 31–2, Bourdieu's emphasis)

This critique of the 'cunning of imperialist reason' then feeds into the critique of the claim to universality, which according to Bourdieu is expressed with particular social force in the efforts of imposition accomplished by economic science in promoting and justifying the neoliberal 'utopia' and the withering away of the State. His intervention on 'The Thoughts of Chairman Tietmayer', delivered in the framework of the Franco-German Encounters at the University of Freiburg in October 1996 (and republished in *Contre-feux*, 1998 [*Acts of Resistance*, 1998]), thus prefigures his text on 'The Imposition of the US Model and Its Effects' (published in *Contre-feux 2*, 2001 [*Firing Back*, 2003]). On this point it develops the project of a *Realpolitik* of reason which would engage the intellectuals in symbolic struggles against the sociodicy of the dominant, and which is not limited to simply adopting a critical position, as Bourdieu explains in an intervention with an evocative title, 'The Myth of "Globalization" and the European Welfare State', addressed to the Greek Trade Union Confederation (GSEE) in Athens in October 1996: 'While one can fight against the national State, one has to defend the "universal" functions it fulfils, which can be fulfilled as well, or better, by a supranational State.'[60] The construction of such an institution, which would be 'relatively autonomous with respect to international economic forces and national political forces and capable of developing the social dimension of the European institutions', is according to Bourdieu capable of forming an effective political project:

Historically, the State has been a force for rationalization, but one that has been put at the service of the dominant forces. To prevent this being the case, it is not sufficient to denounce the technocrats of Brussels. We need to develop a new internationalism, at least

22   *Introduction*

at the regional level of Europe, which could offer an alternative
to the regression into nationalism which, as a result of the crisis,
threatens all the European countries to some degree. This would
imply constructing institutions that are capable of standing up to
these forces of the financial market, and introducing . . . a ban on
backward movement with respect to social gains at the European
level. To achieve this, it is absolutely essential that the trade
unions operate at this European level. Because that is where the
forces they are fighting against are in action. It is therefore necessary to try to create the organizational bases for a genuine critical
internationalism capable of really combating neo-liberalism.[61]

Thus it is at the European level that Bourdieu sees it necessary
to organize a social movement, since this region has a rich tradition of social struggles and militant organizations, trade unions and
associations – the subtitle of *Contre-feux 2* is *Pour un mouvement social
européen* [although the subtitle of the published English translation,
Firing Back, is: *Against the Tyranny of the Market*]. Amplified by
the wide media coverage of *On Television* (1999 [1996]), Bourdieu's
international reputation ensured that his commitment would have a
worldwide impact. He was invited to give lectures in Germany and
Greece, and then in the United States, Korea and Japan. These were
published in the daily press: *Le Monde, Libération, Die Zeit*. In 2001 he
participated in the anti-summit held on 27 January in Zurich, in parallel to the summit at Davos,[62] and in the Continental Social Alliance on
4 April in Quebec, which welcomed the representatives of trade union
organizations and of social movements from thirty-five American
countries, to protest against the Summit of the Americas, which aimed
to extend the law of free exchange to the whole continent.

This critique of the 'new global vulgate' also led Bourdieu to elaborate the first elements of a study of the 'global economic field' (reproduced as Chapter 4.3 of this volume). Here he picks up the analyses of
the logics of unification that he had already posited in his history of
the bureaucratic field,[63] in order to transpose them onto the domain
of the global economy, where the technical and legal limits set by
the nation-states tend to be over-ridden. His model draws attention
to the imbrication of the economic and bureaucratic fields at the
heart of the social logics producing inequalities: 'Integration into the
State and the territory that it controls is in fact the precondition for
domination (as can be readily seen in all situations of colonization).
As I was able to observe in Algeria, unification of the economic field
tends . . . to pitch all social agents into an economic game for which

Introduction 23

they are not equally prepared and equipped, culturally and economically.'[64]

In fact, economic globalization engages social logics which are most often ignored: it is supported by a process of homogenization that follows the dominant norms, that is, the norms of the dominant, which therefore usually suit the interests of the dominant, who are the more open to competition since it takes place on their terms, which explains why it has the effect of reinforcing their domination. Although this text is not a complete analytic exposition of the process, it does show that in a context of internationalization *'unification benefits the dominant'* (p. 139, Bourdieu's emphasis). In this case, as in the case of cultural works,[65] 'globalization' is clearly an imperialism of the universal. And it is the 'universalist potential', borne by a 'global event' like the Olympic Games (whose 'planetarization' is analysed in Chapter 4.1), that finds itself challenged by the invasion of a commercial logic into the field of specific cultural production of athletic display.

The study of 'the unification of the global economic field' must not only take account of the process of 'integration of hitherto compartmentalized national economic universes', but also of the fact that they 'are now organized along the lines of an economy rooted in the historical particularities of a particular social tradition, that of American society, which is instituted both as an inevitable destiny and as a political project of universal liberation'.[66] Analysis in terms of field thus enables us to escape the alternative of a spontaneous globalization generated by supposed 'natural laws' of the market and an imperialism 'remotely controlled' by the United States. The universalist imperialism of the United States is able to impose itself all the more powerfully since 'the dominant economic forces are in fact capable of making (international) law and the great international organizations, which are exposed to the action of lobbyists, operate to their advantage'.[67]

The legal field itself becomes the object of a specific globalization which according to Bourdieu serves as an example of 'paradigm shift' in relations between the national and the international, as he explains in the commentary inspired by Yves Dezalay and Bryant Garth's *Dealing in Virtue*[68] (reproduced as Chapter 4.2 of this volume, in a version complemented by his unpublished notes on the book). Drawing on the theory of fields allows Bourdieu to show that the unification of the legal field arises from struggles among lawyers of different countries fighting to impose legitimate juridical forms. The theory opens the way for a differential analysis of international strategies, reflecting the conversion of the inheritors of national bourgeoisies

24 *Introduction*

who find in the new international space of legal expertise a means of escaping the effects of increasing competition affecting national career opportunities.

Assembling these texts thus reveals the foundations of a coherent programme of research that Pierre Bourdieu himself was not able to develop, but which has been developed by the CSE and others (see 'Guide').

1

Universalism and Domination

1.1

Two Imperialisms of the Universal
On the Strategies of Unification of the Cultural Field[1]

Much of what we can see in the relations between France and the United States is the product of a structure of relations that we need to think of as a confrontation between two imperialisms of the universal. One of the most eminent properties of these two nations, namely their claim to a certain universality, in the political domain in particular, with, for instance, a particular form of constitution and democratic tradition, is part of the political baggage and the symbolic capital that these nations can place at the service of very specific (and very different) forms of imperialism. As always, the sociologist plays the villain here: he disenchants, puts a spanner in the works; he does not fete democracy but questions the social usages that may be made of the democratic idea, which are not always very democratic.

France has the particularity of exercising a form of imperialism which may be characterized as an *imperialism of the universal*: an imperialism that operates above all on the political terrain, but which is also effective in the area of lifestyle and everyday existence, enjoying a legitimacy which it derives from its more or less widely recognized claim to universality. In the struggle for the monopoly of the universal, where the great nations have always challenged one another by invoking whatever is most universal at the time in question, not least through religions (such as Christianity) or ethics declared to be universal, France has had – at least in the modern period – a certain advantage, with its Revolution (whose priority has been contested, and not by accident, on the occasion of the celebration of the French Revolution). France includes in its patrimony the universal Revolution par excellence. The French Revolution, as founding myth of the French Republic, is the universal revolution and the universal model of all revolution. The Marxist tradition has drawn on this to provide the most extraordinary legitimization of France's claim to

28   *Imperialisms*

hold the monopoly of universal revolution. And we are not a little surprised to observe that the Marxists of all the great modern countries – England, the United States, Japan, etc. – have constantly asked themselves whether they have had a true revolution, that is, a French or a French-style Revolution. In so doing, Marx and Marxism have greatly helped to establish the French Revolution as the universal model of revolution.[2] And everyone knows that the leading thinker of the universal, the figure that any discourse on the universal must invoke, namely, Kant, consecrated the French Revolution as the universal revolution.[3] But we could find ever so many more, purely sociological attestations of this quasi-universal recognition of the universality of the particular revolution that was the French Revolution and, thereby, of the nation born of this revolution and consequently invested with a sort of exceptional status. If the French Revolution is the focus of such debates, on both sides of the Atlantic, and not only on the occasion of an anniversary, it is precisely because, through the French Revolution and the idea that we have of it, the key issue is perhaps the monopoly of universality, the monopoly of the rights of man, the monopoly of Humanity, etc.

In this perspective, the French Revolution figures as the legitimizing myth founding France's claim to universality, and thereby to the right to universalize its national culture. Since France has a national culture with claims to be universal, the French feel authorized (or did at least until the Second World War) to indulge in a form of cultural imperialism, which takes the form of a legitimate proselytism of the universal. This is nowhere better seen than in their colonial enterprises, as appears so clearly in a comparative history of the colonizing strategies of the French and the English. French colonization, often conceived as a civilizing and emancipating mission, is characterized by an extraordinary self-confidence, based on the certainty of having the particularity of universality (we often forget today that there was a left-wing colonialism, inclined to view annexation by assimilation as a liberating promotion to the universal).

The imperialism of the universal views itself as a liberating imperialism: there is nothing better than being colonized by France. 'What can I do better for the colonized than make him an alter ego, giving him access to what I am, to this culture that is mine but in addition is universal?' And this is why the claim to the universal is nowhere stronger than in the domain of culture. Now, one of the historical particularities of France, which affirmed itself above all at the end of the nineteenth century, is that for historical reasons it secured another monopoly for itself, that of cultural legitimacy, or, to be more precise, of that other cultural capital, the 'chic', which we can illustrate with two splendid texts by Valéry on Paris, showing triumphal insouciance:[4] we wonder how it was possible to feel universal to such a degree, to the point of being able quite simply to say that Paris is by definition the universal capital of the cultural world. France appears here as a sort of ideology materialized: to be French is to feel the right to universalize your particular interest, this national interest which has the characteristic of being universal. And twice over, in a way: universal in the matter of politics, with the pure model of the universal revolution, and universal in matters of culture, with the monopoly of (Parisian) chic. We can understand how, although its monopoly of the universal is hotly contested, in particular by the United States, France remains the arbiter of elegance in matters of 'radical chic', as they say across the pond; she continues to offer the universe this spectacle of the universal at play, and in particular of the art of *transgression* that makes the political and/or artistic avant-gardes – with their seemingly inimitable manner of feeling always just out of reach beyond the boundaries – able to play with virtuosity on the elusive harmonies among the discord, etc., of political and cultural avant-gardism; it is no surprise that the writer whose name is most directly associated with that acme of radical chic, the review *Tel Quel*, has recently revealed himself to be one of the fiercest defenders of French spelling.[5] No one may touch a language which, by the admission of the Berlin Academy that crowned Rivarol, is clearly universal.[6]

Faced with this French imperialism, which remains the paradigm of universal imperialism, the United States proclaims a rival version which finds its foundation or its justification in the *myth of democracy in America*, elaborated by Tocqueville,[7] who was doubly suited to fulfil this function, since he was French and an aristocrat (for me to be legitimate, I need someone different – a foreigner – to recognize me; if I crown myself – as Napoleon did – instead of asking the Pope to do it, it fails to work). In the struggle for the monopoly of universality, the recognition accorded by others, in particular by other countries, is decisive. And it is no accident for instance if the French are always (even today) summoned (and sometimes volunteer) to crown American universality.

The strong points of the American version of the imperialism of the universal are obviously their constitution, Congress, and unity in pluralism, etc., and when the Americans claim political universalism, it is readily granted them. But for some time now they have also claimed cultural universality, not without success. On this point they particularly wound French sensibilities; although French ambitions

30 *Imperialisms*

of a political order have been blunted, despite some visible vestiges of Gaullism remaining, French claims to cultural universalism are still strong, and we could show that in many areas, including the domain of science, where the universal is measured in Nobel Prizes, the French do their best to remain competitive. The strategies of universalization that all ambitious nations use to justify their domination take on unexpected forms today; for example science itself – with its Nobel Prizes – has become one of the great goals in the struggle for legitimacy within what we might call the global political field; science, and also a form of philosophy based on science. In the struggle for the monopoly of the legitimate domination of the world, the capital, in Valéry's sense,[8] is today Harvard or Chicago, which, in addition to a strong scientific capital symbolized by their Nobel laureates, unite and combine a constellation of talent and a philosophy of action that represents human action as produced by rational calculation and which therefore connects human intent very strongly with scientific rationality, an economic theory strongly formalized and legitimized in the name of mathematics, a philosophical theory of rational decision, etc., and this rationalistic-technocratic complex appears to have quite extraordinary powers of legitimization; science, which is the universal discourse par excellence, becomes the supreme form of ideological apologia.[9] To which we should add that other weapon which is morals, a traditional strong point (all American foreign interventions since 1917 have been covered by the claim to be acting in the name of universalism and in defence of values and morals; and it is worth analysing the strategies of universalization forwarded on the occasion of the Gulf War).[10] The ethical revival that some are celebrating in France today is not unconnected with the progress of American cultural imperialism. One of the domains in which this new cultural imperialism is most clearly seen is that of painting, where it has been splendidly analysed by Serge Guilbaut in a book entitled *How New York Stole the Idea of Modern Art*,[11] in which he describes the very complex process whereby legitimate symbolic domination in matters of painting passed from Paris to New York.

This shows that many of the things written or said about the United States or France or their supporters are the product of a confrontation between two imperialisms, between a waxing imperialism and a waning imperialism, and often no doubt owe much to sentiments of revenge or resentment, although we cannot rule out the likelihood that some of the reactions which we would be tempted to explain in terms of anti-American resentment might and should be understood as legitimate strategies of resistance to the new forms of imperial-

Two Imperialisms of the Universal   31

ism. How should we distinguish between the regressive, nationalist or nationalitarian forms that aim to safeguard protected cultural markets, and the legitimate forms of defence against the destruction of models threatened by monopolistic concentration?[12] Intellectuals, who are the first to be concerned by the imperialism of the universal, embrace an *ambiguous reality*, where they find ample nourishment for their strategic bad faith. This is why what needs to be emphasized in the very summary analysis proposed here is an incitation to vigilance or, better, to *reflexivity*. Many of the arguments about differences or similarities between nations (their political regimes, their educational systems, etc.) are just strategies of universalization designed to defend the symbolic national capital against real or imagined attacks. But things are not so simple, and the ruses of bad faith are countless. The interests linked to the struggle for cultural hegemony in the national space can lead some nationals to become accomplices of the foreigner's cultural imperialism – just as others may take refuge in a retrograde nationalism.

Universalizing individual interests is the prime strategy for legitimization, which is particularly urgent for cultural producers, always led by their whole tradition to see themselves as spokesmen for the universal, as '"functionaries" of humankind'.[13] But although we must always consider with the most extreme vigilance all the strategies oriented towards the unification of the cultural field, still we must distinguish between those that aim at unification through annexation, or, if you prefer, through the imposition of a dominant national model (this is how the cultural unification accompanying the construction of a modern State has usually operated), and those that aim at unification in cultural pluralism. A universal culture cannot avoid involving the universalization of a culture, that is, the *absolutization* of a historical culture, associated with the loss of a part of universality (the same is true for a language). Internationalism, today wrongly discredited for having been exploited by a particularly perverse form of the imperialism of the universal, namely Soviet imperialism, must be rehabilitated, and its truth restored. This calls for the invention of a universal culture that is not the simple product of the universal imposition of an individual culture (a culture that would not be any more universal than what they promise when they tell us that the United States is the 'world's policeman'). In fact, we can only expect to make any progress towards a really universal culture, *that is, a culture composed of multiple cultural traditions unified by mutually shared recognition,* through struggles between imperialisms of the universal. These imperialisms, through the more or less hypocritical homage that they must pay to the universal to impose themselves, tend to make it progress, and at the very least to establish the universal as a potential recourse to be invoked against even those imperialisms that claim allegiance to it.

1.2

The Cunning of Imperialist Reason[1]

Pierre Bourdieu and Loïc Wacquant

Cultural imperialism rests upon the power to universalize particularisms linked to a singular historical tradition by causing them to be misrecognized as such.[2] Thus, just as in the nineteenth century a certain number of supposedly philosophical questions being debated as universal throughout Europe and beyond originated, as Fritz Ringer has shown conclusively, in the historical particularities (and conflicts) proper to the singular universe of German academics,[3] so today numerous topics directly issuing from the intellectual confrontations relating to the social particularity of American society and its universities have been imposed, in apparently de-historicized form, upon the entire planet. These *common places*, in the Aristotelian sense of notions or theses *with which* one argues but *about which* one does not argue, or, put another way, these presuppositions of discussion that remain undiscussed, owe much of their power of persuasion to the fact that, circulating from academic conferences to best-selling books, from semi-scholarly journals to experts' evaluations, from governmental commissions' reports to magazine covers, they are present everywhere at the same time, from Berlin to Beijing and from Milan to Mexico, and are powerfully supported and relayed by those allegedly neutral channels that are international organizations (such as the OECD or the European Commission) and public policy centers and "think tanks" (such as the Brookings Institution in Washington, the Adam Smith Institute in London, and the Saint-Simon Foundation in Paris).[4]

The neutralization of the historical context resulting from the international circulation of texts and from the correlative forgetting of their historical conditions of origin produces an apparent universalization redoubled by the work of "theorization." A kind of fictional axiomatization fit to produce the illusion of a pure genesis, the game of preliminary *definitions* and deductions aimed at substituting the appearance of logical necessity for the contingency of denegated sociological causality tends to obfuscate the historical roots of a whole ensemble of questions and notions that will thus be called philosophical, sociological, historical, or political, depending on the field of reception. Thus planetarized, or globalized in a strictly geographical sense, by this uprooting at the same time as they are de-particularized by the effect of false rupture effected by conceptualization, these commonplaces of the great new global vulgate that endless media repetition gradually transforms into universal common sense manage in the end to make one forget that they have their roots in the complex and controversial realities of a particular historical society, now tacitly constituted as model for every other and as yardstick for all things.

Such is the case, for instance, with the woolly and spongy debate around "multiculturalism," a term which in Europe has been used mainly to designate cultural pluralism in the civic sphere, while in the United States it refers – if in distorted and veiled forms – to the enduring sequelae of the exclusion of blacks and to the crisis of the national mythology of the "American dream" correlative of the generalized increase in inequalities over the past three decades.[5] This is a crisis that the word "multicultural" veils by artificially restricting it to the sole academic microcosm and by expressing it in an ostensibly "ethnic" register, when its principal stake is not the recognition of marginalized cultures by academic canons but access to the instruments of (re)production of the middle and upper classes – and, first among them, to the university – in the context of massive and multisided state retrenchment.[6]

From this example, one can see in passing that, among the cultural products now being diffused on a planetary scale, the most insidious are not apparently systematic theories (such as "the end of history" or its cousin, the tale of "globalization") and philosophical world views (or views claiming to be such, like "postmodernism"), as these are quite easy to spot. Rather, they are those isolated and apparently technical terms such as "*flexibilité*" (or its British equivalent, "employability") which, because they encapsulate and silently communicate a whole philosophy of the individual and social organization, are well suited to functioning as veritable political codewords and mottoes (in this case: the need for firm downsizing and the denigration of the state, the reduction of social protection, and the acceptance of the diffusion of precarious wage labor as a fate, nay a boon).

One could analyze here also, in all of its presuppositions and implications, the strongly polysemic notion of "globalization," which has

The effect, if not the function, of submerging the effects of economic imperialism in cultural ecumenism or economic fatalism and of making transnational relationships of power appear to be a neutral necessity. As a result of a symbolic inversion based on the naturalization of the schemata of neoliberal thought, whose domination has been imposed for some twenty years by the relentless sapping of conservative think tanks and their allies in the political and journalistic fields,[7] the refashioning of social relations and cultural practices in advanced societies after the US pattern – founded on the pauperization of the state, the commodification of public goods, and the generalization of social insecurity – is nowadays accepted with resignation as the inevitable outcome of the evolution of nations, when it is not celebrated with a sheepish enthusiasm eerily reminiscent of the infatuation with America that the Marshall Plan had aroused in a devastated Europe half a century ago.[8]

A number of related themes that recently appeared on the European intellectual scene, and especially on the Parisian scene, have thus crossed the Atlantic in broad daylight or have been smuggled in under cover in the wake of the revived influence enjoyed by the products of American research, such as "political correctness" – paradoxically used, in French intellectual circles, as an instrument of reprobation and repression against every subversive impulse, especially feminist or gay – or the moral panic over the "ghettoization" of so-called immigrant neighborhoods, or, again, the moralism that insinuates itself everywhere, through an ethical vision of politics, the family, crime, etc., leading to a kind of principled de-politicization of social and political problems, thereby stripped of any reference to any kind of domination, or, finally, the opposition, that has become canonical in the regions of the intellectual field closest to cultural journalism, between "modernism" and "postmodernism" which, founded on an eclectic, syncretic, and, most often, de-historicized and highly approximate rereading of a posse of French and German authors, is in the process of being imposed in its American form upon the Europeans themselves.[9]

One would need to grant special attention and to examine in some detail the debate that currently opposes the "liberals" to the "communitarians"[10] (words directly *transcribed* into the various European languages, as with the French *libéral* and *communitarien*, and not translated, from the English) as an exemplary illustration of the effect of *false rupture* and *false universalization* produced by the shift to the register of discourse with philosophical pretensions: *item*, founding definitions signaling an apparent break with the historical particularisms relegated to the background of the thought of the historically

36 *Imperialisms*

situated and dated thinker (how could one not see, for instance, as has been suggested repeatedly, that the dogmatic character of Rawls's argument for the priority of basic liberties is explained by the fact that he tacitly attributes to the parties in the originating situation a latent ideal that is none other than his own, that of an American academic wedded to an ideal vision of American democracy?);[11] *item*, anthropological presuppositions that are anthropologically unjustified but endowed with all the *social* authority of the neo-marginalist economic theory from which they are borrowed; *item*, pretension to rigorous deduction, which allows one to string together in formal fashion unfalsifiable consequences without ever being exposed to the slightest empirical test; *item*, ritual and derisory alternatives between the atomistic individualists and the holistic collectivists – so visibly absurd that the "holistic individualists" have to be invented to accommodate Humboldt – or the "atomistic collectivists"; all of this in an extraordinary *jargon*, a terrible (and terrifying) international lingua franca that allows one to drag along all of the particularities and the particularisms associated with national traditions of *philosophy and politics* without ever taking them consciously into account (as when, for instance, such a French author takes care to write *liberty* in parentheses after the word *liberté* but accepts without discussion such conceptual barbarisms as the opposition between the *procédurel* and the *substantiel*). This debate, and the "theories" that oppose themselves in it, between which it would be vain to try to introduce a political choice, no doubt owes part of its success among philosophers – mainly conservative and especially Catholic philosophers – to the fact that it tends to reduce politics to morality: the vast discourse, skillfully neutralized and politically de-realized, that it has elicited is a timely successor to the great German tradition of philosophical anthropology, this noble and falsely profound discourse of denegation (*Verneinung*) that has for so long formed a screen and an obstacle to the scientific analysis of the social world wherever (German) philosophy could assert its domination.[12]

To turn to a domain closer to political realities, a debate such as that swirling around "race" and identity has given rise to similar, if more brutal, ethnocentric intrusions. A historical representation, born from the fact that the American tradition superimposes on an infinitely more complex social reality a rigid dichotomy between whites and blacks, can even impose itself in countries where the operative principles of vision and division of ethnic differences, codified or practical, are quite different and which, as in Brazil, were until recently considered as counter-examples to the "American model."[13] Carried out by

Americans and by Latin Americans trained in the United States (or in US-sponsored programs in their own country), most of the recent research on ethno-racial inequality in Brazil strives to prove that, contrary to the image that Brazilians have of their own nation, the country of the "three sad races" (indigenous peoples, blacks descended from slaves, and whites issued from colonization and the subsequent waves of European immigration) is no less "racist" than others and that Brazilian "whites" have nothing to envy their North American cousins on this score. Worse yet, Brazilian *racismo mascarado* should by definition be regarded as more perverse precisely on account of being dissimulated and denegated. This is the claim of Afro-American political scientist Michael Hanchard in *Orpheus and Power*:[14] by unthinkingly applying North American racial categories to the Brazilian situation, this book makes the particular history of the US Civil Rights movement of the post-World War II decades, rooted in the unique rigidity and violence of a regime of domination born of a founding contradiction between democracy and racialized slavery unknown in any other society,[15] into the universal standard for the struggle of all groups oppressed on grounds of color (or caste). Instead of dissecting the constitution of the Brazilian ethno-racial order according to its own logic, such inquiries are most often content to replace wholesale the national myth of "racial democracy" (as expressed for instance in the works of Gilberto Freyre[16]) by the militant counter-myth according to which all societies are "racist," including those within which "race" relations seem at first sight to be far less distant and hostile (nay sometimes nonexistent as such). From being an analytic tool, the concept of racism becomes a mere instrument of accusation; under the guise of science, it is the logic of the trial which asserts itself (and ensures book sales, for lack of success based on intellectual esteem).[17]

In a classic article published thirty years ago, the anthropologist Charles Wagley showed that the conception of "race" in the Americas admits of several definitions according to the differential weight granted to descent, physical appearance (itself not confined to skin color), and sociocultural status (occupation, income, education, region of origin and residence, etc.), depending on the history of settlement, intergroup relations, and symbolic conflicts in the different geographic zones.[18] Due to the peculiar circumstances of their colonization, Americans in the United States are alone in defining "race" solely on the basis of descent, and this, only in the case of African Americans: one is "black" in Chicago, Los Angeles, or Atlanta, not by the color of one's skin but for having one or more ancestors identified as black, that is to say, at the end of the regression, as African slaves. The United States is the

38   *Imperialisms*

only modern society to apply the "one-drop rule" conjointly with the principle of hypodescent, according to which the offspring of a mixed union find themselves automatically assigned to the group deemed inferior – here the erstwhile named "Negroes."

In Brazil, by contrast, ethno-racial identity is defined not genealogically but by reference to a *continuum* of "color," that is, by use of a flexible or fuzzy phenotypical principle which takes account of physical traits such as skin tone, texture of hair, and the shape of the lips and nose, to generate a large number of gradational and partly overlapping categories (over a hundred of them were recorded by the 1980 Census).[19] Racial categorization is also qualified by class position (notably income, occupation, and education), and varies strongly by region, with the result that the same individual may receive a different racial designation depending on where he lives and how much money he earns, while two full siblings may be categorized in different "races," two phenomena that are ruled out in the US racial classification scheme. This is not to say that invidious distinctions and deep inequalities pegged to this ethno-racial gradient do not exist in Brazil, for clearly they do; it is to stress that the symbolic construction of "race" in this country has endowed group boundaries and relations with a relative porousness and malleability that the black/white dichotomy fails to capture; in particular, these relations do not entail radical ostracization and exclusionary *stigmatization* without recourse or remedy across the social structure. Evidence for this is provided by the strategies of ethno-racial mobility through marrying up the color ladder pursued by darker-skin Brazilians, the segregation indices sported by Brazilian cities, strikingly lower than those for US metropolitan areas (typical of what in the United States would pass for "integrated neighborhoods"), and the virtual absence of these two typically US forms of ethno-racial violence that are public lynchings and urban race riots.[20] Quite the opposite in the United States, where there exists no socially and legally recognized category of *métis* (mixed-race) following their symbolic eradication in the first decades of the twentieth century.[21] In this case we are faced with a division that is closer to that between *definitively defined and delimited castes* or quasi-castes (proof is the exceptionally low rate of intermarriage to this day: fewer than 3 percent of African-American women aged 25 to 34 contracted "mixed" unions in the 1980s, as against about half of women of Latino origin and four-fifths of Asian American women),[22] a division that one strives to conceal by submerging it within the universe of differentiating visions "revisioned" through US lenses by means of "globalization."

The Cunning of Imperialist Reason

How are we to explain that "theories" of "race relations" that are but thinly *conceptualized transfigurations*, endlessly refurbished and updated to suit current political concerns, of the most commonly used racial stereotypes that are themselves only primary justifications for the domination of whites over blacks in one society,[23] could be tacitly (and sometimes explicitly) raised to the status of universal standards whereby every situation of ethnic domination must be analyzed and measured?[24] The fact that this racial (or racist) sociodicy was able to "globalize" itself in recent years, thereby losing its outer characteristics of legitimating discourse for domestic usage, is no doubt one of the most striking proofs of the symbolic dominion and hold exercised by the United States over every kind of scholarly and, especially, semi-scholarly production, notably through the power of consecration they possess and through the material and symbolic profits that research-ers in the dominated countries reap from a more or less assumed or ashamed adherence to the model issued from the United States. For one may say, with Thomas Bender, that the products of American research have acquired "an international stature and a power of attrac-tion" comparable to those of "American cinema, pop music, computer software and basketball."[25] Symbolic violence is indeed never wielded but through a form of (extorted) complicity on the part of those who are subjected to it: the "globalization" of the themes of American social doxa, or of its more or less sublimated transcription in semi-scholarly discourse, would not be possible without the collaboration, conscious or unconscious, directly or indirectly interested, of all the *passeurs*, "carriers" and importers of designer or counterfeit cultural products (publishers, directors of cultural institutions such as museums, operas, galleries, journals, heads of research centers, etc.) who, in the country itself or in the target countries, propound and propagate, often in utter good faith, American cultural products, and of all the American cultural authorities which, without need for explicit connivance, accompany, orchestrate, and sometimes even organize the process of collective conversion to the new symbolic Mecca.[26]

But all these mechanisms, which have the effect of *fostering* a verita-ble "globalization" of American problems (in the sense of authoritative planetary diffusion), thereby verifying the Americano-centric belief in "globalization" understood, quite simply, as the *Americanization* of the Western world and, by gradual expansion, of the entire uni-verse, these mechanisms are not enough to explain the tendency of the American viewpoint, scholarly or semi-scholarly, to impose itself as universal point of view, especially when it comes to issues, such as that of "race," where the particularity of the American configuration

40   *Imperialisms*

is particularly flagrant and particularly far from being exemplary. One could obviously invoke here also the driving role played by the major American philanthropic and research foundations in the diffusion of the US racial doxa within the Brazilian academic field at the level of both representations and practices, or in another domain of the juridical and moral categories of "human rights" and "philanthropy."[27] Thus the Rockefeller Foundation and similar organizations fund a program on "Race and Ethnicity" at the Federal University of Rio de Janeiro as well as at the Center for Afro-Asiatic Studies at Candido Mendes University (and its journal *Estudos Afro-asiáticos*) so as to encourage exchanges of researchers and students. But the intellectual current flows in one direction only: US categories and problematics (starting with the dichotomous black/white division) travel south, but Brazilian experiences and counterpoints are rarely if ever repatriated north to question the peculiar ways in which the United States has constructed its "race" question and how this construction has in turn been unthinkingly transcribed into the analytical apparatus of its national social science. And, as a condition for its aid, the Rockefeller Foundation asks that research teams apply US criteria of "affirmative action," which poses insuperable problems since, as we have just seen, the application of the white/black dichotomy in Brazilian society is, to say the least, hazardous.

Alongside the role of philanthropic foundations, one must finally include the internationalization of academic publishing among the factors that have contributed to the diffusion of "made-in-the-USA" thought in the social sciences. The growing integration of the publishing of English-language academic books (nowadays sold, often by the same houses, in the United States and in the different countries of the former British Commonwealth, but also in the smaller, polyglot, nations of the European Union such as Sweden and the Netherlands, and in all the societies most directly exposed to American cultural domination) and the erosion of the boundary between academic and trade publishing have helped encourage the putting into circulation of terms, themes, and tropes with strong (real or hoped for) market appeal which, in turn, owe their power of attraction essentially to the very fact of their wide diffusion. For example, Blackwell, the large, half-commercial, half-academic publishing house (what the British call a "crossover press"), does not hesitate to impose titles on its authors that are in accord with this new planetary common sense that it contributes to forging under the guise of echoing it. Such is the case with the collection of texts on new forms of urban marginality in Europe and America assembled in 1996 by the Italian sociologist

The Cunning of Imperialist Reason 41

Enzo Mingione: it was dressed up with the title *Urban Poverty and the Underclass* against the better judgment and will of its editor and of several of the contributors, since the entire book tends to demonstrate the vacuity of the notion of "underclass" – Blackwell even refused to put the term in inverted commas.[28] Faced with the manifest reticence of its authors, it is all too easy for Blackwell to claim that an enticing title is the only way to avoid a high selling price that would in any case kill the volume in question. Thus it is that decisions of pure book marketing orient research and university teaching in the direction of homogenization and of submission to fashions coming from America, when they do not fabricate wholesale "disciplines" such as "Cultural Studies," this mongrel domain, born in England in the 1970s, which owes its international dissemination (which is the whole of its existence) to a successful policy of editorial propaganda. Thus the fact, for instance, that this "discipline" does not exist in the French university and intellectual fields did not prevent Routledge from publishing a compendium entitled *French Cultural Studies*, on the model of *British Cultural Studies* (there are also volumes of *German Cultural Studies* and *Italian Cultural Studies* by rival publishers). And one may forecast that, by virtue of the principle of ethnico-editorial parthenogenesis in fashion today, we shall soon find in bookstores a handbook of *French Arab Cultural Studies* to match its cross-Channel cousin, *Black British Cultural Studies* that appeared in 1997 (but bets remain open as to whether Routledge will dare *German Turkish Cultural Studies*).

Yet all of these factors taken together cannot completely explain the hegemony that US production exercises over the intellectual world market. This is where one must take into account the role of those at the helm of strategies of conceptual "import/export," those mystified mystifiers who can transport unknowingly the hidden – and often accursed – share of the cultural products they put into circulation. What are we to think indeed of those American researchers who travel to Brazil to encourage the leaders of the *Movimento Negro* to adopt the tactics of the African-American Civil Rights movement and to denounce the category of *pardo* (an intermediary term between *branco* (white) and *preto* (black) designating people of mixed physical appearance) in order to mobilize all Brazilians of African *descent* on the basis of a dualistic opposition between "Afro-Brazilians" and "whites" modeled on the US dichotomous divide at the very time when, in the United States, people of mixed origin, including so-called blacks (the vast majority of whom are of mixed parentage), are mobilizing to obtain from the US federal state (beginning with the Census Bureau) official recognition of "multiracial" Americans by ceasing to categorize

42 *Imperialisms*

them forcibly under the single label "black"?[29] Such discordance justifies us in thinking that the recent, as well as unexpected, discovery of the "globalization of race"[30] results, not from a sudden convergence of forms of ethno-racial domination in the various countries, but from the quasi-universalization of the US *folk concept* of "race" as a result of the successful worldwide export of US scholarly categories.

A similar demonstration could be given with respect to the international diffusion of the true/false concept of *underclass* which, through an effect of transcontinental *allodoxia* typical of the uncontrolled circulation of ideas, has been imported by those Old World sociologists most desirous of experiencing a second intellectual youth by surfing on the wave of popularity of concepts stamped with the US seal.[31] To summarize quickly, in this label European researchers hear "class" and believe that reference is being made to a new position in the structure of urban social space, while their American colleagues hear "under" and think of a heap of dangerous and immoral poor people in a resolutely Victorian and racistoid perspective. Yet, Paul Peterson, a distinguished professor of government at Harvard University and director of the Committee for Research on the Urban Underclass of the Social Science Research Council (financed yet again by the Rockefeller and Ford foundations), leaves no grounds for uncertainty or ambiguity when he summarizes approvingly the findings of a major conference on the "underclass" held in Evanston, Illinois, in 1990 in terms that hardly need to be commented upon:

> The term is powerful because it calls attention to the conjunction between the characters of individuals and the impersonal forces of the larger social and political order. "Class" is the least interesting half of the word. Although it implies a relationship between one social group and another, the terms of this relationship are left undefined until combined with the familiar word "under." This transformation of a preposition into an adjective has none of the sturdiness of "working," the banality of "middle," or the remoteness of "upper." Instead, "under" suggests the lowly, passive, and submissive, yet at the same time the disreputable, dangerous, disruptive, dark, evil, and even hellish. Apart from these personal attributes, it suggests subjection, subordination, and deprivation.[32]

In each national intellectual field, *passeurs*, or carriers (sometimes just one, sometimes several in competition with each other), have stepped forth to take up this scholarly myth and to reformulate in these alienated terms the question of the relations between urban poverty, immigration, and segregation in their country. One loses count of the articles and works that purport to prove – or, what amounts almost to the same thing, to disprove – with fine positivist diligence, the "existence" of this "group" in such-and-such a society, city, or neighborhood, on the basis of empirical indicators often badly constructed and badly correlated among themselves.[33] To pose the question of whether there exists an "underclass" (a term that some French sociologists have not hesitated to translate as "sous-classe," no doubt anticipating the introduction of the concept of "soushommes" or *Untermensch*) in London, Lyon, Leiden, or Lisbon, is to suppose at the least, on the one hand, that the term is endowed with minimal analytic consistency and, on the other hand, that such a "group" actually exists in the United States.[34]

Now, the semi-journalistic, semi-scholarly notion of "underclass" is as devoid of semantic coherence as it is of social existence. The incongruous populations that American researchers usually regroup under this term – welfare recipients and the long-term unemployed, unmarried mothers, single-parent families, rejects from the school system, criminals and gang members, drug addicts and the homeless, when they do not refer to all ghetto dwellers in bulk – owe being included in this catch-all category to one fact and one fact only: they are perceived as menacing and living denials of the "American dream" of opportunity for all and individual success. The kindred "concept" of *exclusion* is commonly used, in France and in a growing number of other European countries (notably under the influence of the European Commission), at the intersection of the political, journalistic, and scientific fields with the similar functions of de-historicization and depoliticization by picturing an old and well-known phenomenon – mass unemployment and its sapping social effects on the urban proletariat – as a novel development somehow disconnected from state policies of economic deregulation and welfare retrenchment. All of which gives us an idea of the inanity of the project to retranslate a nonexistent notion into another just as nondescript.[35]

Indeed, the "underclass" is but a fictional group, produced on paper by the classification practices of those scholars, journalists, and related experts in the management of the (black urban) poor who share in the belief in its existence because it is well suited to giving renewed scientific legitimacy to some and a politically and commercially profitable theme to mine to others.[36] Inapt and inept in the American case, the imported concept adds nothing to the knowledge of contemporary European societies. For the modalities of and methods for the government of

44 *Imperialisms*

poverty are vastly discrepant on the two sides of the Atlantic, not to mention differences in ethnic divisions and their political status.[37] It follows that "problem populations" are neither defined nor treated in the same manner in the United States and in the different countries of the Old World. Yet most extraordinary of all is no doubt the fact that, in keeping with a paradox that we already encountered with regard to other phony concepts of the globalized vulgate, the notion of "underclass" which has come to us from America was in fact born in Europe – as was that of "ghetto" which it serves to obfuscate, in keeping with the severe political censorship that weighs upon research on urban and racial inequality in the United States. It was the economist Gunnar Myrdal who coined it in the 1960s by derivation from the Swedish *onderklass*. But his intention then was to describe the process of marginalization of the lower fractions of the working class in wealthy countries in order to criticize the ideology of the generalized embourgeoisement of capitalist societies.[38] One can see here how profoundly the detour through America can transform an idea: from a structural concept aimed at questioning the dominant representation of society emerges a behavioral category custom-made to reinforce that representation by imputing to the "antisocial" conducts of the most disadvantaged responsibility for their own dispossession.

These misunderstandings are due in part to the fact that the transatlantic "carriers" in the different importing intellectual fields who produce, reproduce, and circulate all these (false) problems, while levying in the process their small "cut" of the attendant material or symbolic profits, are exposed to a double heteronomy, owing to their position and to their scholarly and political habitus. On the one hand, they look toward America, the supposed home and hearth of social and scientific (post-)"modernity," but they are themselves dependent upon American scholars who export intellectual products (often soiled and faded) abroad because they do not usually have direct and specific knowledge of US institutions and culture. On the other hand, they lean toward journalism, toward the seductions it offers and the immediate success it procures and, consequently, toward the themes that crop up at the intersection of the fields of the media and politics, right at the point of maximum yield on the external market (as would be shown by an enumeration of the complacent reviews that their works receive in highly visible magazines). Whence their predilection for soft problematics, neither truly journalistic (they adorn themselves with concepts) nor completely scientific (they pride themselves on being in symbiosis with "the actors' point of view"), which are nothing but the semi-scholarly retranslation of the salient social problems of the

The Cunning of Imperialist Reason

day into an idiom imported from the United States (in the 1990s: ethnicity, identity, minority, community, fragmentation, etc.) and which succeed each other according to an order and tempo dictated by the media: youths of the *banlieue*, the xenophobia of the declining working class, the maladjustment of high-school and university students, urban violence, the turn to Islam, and so on. These sociologist-journalists, always ready and eager to comment on current affairs and every so-called *fait de société* in a language at once accessible and "modernist," and therefore often perceived as vaguely progressive (in relation to the "archaisms" of old-line European thought), contribute in a particularly paradoxical way to the imposition of a vision of the world which, surface appearances notwithstanding, is far from being incompatible with those produced and conveyed by the great international think tanks more or less directly plugged into the spheres of economic and political power.

As for those in the United States who, often without realizing it, are engaged in this vast international enterprise of cultural import/ export, they occupy for the most part dominated positions in the American field of power and even, very often, in the intellectual field. Just as the products of America's big cultural industry, like jazz or rap, or the commonest food and clothing fashions like jeans, owe part of the quasi-universal seduction they wield over youths to the fact that they are produced by or associated with subordinate minorities in the United States,[39] so the topics of the new world vulgate no doubt derive a good measure of their symbolic efficacy from the fact that, supported by specialists from disciplines perceived to be marginal or subversive, such as Cultural Studies, Ethnic Studies, Gay Studies, or Women's Studies, they take on, in the eyes of writers from the former European colonies, for example, the allure of messages of liberation. Indeed, cultural imperialism (American or otherwise) never imposes itself better than when it is served by progressive intellectuals (or by "intellectuals of color" in the case of ethno-racial inequality) who would appear to be above suspicion of promoting the hegemonic interests of a country against which they wield the weapons of social critique. Thus the various articles that compose the summer 1996 issue of the journal *Dissent*, mouthpiece of the democratic "Old Left" of New York City, devoted to "Embattled Minorities Around the Globe: Rights, Hopes, Threats,"[40] project upon the whole of humankind, with the humanist goodwill characteristic of a certain strand of the academic Left, not only US "liberal" common sense but the notion of *minority* (we should always keep the English word to remind ourselves that we are dealing with a folk concept imported into theory – and yet again one of European origin)[41] which presupposes precisely that which needs to be demonstrated: that categories cut out from within a given nation-state on the basis of "cultural" or "ethnic" traits have the desire or the right to demand civic and political recognition *as such*. But the forms under which individuals seek to have their collective existence and membership(s) recognized by the state vary at different times and places as functions of historical traditions, and they always constitute a stake of struggle in history. In this manner, an apparently rigorous and generous comparative analysis can, without its authors even realizing it, contribute to rendering a problematic made by and for Americans seem to be universal.

We thus come upon a double paradox. In the struggle for the monopoly over the production of the vision of the social world that is universally recognized as universal, in which it nowadays occupies an eminent, not to say preeminent, position, the United States is certainly exceptional, but its exceptionalism does not reside where the national sociodicy and social science agree in locating it, namely, in the fluidity of a social order that offers extraordinary opportunities for mobility (especially in comparison with the supposedly rigid social structures of the Old World): the most rigorous comparative studies converge to conclude that the United States does not differ fundamentally in this respect from other post-industrial nations, even though the span of class inequality is notably wider in America.[42] If the United States is truly exceptional, in accordance with the old Tocquevillian thematics untiringly reprised and periodically updated, it is above all for the *rigid dualism* of its racial division. Even more so, it is for its capacity to *impose as universal that which is most particular to it* while passing off as exceptional that which makes it most common.

If it is true that the de-historicization that almost inevitably results from the migration of ideas across national boundaries is one of the factors contributing to de-realization and false universalization (as, for example, with theoretical "faux amis"), then only a genuine history of the genesis of ideas about the social world, joined with an analysis of the social mechanisms of the international circulation of those ideas, can lead scientists, in this domain as elsewhere, to a better mastery of those instruments with which they argue without taking the trouble to argue beforehand about them.[43]

Translated by Loïc Wacquant

2

Texts without Contexts

2.1

The International Circulation of Ideas[1]

In order to reflect on the social conditions of the international circulation of ideas, it is possible to use an economics vocabulary that always produces a rupture effect, such as, for example, the notion of intellectual import/export. Without pretending to describe the laws of such circulation – for want of a real inquiry authorizing the use of such pretentious language – we can reconstruct the tendencies of these international exchanges that are usually described in a language that owes more to mysticism than to reason and then elaborate a programme for a science of international relations with respect to cultural matters.

To begin with, we need to consider the history of relations between countries such as France and Germany since the Second World War, and more specifically all the work that has been done, particularly in the political arena, to foster communication and understanding between these two countries. We need an uncompromising historical analysis of the symbolic work that has been necessary to exorcize all the fantasies of the past, at least in a certain segment of the populations of both countries. In addition to the symbolic and practical aspects of the official work carried out by official bodies, we need to analyse the various actions that helped transform the attitudes of the French and Germans, in all their social diversity. In the case of French intellectuals, there was a reconciliation, followed by a fascination with the 'German miracle', and then the current phase of ambivalent admiration, sublimated into a kind of voluntarist Europeanism through which many eleventh-hour workers are trying to find a substitute for their defunct nationalism. But one cannot be satisfied with such considerations, which are as superficial as they are summary.

What can one do today, if one has a genuine desire to further the internationalization of intellectual life? People often have a tendency to think that intellectual life is spontaneously international. Nothing

50 *Imperialisms*

could be further from the truth. Intellectual life, like all other social spaces, is home to nationalism and imperialism, and intellectuals, like everyone else, constantly peddle prejudices, stereotypes, received ideas, and hastily simplistic representations which are fuelled by the chance happenings of everyday life, like misunderstandings, general incomprehension, and wounded pride (such as might be felt at being unknown in a foreign country). All of which makes me think that a truly scientific internationalism, which to my mind is the only possible ground on which internationalism of any sort is going to be built, is not going to happen of its own accord.

Regarding culture, my beliefs are the same as those I hope for everything else: I don't believe in laissez-faire. What I hope to show here is that all too often, in international exchanges, the logic of laissez-faire favours the circulation of the very worst ideas at the expense of the best. And here, as so often, I find myself inspired by that most outmoded of ideas in this postmodern world – a deeply held belief in scientism. And this scientism leads me to believe that if one understands social mechanisms, one is not necessarily master of them, but one does increase one's chances of mastering them, by however small an amount, particularly when the social mechanisms in question rest largely on misunderstanding. There is an autonomous force of knowledge that can destroy, to a certain extent, ignorance. I say 'to a certain extent' because the 'intrinsic force of true ideas' is hit with resistances stemming from interests, prejudices, and passions.

International exchanges are subject to a certain number of structural factors which generate misunderstandings. The first factor is that texts circulate without their context. This is a proposition that Marx noted in passing in the *Communist Manifesto*, an unusual place to look for a reception theory. Marx notes that German thinkers have read French thinkers very badly, seeing texts that were the result of a particular political juncture as *pure* texts, and transforming the political agitators at the heart of such texts into a sort of transcendental subject. In the same manner, many misunderstandings in international communication are a result of the fact that texts do not bring their context with them. For example, at the risk of surprising and shocking you, it seems to me that only the logic of this structural misunderstanding can explain the staggering fact that a Socialist President of a French Republic awarded a decoration to Ernst Jünger.[2] Another example might be the consecration of Heidegger by certain French Marxists in the 1950s.[3] I could equally use contemporary examples. But because I would often be implicated in these examples myself, I shall refrain from doing so, as it might be thought that I was taking advantage of the

The International Circulation of Ideas   51

symbolic power invested in me here today to avenge myself on absent adversaries.

The fact that texts circulate without their context, that – to use my terms – they don't bring with them the field of production of which they are a product, and the fact that the recipients, who are themselves in a different field of production, re-interpret the texts in accordance with the structure of the field of reception, are facts that generate some formidable misunderstandings and that can have good or bad consequences. From this account, which I believe to be objective, one could draw either optimistic or pessimistic conclusions. For example, if someone who is an authority in his own country does not bring that authority with him abroad, then foreign readers and commentators sometimes have a liberty not to be found in the country where the text originates, where a reading might be subject to the effects of symbolic imposition, domination, or even coercion. All this lends some credibility to the idea that foreign judgements are a little like the judgements of posterity. If, in general, posterity is a better judge, it is doubtless because contemporaries are competitors and often have a hidden interest in not understanding, or even in preventing understanding from taking place in others. Foreign readers, like posterity, have in some cases a distance and autonomy regarding the social conditions of the field. In fact, this effect is often slightly illusory, and it does happen that institutionalized authorities, Pascal's 'grandeurs d'établissement',[4] cross frontiers very well, as there is an all-too-real international old-boy network that functions with great efficiency.

So the sense and function of a foreign work are determined not simply by the field of origin, but in at least equal proportion by the field of reception. First, because the sense and function of the original field are often completely unknown, but also because the process of transfer from a domestic field to a foreign one is made up of a series of social operations. There is a process of selection (what is to be translated, what is to be published, who it will be translated by, who will publish it); a process of labelling and classification (often the placing of a label on a product whose label had been removed) by the publishers; the question of the series in which it is to be inserted; the choice of translator and the writer of the preface (who in presenting the work will take some sort of possession of it and connect it with his own point of view and with a problematic inscribed in the field of its reception, only rarely going so far as to explain where and how it fits into its field of origin, as the difficulties presented by such an enterprise are too large); and finally the reading process itself, as foreign readers are bound to perceive the text in different ways, since the issues which are of interest to them in the text are inevitably the result of a different field of production.

The conditions and manner in which texts enter a field of reception is an urgent and important area that needs further research, for both scientific and practical reasons, particularly as our aim is to facilitate and improve communication between different countries. One should study these selection processes and find out who these people doing the selecting (who were recently termed 'gatekeepers'[5] by an American sociologist of science) actually are. Who are the discoverers, and what interest do they have in discovering these things? I am aware that the word 'interest' might shock here. But I do believe that anyone, no matter how well-intentioned, who appropriates an author for him- or herself and becomes the person who introduces that author to another country inevitably has some ulterior motive. It may be sublime, or it may be sublimated, but it should be revealed, as it is clearly a determining factor in what is being done. (I think a little materialism isn't at all out of place here and won't take away the enchantment.) What I am calling 'interest' may simply be a sort of affinity through the occupation of a homologous or identical place in the different fields. To take one example, it is surely not an accident that the great Spanish novelist Benet is published in France by Les Éditions de Minuit.[6] To publish what one loves is to strengthen one's position in a certain field, whether one likes it or not, whether one is aware of it or not, even if that effect was not part of the original intention. There is nothing wrong with this, but it should be more widely acknowledged. Choices which seem pure of other interests, and are mutually agreeable, are often made on the basis of homologous positions in different fields and in fact correspond to homologous interests and styles where the intellectual background or project is concerned. These exchanges can be understood as alliances, and they function in the same way as power relations, hence they might be used to reinforce a dominated or threatened position.

Besides these elective affinities between 'creators' (for which, as you have probably discerned, I feel a certain indulgence), there are also the mutual admiration societies which seem somewhat less legitimate as they exercise a temporal power in a cultural or spiritual sphere, and thus correspond to Pascal's definition of tyranny.[7] One thinks for example of the international establishment and of the series of exchanges that go on between people who hold important positions. A large number of translations can only be understood if they are placed in the complex network of international exchanges between holders of dominant academic posts, the exchanges of invitations, honorary doctorates, etc. The question that must then be asked is what is the logic

The International Circulation of Ideas 53

of choice that makes a certain writer or editor become the importer of a certain thought. Why is writer X published by publisher Y? For there are obviously profits in such appropriation. Heretical imports are often the work of marginals in the field, bringing a message, a position of force from a different field, which they use to try and shore up their own position. Foreign writers are often subject to such instrumental use, and forced to serve purposes which they would perhaps refuse or reject in their country of origin. One can often use a foreign thinker to attack domestic thinkers in this way.

Heidegger is a case in point. Doubtless, many people here today wonder how it was that the French became so interested in Heidegger. There are many reasons of course, perhaps too many, but one particular reason leaps out to the eye: the fact that Sartre held the intellectual field in a stranglehold throughout the 1950s (as Anna Boschetti has demonstrated quite convincingly in her book *The Intellectual Enterprise: Sartre and Les Temps Modernes*[8]). One of Heidegger's main functions for the French was to diminish Sartre's impact, with teachers saying for example that all of Sartre's major ideas were already there in Heidegger, where they were better elaborated. On the one side there was Beaufret, who must have been a contemporary of Sartre's at the École Normale Supérieure, in a position of rivalry with him, taking the *khâgne* classes at the prestigious Henri IV school, preparing students for the rigorous entry exams to the Grandes Écoles, managing to create a sort of status for himself as philosopher by bringing Heidegger to France.[9] Elsewhere, in the literary field, there was Blanchot.[10] And there was also a third category, in the review *Arguments*,[11] the minor Marxist heretics. As straight Marxism was too obviously proletarian, they constructed a modish mixture of Marxism and Heidegger.

Very often with foreign authors it is not what they say that matters, so much as what they can be made to say. This is why certain particularly elastic authors transfer so well. All great prophecies are polysemic. That is one of their cardinal virtues, and explains how they have such general applications and are transmitted so well across cultures and down the generations. Such elastic thinkers are manna from heaven when it comes to serving expansionist strategic uses. After this process of selection and choice, there comes the attaching of a label which finishes the work. Hence, we don't for instance simply get Simmel, we get Simmel with a preface by Mr X.[12] The time is ripe for a comparative study of the sociology of the preface. They are typical acts of the transfer of symbolic capital, or at least this is what they most commonly are, as for instance when we find Mauriac writing a preface for Sollers.[13] The celebrated elder writer in providing the preface is transmitting

54 *Imperialisms*

symbolic capital while at the same time demonstrating that he still has both the ability to recognize new talent, and the generosity to protect an admiring younger generation where his influence is to be discerned. A whole series of exchanges is going on (where bad faith plays an enormous role) which any objectifying sociology would render more difficult. But the direction in which the symbolic capital is circulating is not always the same. For instance, relying on the ruling assumption that the writer of the preface is identified with the author of the book, Lévi-Strauss wrote a preface to Mauss where he effectively appropriated for himself the symbolic capital of the author of the famous essay on the gift.[14]

At the end of all this, the imported text receives another label. The cover of the book acts as a sort of brand name. Seasoned academics have a good understanding of the sorts of covers that different publishers use and even of the sense of the different series published by the publisher in question. One knows what they all mean, and how they fit into the general scheme of scholarly publishing. If, for example, one were to replace a Suhrkamp cover[15] by one from Le Seuil, the sense of the *brand* imposed on the work changes dramatically. When there is a sort of structural homology, the transfer can happen quite unproblematically. But there are often failures here, and writers fall awkwardly by the wayside as a result, sometimes simply by chance, sometimes by ignorance, but also often because they are unwittingly objects of a process of appropriation. In such cases, even the cover itself is already a symbolic imposition. Since, to my mind, Le Seuil was basically a left-wing Catholic publisher and identified at that time with personalist thought, Chomsky found himself with a new brand name, as a result of a typical expansionist project. For Le Seuil to publish Chomsky,[16] in an environment where Ricoeur's[17] influence was extremely powerful, was to combat what was known as 'subjectless structuralism' with a creative, generative subject. And by the insertion of a book into a series, by the addition of a preface, by the contents of that preface, and by the position of the author of the preface, a whole series of transformations take place, whose end result was to considerably alter the sense of the original message.

In reality, the structural effects which (thanks to ignorance) make possible all sorts of transformations and deformations linked to the strategic use of texts and authors are constantly going on, independently of any intention to manipulate information. The differences are so great between historical traditions, in the intellectual field per se as well as in the ensemble of the social field, that the application to a foreign cultural product of the categories of perception and appre-

The International Circulation of Ideas 55

ciation acquired from experience in the domestic field can actually create fictitious oppositions between similar things, and false parallels between things that are fundamentally different. To demonstrate this, one could analyse in detail the links between French and German philosophers since the 1960s and show how similar intentions have resulted, through reference to starkly different intellectual and social contexts, in the adopting of apparently opposing philosophical positions. To put this in a more striking but more fanciful manner, one might ask oneself whether Habermas would not have been much closer to Foucault than he appears to be, if he had been trained and brought up as a philosopher in France of the 1950s to 1960s, and whether Foucault would not have been much less different from Habermas, had he been trained and brought up as a philosopher in Germany at the same time. This is to say, by way of an aside, that both thinkers, while appearing to have great freedom in their contexts, are in fact both deeply marked by the context in which they found themselves, partly because (through their hegemonic intentions) they came into conflict with the intellectual traditions particular to their own countries, which were of course profoundly different.

Another instructive example. Before becoming self-righteously indignant, like certain German scholars, at the use to which certain French philosophers (notably Deleuze and Foucault) have put Nietzsche, one must understand the function that Nietzsche – for Foucault the Nietzsche of *The Genealogy of Morals* – fulfilled in a certain field of academic philosophy which was dominated at the time by a sort of subjective, spiritual existentialism.[18] *The Genealogy of Morals* offered a sort of philosophical guarantee and philosophical respectability both to apparently old-fashioned scientific, positivist ideas (incarnated in the fading image of Durkheim) and to the sociology of knowledge and the social history of ideas. Thus, in an effort to combat ahistorical rationalism by founding a historical science of historical reason (complete with the idea of 'genealogy' and a notion like that of the *episteme*), Foucault was thought to be contributing to a movement which, when viewed from Germany, where Nietzsche had a totally different meaning, appeared to be a restoration of irrationality, against which Habermas, among others (like Karl-Otto Apel, for instance), set up his whole philosophical project.

The opposition is considerably less radical than it first seems, between, on the one hand, the rationalist and historicist approach that I pursue (with the idea of a social history of reason, or of the scientific field, as the place of the historical genesis of the social conditions for the production of reason) and, on the other hand, a neo-Kantian rationalism, which attempts to transform itself into a scientific sort of reason by basing itself on linguistic arguments, as in Habermas and Apel. A rationalist relativism and a sort of enlightened absolutism can be of great mutual assistance in the defence of the *Aufklärung*,[19] perhaps because they express the same intention through another system of thought. Of course, I exaggerate a little here. But I do believe that these differences are not as great as they have long been imagined to be, by people who fail to take account of the deforming prism effects (as much on production as on reception) generated by the national intellectual fields and their imposition of categories of perception and thought.

This is why today's direct discussions (which constitute already an advance on the earlier period, when European scholars communicated only through an interposed America) so often remain artificial and unreal: the effects of *allodoxia* resulting from the structural mismatch between contexts provide inexhaustible resources for the polemics of bad faith and the mutual condemnations of self-righteousness in which mediocre and irresponsible essayists, such as the inventors of the myth of 'la pensée 68'[20] or the righteous denunciators of 'cynicism', excel. One could think of the propensity of petty intellectuals to set themselves up as vigilantes, or, more accurately, as Fouquier-Tinville[21] and Zhdanov,[22] on the right or on the left, who, as we saw in connection with the 'Heidegger affair',[23] replace the logic of critical discussion, committed to understanding the reasons – or causes – for opposing thought, with the logic of the trial.

The logical *Realpolitik*[24] of which I am a ceaseless advocate must above all have as its aim an intention to work towards the creation of social conditions permitting a rational dialogue. In this context, this means working at raising awareness and knowledge of the ways in which different national fields function, for the greater the ignorance of the original context, the higher the risk that the text will be used in a different sense. This project will only appear banal so long as we fail to enter into the details of its realization. The aim must be to produce a scientific knowledge of the national fields of production and of the national categories of thought that originate there, and to diffuse this knowledge as widely as possible, notably by ensuring that it forms a component of studies of foreign languages, civilizations and philosophies. To give an idea of the difficulty of the enterprise, one could do worse than begin by examining the attitudes to be found among specialists in these fields. All too often, the so-called specialists in international exchanges have developed their own private sociologies to explain differences between national traditions. Germanists and

Romance-language specialists, for example, constantly produce and reproduce views which have their basis in ill-thought-out half-truths: people who 'know them pretty well', 'who aren't so easy fooled,' who 'find them awful, but love them all the same'. Such convictions are particularly common among specialists of foreign civilizations (like 'orientalists' or 'japanologists') and betray attitudes which result in a sort of condescending amusement which is ultimately quite close to racism.

Freedom regarding national categories of thought – through which we think about the differences between the products of these categories – can result only from a sustained effort to think out those categories and render them quite explicit. It can only come from a social history and a reflexive sociology which would be critical in the Kantian sense, whose goal would be a scientific socio-analysis to illuminate the structure of a national cultural unconscious. Through a rigorous historical anamnesis of the different national histories, and above all through a history of the educational institutions and the fields of cultural production, it would unveil the historical foundations of various categories of thought, and the problematic areas that social actors unwittingly reveal ('it is history which is the true unconscious' as Durkheim said[25]) through acts of cultural reception or production.

Nothing is more urgent than to undertake a comparative history of the different disciplines, along the lines of what has been done for ethnology under the direction of Isaac Chiva and Utz Jeggle.[26] Indeed, only a comparative history of the social sciences can liberate us from the modes of thought inherited from history, by providing the means to ensure a conscious mastery of scholastic forms of classification, of the unthought categories of thought, and of obligatory problematics. As one clearly sees in the case of anthropology, comparison makes everything that was held to be necessary appear arbitrary or tied to the context of a contingent tradition: the very words ethnology or *Volkskunde*, which designate the discipline, are laden with a whole past of implicit traditions, which means that these two theoretically equivalent terms are separated by the entire history of the two fields. An adequate understanding of the objects and programmes of research undertaken in these two disciplines would enable us to understand the entire history of the relationship they have maintained with the political field, and which is encapsulated in the difference between the French 'populaire' (Musée des arts et traditions populaires) and the German *Volk* or *völkisch*,[27] between a tradition of the left, linked to the State and defended against a right-wing tradition, devoted to folklore and the people in the manner of Le Play,[28] and, on the other hand, a

58 *Imperialisms*

conservative tradition, identifying the people with the nation and the *Heimat*[29] or the peasant *Gemeinschaft*.[30] It would also mean understanding the discipline's position in the nation's hierarchical space of disciplines: in France, on the side of the positive sciences, somewhat despised; in Germany, on the side of German Studies ('germanistique'). And it would mean examining all the differences that arise from these principal oppositions.

The teaching system is one of the places where, in differentiated societies, systems of thought[31] are produced and reproduced. It is the equivalent, albeit more refined, of the 'primitive forms of classification' that Durkheim and Mauss, as consistent Kantians, inventoried for societies lacking writing or teaching institutions.[32] The structural oppositions between dry and wet, east and west, cooked and uncooked, listed in the table of categories of so-called 'archaic' understanding, correspond to the oppositions between explaining and understanding, or between quantity and quality, which the collective history of an educational system and the individual history of a school career have deposited in the cultivated understanding of each of the completed products of the educational system.

These systems of opposition include invariants (such as the oppositions mentioned above, which through a philosophical teaching deeply dominated by the German tradition – in which, if we are to believe Fritz Ringer,[33] they were constituted – have penetrated French teaching); they also include national variations. Or, to be more precise, the dominant traditions in each nation can give inverse values to the terms of the same oppositions, as for example to all the secondary oppositions that gravitate around the central opposition, so important in German academic thought, at least until the Second World War, between *Kultur* and *Civilisation*, and which serve to distinguish the noble and authentic Germanic tradition from the adulterated and superficial French tradition: the opposition, precisely, between the profound or serious and the brilliant or superficial, or the opposition between content and form, between thought or feeling and style or wit, between philosophy or philology and literature, and so on.[34] An opposition that France's dominant tradition (which reconciled Henri IV's *hypokhâgne*, the heart of the school system, with Alain and Valéry's *La NRF*[35]) took up, but reversed the signs: depth became heaviness, the serious became scholastic pedantry, and the superficial became French clarity. You need to bear all this in mind to understand that Heidegger is a close approximation of Alain, and vice versa, whereas the former may have been perceived and used in France as the perfect antithesis of the latter.

The International Circulation of Ideas 59

And in fact, by one of those tricks of historical reason that make access to intellectual freedom so difficult, the mythical opposition between the two traditions, German and French, was as much imposed on those who rebelled against it in each country as it was on those who naively took it up on their own account, on those who intended to find a form of freedom from imposed forms of thought by simply reversing the sign of the dominant opposition, accepted as it was by satisfied nationalists. Thus, throughout the nineteenth century in Germany, and even today (how else can we explain the success of certain post-modernists?), many young progressive intellectuals sought in French thought the antidote to everything they detested in German thought, while young progressive French intellectuals did the same in the other direction – which left little chance of meeting each other along the way.

If there is no question of denying the existence of profound intellectual nationalisms, based on what are perceived as important intellectual national interests, there is also a less obvious point worth noting. The international struggles for domination in cultural matters and for the imposition of the dominant principle of domination – I mean by this the imposing of a particular definition of the legitimate exercise of intellectual activity, for example the German valorization of ideas of *Kultur*, depth, philosophical content, etc., over what they saw as the French stress on *Civilisation*, clarity, literature, etc. – inevitably find their roots in the struggles within each national field, in struggles where the dominant national definition and the foreign definition are themselves involved. They are not simply arms in a struggle but are also themselves stakes of a struggle.

We can say why such conditions make philosophical confusion and misunderstandings more the rule than the exception in the international scene, as another example could show. A considerable amount of intellectual independence and theoretical lucidity is necessary to understand that Durkheim, revolting against a dominant intellectual order which included men like Bergson, is actually in the same camp as Cassirer (who in *The Myth of the State*[36] made an explicit link between his 'symbolic forms' and Durkheim's 'primitive forms of classification'), while Cassirer was a target against whom Heidegger developed a variation of Bergsonian *Lebensphilosophie*.[37] One could multiply almost indefinitely such chiastic effects, which, by favouring alliances or rejections equally based on misunderstanding, work to prevent or minimize the accumulation of the historical assets of the internationalization (or the denationalization) of the categories of thought, which is the primary condition for a true intellectual universalism.

Translated by Richard Shusterman

UNTRANSLATABLE

Like people, nations are separated from one another by their history, and also by their present interests, often connected with this history. Volker Braun's *Iphigenia* bears witness to this profound alienation, which sometimes borders on the incommunicable: far from the vaguely conciliatory considerations generated by ritual encounters where the inevitable representatives of the different European nations come to profess their ecumenical convictions, this obscure text, sometimes as opaque as anything by Aristophanes, comes to remind all of us, whether without or within reunified Germany, lest we forget, of everything that each tradition owes to its singular history and its more or less universalized internal references (here Goethe and Brecht, etc.), with its past or present debates, and the text even does so in the very form used, a cryptic language that has survived its long apprenticeship in the art of cheating the censors.

Accustomed for many years to the kind of covert comprehension that we glean from texts proclaimed as universal as a direct effect of this factitious comprehension – and among which we must include the most universally recognized classics, from Homer to Marx, who spoke rashly of 'the eternal charm of Greek art', or from Chekhov to Joyce and Beckett – we no longer know how to handle the historical opacity of such works and of those who produced them. And when sometimes we are confronted by it, in the form perhaps of the *untranslatable*, our immediate reaction is to dissipate it, in the name of 'respect for difference', our fashionable variant of the taste for 'toleration' dear to Enlightenment philosophers. And yet this indulgent acceptance of lifestyles or practices tacitly considered unpleasant or blameworthy, which always implies a certain condescension, is far from genuine comprehension, which supposes knowledge and acknowledgement of the historical foundations of the difference: here this is affirmed in the confrontation of viewpoints on the historical reality of Germany, whose reunification obliges us more than ever to experience the divisions that partition for more than a generation has inscribed lastingly in people's social and mental structures. Volker Braun is right: Germany is the country that, like the house of Atreus, is forever separate from others and divided against itself by the history of its misfortune and its crimes. Like all countries. But at least this one is aware of it.

This note by P. Bourdieu appeared in Liber, *10 June 1992, p. 2.*
Translated by Peter Collier

2.2

Programme for a Sociology of the International Circulation of Cultural Works

The method

I would like to spell out some guidelines for our procedure. As most of you know, this meeting is not an ordinary colloquium.[1] It is not about presenting formal exposés before eminent colleagues, but about trying to explore a largely uncharted terrain together. The mode of exposition and the style of speaking must match our intellectual intentions: we should speak without preamble and without oratory precautions, briefly and informally. Those of you who are not specialists in the problems that we are to discuss – which is the case for most of you: I don't know if there are any specialists, since the problem is fairly new – should not feel inhibited by any kind of collective censorship. You should just say whatever the topic has inspired you to think. (. . .) The main intention of this meeting, then, is to elaborate the problems, and establish a research programme. Research into international problems is terribly under-developed, for so many reasons. One way to help bring it into being is to place in the same room, for a certain period of time, a certain number of people who will be invited to think about the problems that they find in their own country, while listening to the others speaking of theirs: it is a process of practical comparatism. The thoughts provoked by this confrontation need to be expressed, however imperfect or provisional the form of that expression may be. (. . .)

The starting point of this meeting is a recent encounter I had with Joseph Jurt in Freiburg, where I had been invited to speak on the occasion of the creation of an institute devoted to France.[2] We had started to elaborate a little on the problem of the international circulation of works and ideas, etc. We had expressed the idea that the problem was too little studied or in any case studied in fragments and never as a

62   *Imperialisms*

whole subject. And we formed the project of this colloquium bearing in mind the definition that I have just formulated.

The global objective: to construct an object of study that you might call 'cultural import/export', or 'the field of international cultural relations', or again, 'the logic of the international circulation of works'. In my opinion this object needs to be constructed, although as soon as we start, we shall find that there is a whole pile of material ready and waiting to be used. For there is traditional research on the circulation of translations, students, professors and grants, etc., a whole lot of research that we can draw on as soon as the object of study is constructed.

Taking stock

As a first move, we need to take stock. Our enterprise includes a descriptive phase: we need to report on the current state of exchanges in a country, and to do that we need to find helpful indicators enabling us to measure the flow in each direction, etc. Obviously we think immediately of the translations that we need to analyse in detail by categories (human sciences, literature, natural sciences, etc.) and by country. In France there are already statistics for this problem by category and by country, but we don't have double cross tabulation.

We need to take stock of the statistics available and, observing best practice, record the indispensable information on the conditions regulating the establishment of these statistics (who designed them, how, under what conditions, customs records, etc.). This preliminary critical work is indispensable if we are to avoid comparing things that are not comparable when constructed according to different principles. In international research, nine times out of ten it all falls apart as soon as you compare statistics, if you haven't done this critical work.

We need to interpret these flows and try to understand their principles, and this will be the second phase; but obviously the two phases will constantly intermingle when we are discussing the mechanisms involved. Having drawn up a balance sheet using a certain number of indicators, we can start to look for the mechanisms that explain things. Following the same logic, we could proceed to compare non-national pantheons of authors in order to see – either on the level of the whole history of a country or at least for the postwar period – who are, for example, the German authors most translated into Italian and French, etc.

Another indicator of international exchanges: the translators, their number, their status, and, more precisely, their material and symbolic remuneration. How are they paid in theory and in practice? Do their names figure on the cover or the title page, etc.? Do authors who quote translations give the translators' names? Are some translators famous? Do famous authors publish translations? How professional are the translators (are they academics or full-time translators)? Do they belong to a trade union or an association? Are there regulations controlling access to the profession, etc.? We would also need to analyse State subsidies for translation, in both directions.

Another indicator: the existence of critics specializing in a [foreign] nation's books. What place is reserved for them (relative prestige compared to that assigned to critics of national works)? Are foreign books reviewed as soon as they appear in their native language, or do the reviews start to come in only when the works enter the national market in translation? Are there channels devoted to non-national works (publishers, specialized reviews)?

The search for mechanisms (1): national field and international field

Does an international field exist? Does it exist to the same degree in the different domains? For instance, in mathematics there is undoubtedly a unified field, but, at the other extreme, does one exist to the same degree in law? The case of sociology is interesting,[3] because it is doubtless situated between the two poles, but more on the side of law, because of the connections that link the issues raised by sociologists and their methodology to the national political conditions; [nevertheless] there are effects of imperialism and domination that may still be operative. (One of the surest indicators of the degree of internationalism of a scientific discipline might be the degree to which its producers are obliged to use an international language, today English.)

Where a field does exist, we can observe field effects: In what ways does the (international) field have determining effects on the producers (e.g. making one publisher take on an author to prevent another from having him)? What is the relationship between the national subfield and the international field? What is the relative autonomy of the national field within the international field? How is it secured? By a conscious and intentional protectionism or by the fact of the inertia linked to the workings of the academic institution; or, again, by the isolating effect exercised by the language (which would be the difference between France and England in their relations with the United States)?

64 *Imperialisms*

We need to reserve a particular place for the great transnational linguistic markets, anglophone of course, but also francophone, with the Belgian Walloons, the francophone Swiss and the Quebeckers: in these cases, we can measure the effects of the purely national logic (academies, national cultural institutions such as theatres, for example) in relation to the forces of the linguistic and cultural transnational field. The cases of Belgium and Switzerland, linguistically and culturally divided, with each linguistic and cultural zone obliged to refer to an external legitimacy (the Walloons to France, the Flemish to Holland), present a sort of experimental situation: can the State effects counteract the field effects? It's the same for Quebec, subject to an effect of *double domination*, with the United States on one side and France on the other, and able (or obliged) to use one domination to counteract the other.

We could analyse in the same perspective the relations of domination at the heart of the greater Hispanic area: the effects of linguistic nationalism that may give Spain an opportunity for *symbolic aggrandizement*, or enlargement (they can annex a South American Nobel Prize in the name of linguistic unity).

If we admit that there is a field, what are the field effects that act on the circulation of works? We can speak of symbolic power relations which make certain nations statutorily dominant in certain markets, so that certain writers are 'in a conquered land' in certain markets, while others must single-handedly fight veritable campaigns to 'conquer the market'. (I am thinking of the young American historian who, after a 'tour' of France in the 1970s, told me that the French historians welcomed him with respect and consideration, and slipped offprints of their works under his hotel door at night, etc.) Insofar as they belong to a more or less globally prestigious nation, each author shares in the specific *national symbolic capital* of their nation (which may vary according to the discipline: literature, science, human sciences, etc.).

The search for mechanisms (2): the accumulation of national symbolic capital

How does this symbolic capital accrete? In general it comes from afar: there are all kinds of trailblazers. And we should draw up a map of the main cultural pathways, for example the great traditional highroads of literature and sociology. I think of Auguste Comte, who opened the way in Brazil for the interwar historians and ethnologists, Braudel,

Bastide and Lévi-Strauss, who in their turn opened the way for the philosophers and sociologists of the 1970s, etc. It goes without saying that a number of these well-trodden routes are often the lasting result of linguistic and cultural colonization (between France and the countries of the Maghreb or black Africa, between England and the Indies, between Spain and Latin America). But we also need to ask how and why they continue, and in whose interest they do so.

How should we measure a symbolic national capital? In fact, we should take into account and agglomerate the whole range of specific capitals, literary, scientific, etc., which may or may not be correlated, each country having its *own profile* of national cultural capital (e.g. we might think that France would have a histogram with a very high bar for its literary and artistic capital, a medium-sized one for its capital in social sciences and a low one for scientific capital). The symbolic value attributed to a nation and a national language varies according to the field: for instance, throughout the nineteenth century, French remained the language of the arts and literature – which even today very often makes it the prerogative of women, as in Japan – while English was the language of trade. Our spontaneous intuition of the 'cultural weight' of a particular country is no doubt an intuition of the volume and structure of the symbolic capital that it possesses.

We need to find indicators, proceeding no doubt as I did some years ago[4] when I wanted to construct the indices of national cultural capital in painting, which were indispensable in giving an account of the national differences recorded, other things being equal, in the cultural practice of visiting museums. We might think of the number of Nobel Prizes (in literature and other disciplines), the flows of translation, and the contribution of foreign authors, etc. In fact, symbolic capital is a *fact of belief* (think of the economists' 'speculative bubbles'); the critics, then, doubtless play a decisive part in establishing and maintaining it (we think something is important because a lot of important people think and say that it is important: cf. the 'reputational method' of the sociologists of power); more generally, the literary and artistic but also the scientific worlds obey this reputational logic, that of the mutual admiration society, of networks of reciprocal consecration, of 'invisible colleges',[5] etc. But the critics are capital, because it is they who help to constitute something's *importance* (submitting consciously or unconsciously to the prevailing state of symbolic power relations: it is likely that they won't discuss a Bulgarian novelist in the way they would a German novelist; there are contamination effects). The symbolic power relations do more than structure the strategies of the agents (authors and critics, etc.); they are also a focus of individual and

66   *Imperialisms*

collective struggles (see Guilbaut's book on the transfer of domination in painting from Paris to New York[6]).

The search for mechanisms (3):
the agents of import/export

We should analyse the whole set of agents engaged in these struggles (the active participants): the State with its cultural policies to protect national production and aid exports (here analysing also the recruitment and training of the agents of cultural exportation), not forgetting the role of associations or foundations (cf. the role of American foundations in the dissemination of American social sciences after the Second World War[7]); the dealers or the publishers; the professors and all the educational institutions; the critics and the writers, etc. In describing the international space, we need to distinguish exportation from importation, because the two sets of agents are not identical (although in the publishing houses, for example, the same agents are employed for the sale and purchase of rights[8]), or, at least, they do not follow the same operational logic. Thus the State does not behave in the same way at all towards importation as it does towards exportation. On the one hand, then, the *agents of exportation*: agents of the State or of semi-official agencies that support exportation (DAAD for Germany,[9] which provides support for translation, e.g. translations into French of the major German scholars of Romance studies: Auerbach, Spitzer); cultural institutes and agencies; lectures and lecturers, etc.; publishers (sale of rights, copublication). On the other hand, the *agents of importation*: firstly the trade professionals (books are commodities and economic considerations doubtless weigh heavily in their choice – this to correct my Freiburg paper which foregrounded the intellectual motives of choice[10]), those in charge of foreign rights (often women and of foreign origin).

How are these selectors selected? How are they trained? Where do they get their categories of perception of foreign literature from, their *national stereotypes* of literature? These are questions that need to be specified by domain, genre and discipline, etc. We might suppose that Brazilian authors who conform to the stereotype of Brazilian literature would cross the frontier of translation more easily than those who differ (even if they do so with the intention of cleaving closer to the model of the national literature of the country importing them). The differential reception in France of Walloon writers as opposed to Walloons following the fashion for Flemish 'regionalism' is typical of this 'misunderstanding'. It may thus happen that writers who claim to be regionalist in their own country are perceived and welcomed as being more 'universal'. And we should therefore submit this notion of *universal literature* to scrutiny. If what the Germans like most in France is what appears most exotic to them, and vice versa, then a universal literature could be a meeting point for exotic extremes. But things are doubtless more complicated.

To this we should add the series editors (who are often members of international networks), the selection committees and the translators, who often have a monopoly of access to the original book and its discovery, etc. Publishing decisions are the outcome of very complex collective procedures, even if there is no selection committee. The selection committees may be institutionalized or not, their proceedings more or less codified. But what is certain is that, even in those cases where institutionalization is weakest, there is still a more or less widespread network of advisers and consultants. In each case, we should seek to find the specific interests that lead each of these categories of agents to favour the translation and publication of certain works, and to give them precedence over others. In this context we should pay particular attention to the cosmopolitans, who are the privileged agents of circulation (and take particular note of members of transnational political or religious organizations, such as the Communist Party or the Roman Catholic Church, for instance), and to the émigrés who can transfer their original skills to sell them on another market. In short, we should determine who has an *interest in the foreign*, and in importing from abroad, who has an *interest in the international*.

There is a case for examining how the State regulates its international cultural relations, in particular in matters of importation: What are its criteria for choosing between the possible borrowings? It may for instance make selective use of foreign products in order to compose a national identity (this is often the case with new nations, who may go for the option of eclecticism to avoid domination by a single country).

The search for mechanisms (4): the strategies in the international field

We may suppose that the position of each of these agents in the structure of their national field helps to orient their strategies in the international field. For example, a small publisher has an economic interest in launching foreign authors: since the cost of acquisition of the rights is relatively low, they can build a reserve of famous authors

68 *Imperialisms*

in a shorter time and at lower cost than that involved in discovering young national authors (e.g. in France: Actes Sud, Rivages, Quai Voltaire, Christian Bourgois).[11] In general, we would need to establish the connections that link the strategies of different publishers in publishing foreign authors with the position that they hold in the field. And likewise for the authors: Do they behave as imitators of the dominant models (cf. the European sociologists who act as sales representatives for the dominant sociology of the United States) or do they go in for resistance? Do they practise a selective, liberating borrowing, either from the dominator or from other dominated agents (like the African writers who claim allegiance to the South American model)?

We should also examine the mechanisms designed to ensure the reproduction of the structures of the international field, the structural factors of inertia that tend to perpetuate relations of domination. Here we should note *the role played by the infrastructure specific to the field of cultural reproduction*, that is, the University, which is the producer of the producers and consumers. In the specific infrastructure of literature in particular, there is the language, which is doubtless one of the principal factors of the unity of the field. But there is above all the national university, which is the source of the production and reproduction of the producers and consumers of national culture, and makes an essential contribution, through the teaching of languages in particular, to the assimilation of foreign works. This is where we need to study the teaching of foreign languages and the place reserved for them in the syllabus and the timetable, etc. (cf. Picht's thesis),[12] and, at the same time, the interests involved in the mastery of a foreign language and culture.

The possession of a linguistic capital is the basis of a lasting interest in and attachment to the very existence of a foreign culture; it is accompanied by an openness for cultural models, and institutional ones in particular (the nineteenth-century German style of seminar). There is a sort of structural inertia in the relation to foreign languages which results in particular from the fact that the holders of transnational linguistic and cultural competence work, most often entirely in good faith, to perpetuate the conditions favourable to ensuring a satisfactory return on their investment, maintaining teaching commitments, defending the culture of their chosen country, translations, etc.; their attachment is maintained at least during their lifetime, and it is not unusual for them to transmit it to their offspring (there is a hereditary Germanophobia or Francophilia). There are also the effects of *hysteresis* which affect the presentations of foreign countries; this is the result of very diverse factors, such as the fact that information wanes with distance travelled while magical admiration (*e longinquo reverentia*) waxes; or the fact, already very apparent in international circulation, that articles have a more restricted circulation (limited to *the realm of specialists*) than books, and are much less translated than the latter.

We should use the same logic to study all the transnational migrations of an academic nature: circulation of professors, lecturers and students (Fulbright scholarships, etc.). We should study the cosmopolitan figures (polyglot and polycultural), the voluntary émigrés who are spontaneous importers, and the forced émigrés who are proselytes by vocation, because it is for them a way of recouping their capital.

Nationalism and internationalism

One of the functions of research is also to direct action. From an analysis of the functioning of the international fields we may derive the principles of a policy of internationalization, the foundations of a methodical internationalism. I also think that in principle intellectual life gains from being as international as possible. However, in the current state of affairs, culture and language unite those who share them, but do so by separating them from others. Which means that analysing obstacles to circulation, such as the factors motivating protectionism and isolationism, etc., seems to me to make a positive contribution to internationalizing intellectual life and establishing conditions favouring a genuine cultural cosmopolitanism.[13]

I am struck by the tight bonds that unite on the one hand the formation of the State and on the other hand the establishment of a national language and literature (and also, in the nineteenth century above all, of a national social science, often thought of as bound to contribute to the construction and management of the nation). I think that writers are among those most responsible for nationalism – an educated, well-bred nationalism, of course, which only makes it the more pernicious. It is in fact subtly diffused in the schools, in the guise of the cult of our national literature (for those in any doubt, I recommend reading the positions taken up only recently by our writers, ranging from d'Ormesson to Sollers, on French spelling).[14] Recently I read two texts on Paris written by Valéry,[15] which are a perfect illustration of this literary patriotism and nationalism, which needs to be analysed and understood, in the hope, perhaps, of uprooting it.

In order to communicate the force of this intimate communion in a shared literary culture, I would like to invoke a literary anecdote: there are two lovers, German of course, it's raining, they are melancholy,

70 *Imperialisms*

and they express the ultimate depths of their feelings by saying the single word 'Klopstock'.[16] There are these extreme emotions which can only be expressed through a reference to something which is part of the national heritage. We need to realize that when we work on literature we are dealing with things of this type, ineffable, intimate, sacred, untouchable. Literature makes a very considerable contribution to the construction of the *national cultural unconscious* (following this logic, we should study children's books). But there is no contradiction in saying that at the same time the reference to the foreign (positive in the case of borrowings, or negative where there is rejection, as between France and Germany) can be a determining element in the construction of a national identity. As both weapon and target in national struggles, the foreign fulfils all sorts of functions, that of the principle of legitimization (we often suppose that consecration by the foreign is more 'universal', closer to the viewpoint of posterity), or that of instrument of criticism and defamiliarization (the dominated in a national field – avant-garde publishers and writers, etc. – can borrow from foreign models that allow them to challenge the national orthodoxy), by acting as a repellent (Revolutionary France for England), or as a source of profits associated with the overt or covert (plagiaristic) borrowing authorized by a linguistic monopoly or by the (outright) monopoly of importation, etc.

Finally, we should approach the problem of all the misunderstandings linked to the *gap between the field of production and the field of reception*, and to the fact that texts circulate without their context, often with considerable delay – which means that a *temporal slippage* comes to aggravate the cultural slippage. I may say in passing that the creation of *Liber*[17] was basically inspired by the intention to reduce both forms of gap at once, by unifying the space of discussion (and therefore the problematics involved) and by synchronizing the intellectual debates which today in the different countries are often mistimed and misinterpreted when they happen. The fact that works circulate with a delay has very important effects and forms a considerable obstacle to the unification of the space of discussion: the implicit references (in a discussion of, say, positivism, historicism or postmodernism) are profoundly different, to a large extent because the spaces of position-takings, which provide implicit guidelines for individual standpoints, are profoundly different from one country to another, causing formidable misunderstandings. Among the aims of the sociological work that we are undertaking, there may be, in addition to the scientific aims, that of contributing to the unification of the intellectual field, and thereby of the problematics concerned.

Programme for a Sociology...

We should in fact admit that most often what we know and like from abroad are *artefacts* produced in and by the two gaps that I have indicated. The re-creations thus created can doubtless be liberating, and I would dare say universalizing (I think of the rereading of Nietzsche in France in the 1960s,[18] or the rereading of Weber in the same period);[19] they can make these works attain a higher degree of universality by stripping them of all connotations linked to their national and historical roots, by bathing them in a gaze cleansed of all the pre-notions and prejudices born of familiarity with the social and political position of the author or the social usages that their work has been subjected to, or the more or less unjust representation that its opponents or enemies have made of it. Being less directly in competition with the author and equally being freer from the *specifically social* constraints of the national field – in particular from the authority effect – the foreigners are, paradoxically, often able to deliver a more 'comprehensive' judgement than the natives, despite the effects of the twofold gap.

I have spoken in defence of creative misunderstanding, but the *structural misunderstanding* resulting from the twofold gap is no doubt most often *destructive*. It is not certain that it is the best works that circulate easily and most rapidly (witness the differential reception of Sombart and Weber in France),[20] and we might think that, even more than in the national market, the fast-circulating works that match the expectations (or prejudices) of the 'gatekeepers', not to mention works deliberately prepared for international circulation (as in the cinema), circulate more freely than difficult works closely connected – in the best cases – with the historical achievements of their historical tradition. It is not certain that the universal culture of tomorrow should be made up of those international *best-sellers* which are the universal precisely because they ignore particular problems; and we might simply hope that a better knowledge of the mechanisms of the international circulation of works could help to bring to universal attention works which, despite their structural *allodoxia*, and although laden and even overburdened with particular issues, have only been able to gain and express the share of the universal that they have to offer to humankind through the particular and even bizarre aspects of a historical situation.

FINAL DISCUSSION

I would like to thank all the participants. I have been impressed by the quality of the work they have accomplished in so little time, without being specialists in this domain (since this domain does not exist, there can be no specialists), collecting statistics and information, etc. I think that one of the objectives which I had in mind, that is, a fairly systematic review of current data, has been successfully achieved. One disadvantage of the formula: some years ago I proposed the creation of these short seminars with the idea that, as opposed to those colloquia where it is often said that what is most interesting is what happens in the intervals between sessions, we could have colloquia where there would be no intervals. But for that kind of seminar to work, and for us to accomplish in two days what sometimes is not resolved in a week of rather tedious colloquium papers, for the formula to be perfectly efficacious, the papers would have to be submitted in advance, for everyone to read them, so that the speakers would speak for ten minutes or a quarter of an hour, to repeat the gist of what they had written and stimulate debate. Knowing that the others had read you, you could even discuss something quite different, in a kind of metadiscourse, saying things that you didn't dare write, to engage a lively debate. Here we have been somewhat frustrated, because it was indispensable to gather and accumulate the information in the first place, which was only possible at the expense of some of the discussion.

Second point: It seems to me that the contributions have expanded the area of debate. Everyone has constructed their object of study as they saw fit, and I think that certain communications, like that of Martin Chalmers, for instance,[21] have situated the rather limited problems of translation in a sort of global cultural geopolitical sphere. They have reminded us that we cannot separate cultural politics and translation policies from the totality of the political problems that confront modern societies; whereas when we specialize, for instance in the problem of the circulation of translations or the problem of reception, we tend to limit ourselves to the purely literary dimension, as if it were possible to treat it as completely autonomous. In several of the analyses of national situations – I think of the Brazilian, Romanian, Hungarian or Greek cases – we see clearly how the politics of the State goes hand in hand with cultural politics and how, in particular in the cases of Romania and Brazil, we cannot understand the construction of a national culture without taking into account the national usage of the international. (. . .)

A question (not transcribed) from Agnès Renyi[22] on the problem of the third world and the specific domination of the third world by East European countries. Bourdieu continues:

I would emphasize what you have said even more strongly, to try to give it a more general application. The first point is very important and, in the case of Hungary, is plain to see: not only because you know how to look, but also because it is more apparent in this particular case. This is another property of international collaboration: we take the same object of study, but there are some places where it is easier to read. And the question that looms in one country can be immediately raised in other countries. There is a monopoly of the international, and just as the religious field is the site of a struggle for the monopoly of the legitimate appropriation of religious goods, so the international field is the site of a struggle for the legitimate appropriation of the legitimate usage of the international, to see who has the right to translate, who has the right to say which foreign products are good, to say that in the United States the three sociologists who matter are X, Y and Z.[23] Who can say this with some chance of being heard? This monopoly of the international is unevenly distributed. It is linked to linguistic competence, and the ability to travel – two things which are in any case linked; it is linked to the ability to travel when young, in childhood, therefore linked to social class. Which has important consequences: not everyone can choose to be a cosmopolitan. Which makes cosmopolitanism and internationalism somewhat ambiguous. The knee-jerk reaction (and reactionary forms) of nationalism which, like Hungarian populism, are rooted in a rejection of internationalism, are understandable, however inexcusable. They constitute one of the defences of the dominated in the intellectual field. The likelihood of speaking a foreign language is one of the properties most strongly linked with social milieu. Which means that there is a very strong bias in international exchanges.

The great cosmopolitan writers are almost inevitably scions of the most privileged milieux. There is a cosmopolitanism *de luxe* which we should not confuse with the internationalism of the poor. I think that one of the fundamental principles of intellectual divisions, one of the most important variables for understanding the position of an intellectual in the intellectual field, is their access to the international market, and, more precisely, the form of this access. Which countries do they visit? Do they travel East or West? For these properties are strongly linked to very persistent social characteristics, such as class accents which outlive cultural realignment, or shyness, with the fear of speaking in public, especially in a foreign language. There are people who manage to have an international existence simply because they were born in the right milieu, because they speak foreign languages. I am thinking of some Brazilian examples, but you could find some in every country. There are people who exist in the international market only because they know how to export themselves; they may have little to export, but they export it everywhere.

Interventions (not transcribed) by Afranio Garcia, Mihai Gheorghiu, Martin Chalmers, Yves Winkin. Bourdieu responds:

The problem of internal exile is raised in connection with academic or *freelance* translators. It is often said of ethnologists that they go abroad because they are ill at ease in their own society. We should try to understand in this perspective the choice of being a translator, translation as a refuge, internal exile in tyrannical countries . . .

The benefits of this 'international capital' depend a lot on the structure of the national field, which changes over time. For instance, thirty years ago in France, the fact of being international was doubtless not very positive. If people exported themselves, it was really because they had not found a place for themselves in Paris, which they thought was the best place in the world. So what were they going to do somewhere else? We can understand in this perspective certain borrowings from abroad. I am thinking of linguistics; it is a special case, but I think that it helps us to understand many things. Philology was a typically national science; it was not very old, it had been created in the nineteenth century after the German model, but it was considered the heart of the French university, with the *agrégation* in grammar. The people who did philology were at the absolute peak (alongside philosophy). Then linguistics arrived. Who did linguistics? People like Martinet,[24] who were extremely low, seen from the viewpoint of the national hierarchy – Anglicists, poverty stricken in terms of national values. For this reason, they could import the international. I say this to remind you that the benefits of the international vary according to the state of the field and the position of the field of the national specialism in the international field. At the moment, we are seeing a kind of inversion: it seems to me that we are tending now to over-value the international.

Marie-France Garcia: In the case of Brazil, to move to France is reactionary, because it is a dominant country. Bourdieu's reply:

One of the important variables is the degree of autonomy of the scientific field from the political field. The political field helps to define the relative value of the different nations in their international relations.

2.3

Does Belgian Literature Exist?
The Limits of a Field and Political Frontiers[1]

The whole question lies in the wording: Should we say Belgian literature or 'Belgian' literature, French-language Belgian literature or French literature from Belgium? This debate asks the key question: Does Belgian literature exist?

This problem interests almost exclusively writers of Belgian nationality, whose attitude depends on the position that they hold within the French field: for everything seems to indicate that they are all the more inclined to defend the idea that the literature produced by Belgian writers is an integral part of French literature, the more recognized in the French field they are (this can be seen for instance in the argument that opposed the nationalist journal *L'Art moderne* to the *Groupe du lundi*, the journal of Charles Plisnier and Grégoire Le Roy, among others[2]). It all seemed to show that any writer of Belgian nationality (like any writer from provincial France) was caught hesitating between two strategies, and therefore two literary identities: a strategy of identification with the dominant literature or a strategy of retreating into the national market and claiming Belgian identity. The second strategy becomes the more imperative, the more the chances of success in the first diminish.

Another index of heteronomy: Belgian writers dispose of a whole set of specific institutions – publishers, reviews and theatres – but they do not have their own *specific institutions of consecration* (Ghelderode, for instance, had to wait for one of his plays to be produced in Paris at the Théâtre de l'Oeuvre before he was recognized in Belgium), as if the writers and the educated public did not believe in their own national institutions, that is, in the value of their judgements. We can understand that, under these conditions, writers recognized by the only acknowledged institutions, the Parisian ones, show no interest in the creation of a field with a national (or local) base. We can also understand that the debates and movements and the like remain very strictly 'under the influence': the dependence is in the structures but it is also present in the mind, and it is this that, as one commentator says, 'discourages the publishers, anaesthetizes the critics, paralyses the theatrical producers and drives the best talents into exile'.

The French-language writers of Belgian nationality are thus faced with the alternative of identifying with the dominant model – which, when successful, deprives them of their national identity – or being excluded in alterity. A purely negative alterity, a simply diminished being, in the case of the Walloons who, although dominant (at least until recently) among the national writers, and bound to reproduce the opposition between France and Belgium in their confrontation with the Flemish, are dominated in the field of French literature. Proud of their share of 'French virtues' (such as 'musicality', 'sensibility', 'delicacy' and a 'sense of nuance'), they affirm their superiority over the Flemish (seen as 'colourist', 'materialist' and 'instinctive'), but they find themselves rejected in the name of a similar opposition, that of body and soul, by the Parisian world which treats them as pale, provincial imitators or foreign barbarians.[3] And all this with less chance than the Flemish, who are doubly dominated by the Walloons (and the French) as well as the Dutch, of being able to take refuge in an assumed alterity (paradoxically, the Belgian writers 'best known' – as Belgian – are in fact nearly all Flemish). This alterity can in fact be positively configured, as a fertile difference, at the expense of a change of sign which transforms the barbarism and roughness of the provincial or the foreigner into literary exoticism. It is once again the logic of the French field that creates the Flemish writers, and it is through and in relation to this logic that a Verhaeren, a Maeterlinck or a Ghelderode, for instance, who were sufficiently integrated into the French field to be alert to the inferior status of the Dutch field (at least at that time), are established and establish themselves as both recognized – as symbolists, for example – and different, but enjoying a difference with recognized literary significance.

This legitimate difference is none other than the 'literary temperament' which is invented, by a veritable *collective labour*, in the relation between the dominated writers and the central institutions. A representation of Flemish painting, simplified to the point of stereotype, with its festivals, household scenes, orgies and processions, serves as a basis for the construction of a literary image of the 'Flemish soul', a combination of mysticism and sensuality; this cultural invention, derived from a cultural tradition, becomes a *natural* principle, rooted in the soil of a 'Flemish literature' endowed with the same properties. And these

78 *Imperialisms*

properties are all the easier to find in the literary works because the artists for their part can fall back on the myth of the 'home grown', or reverse the sign of the stigma or insult, to fabricate a 'literary temperament' for themselves matching the literary image of their 'regional temperament'. Thus it is with reference to the French field, its landmarks and its 'beacons' (Victor Hugo, in whom he sees a demi-barbarian, and above all Baudelaire and Mallarmé) that Verhaeren[4] marks out his difference, with a 'Flemish temperament' arising, not from the 'home grown', but from the literary representation of that 'home grown'. The field effect is even more obvious in the case of genuinely regionalist writers such as Charles de Coster,[5] a keen reader of Rabelais, and, after him, Lemonnier,[6] who invented a Flemish literature, close to the people and free from decadent refinement, but at a moment when the prestige of naturalism favoured the success of the kind of exotic realism that provincial writers are encouraged to cultivate.

Thus everything leads to the conclusion that there is no Belgian literary field in the strict sense of the term, and Belgian authors writing in French, similar in this to our provincials, often remain subject to the laws of the French literary field. That said, it is the political frontiers, with their arbitrary jurisdiction, that determine where the discontinuities in the continuity of the field of forces lie, and political independence – which endows the writers and artists with national institutions, academies, universities, associations, reviews, theatres and journals, etc. – is not entirely without effect, if only because these institutions offer a protected market where the impact of competition in the literary field is particularly mitigated.[7] But we may wonder whether this doesn't result in a *structural gap* between the hierarchies in the French literary field and the hierarchies at the heart of the national institutions, which are bound to be dominated by agents who are, or who are perceived to be, the product of a negative selection, and whether this gap, through its effects (such as mistrust of the national institutions of consecration), might not reproduce the relation of symbolic dependence which produced it in the first place.[8]

3

A Relational Comparatism

3.1

Passport to Duke[1]

Marx articulates an intuition in passing in *The Communist Manifesto* according to which texts circulate without their context. It follows that texts such as mine, produced in a definite position in a definite state of the French intellectual or academic field, have little chance of being grasped without distortion or deformation in the American field given the considerable gap that separates these two fields, notwithstanding their apparent growing interpenetration.

Now this gap is most often ignored. For instance, French authors such as Foucault, Derrida, or Lyotard who have been "incorporated," more or less completely, and according to very different modalities, in this or that subsector of the American academic field (in literary studies more often than in philosophy, their originating point in France), were embedded in a whole network of relations. These *objective* relations, irreducible to personal interactions, which united them to each other as well as to a whole series of institutions (for instance disciplines whose structure, history, and hierarchy are not the same on the two sides of the Atlantic) and to an entire galaxy of agents (philosophers, social scientists, writers, artists, journalists, etc.) most of whom are unknown in the United States, helped shape the creative project of which their work is the expression. Transformed into isolated asteroids by international import which typically tears them from the constellation of which they are but elements, such French authors (I fear I am about to enjoy, or suffer from, such a strain of "French flu," as my late friend E. P. Thompson used to say) become available for all manners of interpretation as they may be freely subjected to categories (such as the faddish opposition between modern and postmodern, hardly ever invoked in France) and problematics specific to the American field.

This is where being present in person can play an irreplaceable role. The questions, inevitably ambiguous, on the relations that the guest

82 *Imperialisms*

speaker may entertain with other absent authors ("What do you think of Derrida?," or, to be more precise, "I read that you recently led a series of political interventions with Derrida, what are we to make of this?"), such questions, and many others you might have in mind, can trigger so many explicit or implicit position-takings – as would no doubt be the case if I were before you at this moment: an amused and somewhat ironic smile for Lyotard, a loud silence concerning Baudrillard. Such position-takings would at least allow you to see how the invited author situates himself, consciously, in relation to other authors.

This is all very well but would it suffice to overcome the structural disjuncture to which I was referring at the outset? I do not believe so. Having dealt, through a series of negative clarifications, with all of the misunderstandings that result from the effect of *allodoxia* produced by the distance (and not only geographical) that separates national intellectual fields, and having cleared up interferences between the historical traditions these have engendered, I would still have to effect two *apparently* contradictory operations in order to achieve better communication with you.

First I would have to show the coherence and empirical adequacy, that is, the *scientificity*, of the theory, or the *system of relational concepts*, I have developed and which can be engaged in the construction, at once theoretical and empirical, of objects phenomenally very different and typically assigned to different disciplines (history of literature, history of sciences, history of philosophy, history of art, and so on. I could enumerate here the diverse and manifold disciplines represented at this conference, much to my satisfaction). Second I would outline the structure of the field, and the corresponding space of possible theoretical stances (that is, the system of negative and positive determinations), within which this conceptual framework has been constructed and to which it owes its virtues but also its limitations, some of them unapparent to me in spite of all my efforts to shun national particularities and particularisms through a deliberate (and early) commitment to scientific internationalism.

On the second point, the structure of the academic field and the relations it entertains with the literary, artistic, and political fields in France (relations that are profoundly different from their counterparts in the United States), I can refer you to my book *Homo Academicus* and in particular to the "Preface" to the English-language translation (Stanford: Stanford University Press, 1988, orig. 1984). In it, I try, based on the diagrammatic mapping of a multifactorial correspondence analysis, to uncover the characteristics of the position occupied by the main contenders in the French academic field, which comprise

Passport to Duke

those authors best known in the United States, Foucault, Derrida, Barthes, and many others, me included. I show how, taking into account variations produced by discrepancies in social and academic trajectories, this structural location is at the root of the critical, anti-institutional stances these authors took in their works. To gain a more thorough understanding of commonalities and differences between them, you could read a paper entitled "An Aspiring Philosopher" ("Un aspirant philosophe: Un point de vue sur le champ universitaire dans les années 50," in *Les enjeux philosophiques des années 50*, Paris: Éditions du Centre Pompidou, 1989, pp. 15–24), where I try to specify, through a sort of retrospective self-analysis, the dispositions (or, more precisely, the intellectual ambitions and pretensions) associated with being a philosophy student in a French elite school, the École normale supérieure, around the time of its apogee. You will also find in this paper instruments to understand one of the factors which, along with my social origins, separates me most neatly from the most famous of my contemporaries: namely, the choice I made to leave the *superior caste* of the philosophers and turn first towards anthropology (with my field work in Kabylia) and later – an even more grievous derogation – towards the sociology of work (see *Travail et travailleurs en Algérie*, 1963) and the sociology of education (with *The Inheritors* and *Reproduction*, published in 1964 and 1970 respectively), at that time two of the most despised subsectors of a pariah discipline. I effected this reconversion precisely during that period, the sixties, when those who would later discover, no doubt due partly to the sociology of education and of science, the question of power in academic and scientific life were surfing on the structuralist tide.

It is an understatement to say that I did not partake of those semiologico-literary fads exemplified in my eyes by Roland Barthes and, at the intersection between the scientific and literary fields, the fanatics of *Tel Quel*, mixing Mao and Sade (in those years, virtually all French intellectuals, Simone de Beauvoir included, wrote their dissertation on the author of *Justine*); Sollers, Kristeva, and their little coterie of minor writers with grandiose pretensions tried to institute, in the intellectual field, the aestheticist cult of gratuitous transgression, erotic or political (on this point, see my "Sollers *tel quel*," *Liber, revue européenne des livres*, 21–2, March 1995, p. 40). I was scarcely more indulgent towards those who, cumulating the prestige of philosophy, preferably Nietzschean as with Deleuze and Foucault, or Heideggerian in the case of Derrida, and the aura of literature, with the compulsive and compulsory reference to Artaud, Bataille, or Blanchot, contributed to blurring the frontier between science and literature, when they

84   *Imperialisms*

did not go so far as to breathe life back into the dullest commonplaces that the arrogance of philosophers has produced against the social sciences and which periodically take them to the brink of nihilism (for excellent demonstrations on this, I can refer you here to two books by my companion in *resistance*, Jacques Bouveresse: *Le philosophe chez les autophages*, Paris: Éditions de Minuit, 1984, and *Rationalité et cynisme*, Paris: Éditions de Minuit, 1989).

This is why I am more than a little surprised when I see myself placed, through a typical effect of *allodoxia*, on the side of those so-called "postmodern" writers whom I have ceaselessly fought on intellectual grounds, even when I might have shared political grounds on account of the fact that, as I noted earlier, we have similar subversive or anti-institutional dispositions linked to the propinquity of our positions in academic space.

This leads me on to the second point of my intended demonstration, namely the space of theoretical options in relation to which my own specifically scientific project (founded upon a total social break with the mundane games of literary philosophy and philosophical literature) was constituted. It is clear that if I reacted forcefully against the authors most directly engaged in the semiologico-literary fashion of the time, and if I quite consciously denied myself the benefits of the accelerated international circulation of ideas that the latter have enjoyed, thanks to the prestige still accorded to Parisian literary avant-gardes, in particular via the French departments of select American universities, I was actively engaged in confronting structuralism as incarnated by the Lévi-Strauss of *The Elementary Structures of Kinship*, *The Savage Mind*, and *Mythologiques*, and this in my research practice rather than solely at the level of discourse (as with philosophers, save for Foucault). In the prologue to my book *Le sens pratique* (*The Logic of Practice*, 1980/1990), I draw out the intellectual context of my research work during the sixties and try to show, in the first two chapters of that same book, how I strove to overcome the opposition, still salient in all the social sciences today (for a discussion with reference to history, see my interview with the German historian Lutz Raphael in *Actes de la recherche en sciences sociales*, 106–7, March 1995, pp. 108–22), between objectivism, represented in exemplary fashion by Lévi-Strauss, and subjectivism, taken to its outer limits by Sartre. The concept of *habitus* is intended to give a stenographic expression to the overcoming of this antinomy.

But to understand the other instruments I employ in my analyses of cultural works, law, science, art (as with my work in progress – for much too long now – on Manet), literature (cf. my study of Flaubert and, more recently, Baudelaire), philosophy (with the study of the German philosophical field in Heidegger's time), one would need to draw out the totality of the space of theoretical contributions to the analysis of symbolic power that I have been led to cumulate and to synthesize, step by step, to resolve the problems posed, very concretely, by the analysis of Kabyle ritual or religious practices or of the literary and artistic productions of differentiated societies (I presented a sort of simplified synopsis of these theories for the first time in 1972, at the University of Chicago, before an audience of positivistically inclined, and thoroughly befuddled, sociologists: see "On Symbolic Power," reprinted in *Language and Symbolic Power*, Cambridge: Polity, 1991).

The concept of literary field, as a space of objective positions to which corresponds a homologous space of stances or position-takings (which operates as a space of possibles or options given to participants in the field at any given moment), was itself elaborated in relation to a space of different possible approaches to literary works, which are opposed to one another, and to which it is opposed at the same time as it annexes and integrates them in a non-eclectic manner (you will find a map of this space of theories of literary or artistic products in "Principles for a Sociology of Cultural Works," in *The Field of Cultural Production: Essays on Art and Literature*, New York: Columbia University Press, 1993, as well as in *Les règles de l'art*, Paris: Éditions du Seuil, 1993, pp. 271–92; translated as *The Rules of Art*, Cambridge: Polity, 1996).

If I had the time, I could show you how one can critique symbolic structuralism, as conceived by Foucault and the Russian Formalists, and yet preserve its achievements (the idea of a space of strategic possibilities or intertextuality) within a framework that transcends the opposition between internal analysis (text) and external analysis (context) by relating the literary (philosophical, juridical, scientific, etc.) field in which producers evolve and where they occupy dominant or dominated, central or marginal, positions, on the one hand, and the field of works, defined relationally in their form, style, and manner, on the other. This is tantamount to saying that, instead of being one approach among many, an analysis in terms of field allows one methodically to integrate the achievements of all the other approaches in currency, approaches that the field of literary criticism itself causes us to perceive as irreconcilable.

Lastly, I would need to show you how an analysis armed with knowledge of the general properties of fields produced by the theory of fields can discover in each of the various fields (for instance, the literary field or the field of painting) properties that the naive (and native) vision would overlook. Such an analysis can bring to light, thanks to

methodical comparison made possible by the notion of field, properties that uniquely characterize the functioning of each of the different
fields, which leads in particular to refuting the conflation between the
scientific field and literary field fostered by a certain "postmodern"
vision of literature and science (I think of the nihilistic critiques of
the social sciences that have proliferated recently in the name of the
"linguistic turn").

As I tried to demonstrate in what would seem to be the most unlikely
case, that of sociology (see "La cause de la science," *Actes de la recherche
en sciences sociales*, 106–7, March 1995, pp. 3–10), if science, even the
purest science, presents a number of structural and functional traits in
common with the political field, it remains that it has its own *nomos*,
its (relative) autonomy, which insulates it more or less completely from
the intrusion of external complaints. This explains that truths produced in this relatively autonomous field can be historical through and
through, as is the field itself, without for that being either deducible
from historical conditions or reducible to the external conditionings
they impose. This is because the field opposes to external forces the
shield, or the prism, of its own history, warrant of its autonomy, that
is, the history of the "languages" (in the broadest possible sense of the
word) specific to each field or subfield.

These are some of the arguments I would have liked to make before
you, had I been able to travel to Duke University and to be there with
you on this day. I would have liked also to tell you how grateful I am
for the interest you have shown in my work, and this in the manner
which pleases me the most: by treating it as an intellectual machinery
capable of generating new products and thus by working together to
design whatever improvements are needed.

Paris, March 1995
Translated by Loïc Wacquant

3.2

Social Structures and Structures of Perception of the Social World[1]

They would like, by all means, to convince themselves that the striving after English happiness, I mean after COMFORT and FASHION (and in the highest instance, a seat in Parliament), is at the same time the true path of virtue; in fact, that in so far as there has been virtue in the world hitherto, it has just consisted in such striving.

F. Nietzsche, *Beyond Good and Evil: Prelude to a Philosophy of the Future,*
trans. H. Zimmern, §228 (Project Gutenberg ebook, 4363, 2013).

It would be too easy to link ethnocentrism and naive evolutionism, which lead a number of American sociologists to describe foreign countries in terms of privation, directly to the imperialist position of their nation and to the profound nationalism fuelled by the necessity to integrate immigrants symbolically or the tendency of the immigrants themselves towards hyper-identification.

Among all the mediations that ought to be analysed (such as the specific position of academics in the structure of the field of power), there is one that is particularly important for the philosophy of knowledge, but which is most likely to escape us. The evolutionist model, which encourages us to see different societies as so many stages on the path leading to American society, and which Parsons,[2] like the thoroughgoing ideologue he is, has once more the merit of explicitly and systematically formulating, might owe its particular force and its concrete form to the fact that it involves projecting onto the contemporary world the structure of American society: a structure at once *synchronic*, that of the hierarchy of the ethnic groups, which entertains a complex relationship with the hierarchy of the classes (and which thus

88   *Imperialisms*

finds itself predisposed to fulfil a *euphemistic* function of neutralizing
the reality of the classes), and *diachronic*, that of the *historic order of
arrival* of the groups of immigrants. The correspondence between the
two hierarchies is more or less perfect, if we leave out the blacks, who,
arriving last on the labour market, do not hold a synchronic position
corresponding to their diachronic rank.

The social structure adopted as mental structure tends to organize
perception of the social world, both inside (with all the forms of racism)
and outside. Inside, it leads people to identify American society with
the ethnic class that is *at its summit*. And all the more strongly no
doubt because, depending on the position you hold in this structure,
you aspire more strongly to identify with or be identified with the
summit. Just as every soldier of year II of the French Revolution
carried a marshal's baton in his knapsack, every American, even those
of Italian origins, harbours within themselves a virtual **WASP** (White
Anglo-Saxon Protestant). Most of the studies of mobility have no
function other than to confirm this 'American creed', the equality of
opportunity. American society, as Parsons describes it, thus accumu-
lates all the properties of its summit, through a sort of unreflecting
universalization of Bostonian privilege.

At the peak of the ideological hierarchy, as at the peak of the social
hierarchy, we find the 'English happiness', the British political tradition, the measure of all democracies (cf. Lipset), the Anglo-Germanic
university tradition, the model of all meritocracies (cf. Bell), the spirit of
enterprise and the typically puritan taste for success and achievement.
At the bottom of the hierarchy, at the lowest level of the thinkable and
nameable, is Italy, the black and the red, a diabolical combination of
Catholicism and communism, a double negation, that they would like
to convince themselves is temporary, of the ideal achievement. Just as
the future of all Americans is contained in the WASP, so all nations are
in the process of evolving towards America, or more precisely towards
the Waspish truth of America.

English happiness

I quote Lipset:

> I would suggest, however, the alternative hypothesis that, rather
> than being a source of strain, the intransigent and intolerant
> aspects of Communist ideology attract members from that large
> stratum with low incomes, low-status occupations, and low edu-

Social Structures and Structures of Perception 89

cation, which in modern industrial societies has meant largely, though not exclusively, the working class. The social situation of the lower strata, particularly in poorer countries with low levels of education, predisposes them to view politics as black and white, good and evil. Consequently, other things being equal, they should be more likely than other strata to prefer extremist movements which suggest easy and quick solutions to social problems and have a rigid outlook. ... In a country like Britain, where norms of tolerance are well developed and widespread in every social stratum, even the lowest class may be less authoritarian and more 'sophisticated' than the most highly educated stratum in an underdeveloped country, where immediate problems and crises impinge on every class and short-term solutions may be sought by all groups. ... The instability of the democratic process in general and the strength of the Communists in particular, as we have seen, are closely related to national levels of economic development, including national levels of educational attainment. The Communists represent a mass movement in the poorer countries of Europe and elsewhere, but are weak where economic development and educational attainment are high. The lower classes of the less developed countries are poorer, more insecure, less educated, and relatively more underprivileged in terms of possession of status symbols than are the lower strata of the more well-to-do nations. In the more developed, stable democracies of Western Europe, North America, and Australasia the lower classes are 'in the society' as well as 'of it' – that is, their isolation from the rest of the culture is much less than the social isolation of the poorer groups in other countries, who are cut off by abysmally low incomes and very low educational levels, if not by widespread illiteracy. This incorporation of the workers into the body politic in the industrialized Western world has reduced their authoritarian tendencies greatly, although in the United States, for example, McCarthy demonstrated that an irresponsible demagogue who combines a nationalist and anti-elitist appeal can still secure considerable support from the less educated.[3]

And now Bell:

On its positive side, equality meant the chance to get ahead, regardless of one's origins; that no formal barriers or prescribed positions stood in one's way. It was this combination of attributes – the lack of deference and the emphasis on personal achievement

90   *Imperialisms*

– which gave 19th-century America its revolutionary appeal, so much so that when the German '48ers came here, including such members of Marx's Socialist Workers Club as Kriege and Willich, they abandoned socialism and became republicans.[4]

From Lipset writing on the authoritarianism of the popular classes at Bellah to LaPalombara writing on Italy, from Lerner describing the withering away of 'traditional societies' to Lazarsfeld describing the prehistory of empirical sociology,[5] and including all the specialists of 'international studies of the elites', who hand out the same equally irrelevant questionnaire everywhere, from the United States to Tunisia, from Poland to Germany, or from Bolivia to Peru,[6] 'official' American sociology speaks in fact only of American society, that is, of the social unconscious of the American sociologists.

Ideology as a cultural system: such is the title of an article by Clifford Geertz,[7] whose high citation rating attests to the fact that it expresses profoundly one of the cultural credos of American sociologists and their society. If I were not afraid of appearing to accept the implicit assumptions of culturism, and in particular its bracketing out of the political functions of domination and domestication that cultural phenomena enact, I would suggest the opposite: *Cultural system as ideology*. It is in fact the social structure that, through the mental structures it produces, functions as the generating principle of ideology.

The America of the immigrants as a hub of universal attraction

Daniel Lerner's book, *The Passing of Traditional Society*,[8] represents an extreme case of all the studies devoted to the problem of 'modernization'. The 'theory' of social change that we find in it is based on an empirical enquiry that constitutes the apotheosis of the scientific artefact: a sample of 1,600 individuals chosen from Middle Eastern countries whose rate of literacy varies from 10 per cent to 30 percent (except for Lebanon), are given 117 questions, of which eighty-seven concern their attitudes towards the 'mass media' – cinema and press (sixteen questions), radio and television (and more precisely their aptitude to 'identify with' the messages broadcast) – and two concern their work and socio-economic status, variables which moreover will more or less never be taken into account afterwards in analysing the results. The results thus produced are submitted to an analysis of latent structure which reproduces, in scientifically legitimized form, the latent structures of the questionnaire, that is, the attitude of the researcher, and

Social Structures and Structures of Perception 91

on this basis they construct a 'theory of modernization': thus it is that the irresistible psychological attraction of modern (that is, American) civilization becomes the model of all social change.

I quote Lerner:

> The model of behaviour developed by modern society is characterized by empathy, a high capacity for rearranging the self-system on short notice. Whereas the isolate communities of traditional society functioned well on the basis of a highly constrictive personality, the interdependent sectors of modern society require widespread participation. This in its turn requires an expansive and adaptive self-system, ready to incorporate new roles and to identify personal values with public issues. This is why modernization of any society has involved the great characterological transformation we call psychic mobility.[9]

And even more naively expressed:

> The media teach people participation of this sort by depicting for them new and strange situations and familiarizing them with a range of options between which they can choose. Some people learn better than others, the variation reflecting their differential skill in empathy . . . Empathy endows the person with the capacity to imagine himself as proprietor of a bigger grocery store in a city, to wear nice clothes and live in a nice house, to take an interest in 'what is going on in the world' and to 'get out of his hole'. With the spread of curiosity and imagination among a previously quietistic population come the human skills needed for social growth and economic development.[10]

'Modernity' being defined as a 'participant style of life', we can identify its 'distinctive personality mechanism as *empathy*'[11] and see in the 'media exposure', which is supposed to increase empathy by giving it an opportunity to exercise itself, one of the determining factors of the transformation of dispositions. 'Urban residence, schooling, media exposure then train and reinforce the empathic predisposition that was already present.'[12]

'The importance of media exposure, in our theory, is that it enlarges a person's view of the world ("opinion range") by increasing his capacity to imagine himself in new and strange situations ("empathy").'[13] In fact it is sufficient to *show* modern civilization, the image of happiness fulfilled, to impose it. 'The modernizing individuals', writes

Daniel Lerner, 'are considerably less unhappy – and the more rapidly the society around them is modernized the happier they are. ... Traditional society is passing from the Middle East because relatively few Middle Easterners still want to live by its rules.'[14]

3.3

The Specifics of National Histories
Towards a Comparative History of the Relevant Differences between Nations[1]

History and the explanation of the present

This seminar intends to be a genuine research seminar with all the uncertainty, difficulty and possible confusion that this implies. We want to attempt to reflect on ways of mobilizing history in our research into a certain number of problems in a certain number of European countries. We could say as Durkheim did that history has the aim of providing the means to understand the present, in other words that history is subordinated to understanding and explaining the present. But this historical research oriented towards the present must try to escape the dangers of teleology and avoid serving up pseudo interpretations-explanations of the present: 'However far back we go in the past', Durkheim reminds us, 'we never lose sight of the present. When we describe even the most primitive forms of the family, it will not be simply to satisfy our curiosity, however legitimate, but to gradually arrive at an explanation of our European family.'[2] Thus 'it will not be simply to satisfy our curiosity, however legitimate'. Accepting this assumption that 'we start out from the present' means taking a considerable risk: we risk imposing on the past problems which were not raised in the past, imposing an ethnocentric view or at least normative questions that have no bearing on the past. There are retrospective revolutionaries everywhere, for it is so easy to cast an inquisitorial, indignant gaze over the past in order to distribute praise and blame.

We need to start out from the present, but in order to put questions that are subordinate to a programme of research, that is, a more or less coherent programme of hypotheses associated with a more or less coherent system of methods and techniques of validation or refutation

94 *Imperialisms*

of these hypotheses. Everyone will moderate this research programme in their own fashion, and there will be small slippages, perhaps even contradictions and oppositions. The programme will be developed in more detail as it makes progress towards its fulfilment.

I now come to the enterprise of comparative European research, which is practised in the framework of the Centre for European Sociology. From its origins in the 1960s, the Centre has striven to undertake research that is transnational and comparative. There have been all sorts of experiments, such as the enquiries into museums published in *The Love of Art*, with its subtitle *European Art Museums and Their Public*.[3] This was an enquiry carried out in five European countries at the cost of enormous difficulties of every kind, not only scientific, but technical, administrative and political. The enquiry enabled us to learn a lot about the comparability and incompatibility of statistical information. There have been other experiments in different guises, more monographical, but this comparative concern was always present (thanks to financing from the European Community, it is possible today to undertake major European research into State policies).

In the first confrontations that we had with Greek, Dutch, Belgian and German researchers, we noticed that a certain number of differences in practices which we observed, in forms of delinquency for example, could be linked to profound historical differences.[4] On the one hand there were differences in legislation that were relatively easy to grasp, since we were dealing with things that were declared, patent, codified and recorded in law. And on the other hand there were differences much more difficult to grasp, which are linked for example to religious traditions, or the 'aftermath' of some historical trauma, transposed into dispositions. These might be the government of the colonels in Greece, or perhaps the Occupation and the Resistance in France, long-lasting after-images of historical events or actions that we are obliged to consider still operative in order to understand certain differences. There is a third, even more unconscious level, the profound differences in 'mentality' (a very dubious concept), in the historical unconscious or the historical transcendental, in short, the habitus. How do we handle all this? The majority of the research financed by Europe is not concerned with these problems, and nobody is asking us to take them on. But if we don't, our comparatism will be amateur, and we will be in danger of finding false differences and false similarities, of being dazzled by *curiosa* devoid of interest.

So, for the first phase, how do we try to objectify these differences in the realm of the deep historical unconscious? It would seem that family structures are very important from this point of view. We can make a tentative use of multiple correspondence analysis to try to grasp this. The idea was to take national and if possible regional statistics of the indicators of family integration. Obviously there is a danger of comparing the incompatible. There is a service called Eurostat which collects the statistics that the different nations have produced without submitting them to any minimal preliminary critique, such as a critique of the conditions of administration of the questionnaires, of the categories into which the data is divided, etc. Once this preliminary triage has been done, we can try to select indices of integration or *anomie* (marriage, number of children, divorce, celibacy, cohabitation among generations, rate of suicide, delinquency, etc.). Then economic indicators, level of unemployment, if possible by social category, age and income, etc., and educational indicators (by levels). An analysis of this type could give us a sort of map of the deep, hidden structural principles of differentiation which we then have to bear in mind when interpreting anything, especially anything connected with integration. In other words, it would be a map of the national or regional unconscious minds.

Obviously this map would be there to act as a wake-up call, but it would also be there to act as a motor to throw up problems. To interpret this multiple correspondence analysis, we would need to answer a whole host of questions (for example, why does Bavaria which is Catholic have a higher divorce rate than Rhineland?). The variables that we could introduce into the analysis, and that we could insert into its interpretation, will very often be historical variables. In other words, this programme of structural description of the space of national and regional unconscious minds will produce a research programme into the specifics of national history capable of explaining these differences. We can easily see that, following Durkheim's recommendation, we start out from the present and we put questions to the past, looking for explanation. We are not driven by purely erudite curiosity but seeking to explain why things are the way they are.

What should be the nature of a history capable of tackling these issues? Firstly, by definition, it cannot be a national history. And it cannot be a juxtaposition of national histories, like for example those 'histories of European literature' written by four dons from four countries who merely juxtapose their national traditions. At the same time we should shed our obsession with deeds from our national past, with everything lodged in our national memory and its logic of anniversaries and systematic celebrations. This abandonment of the national point of view, and more profoundly of the national view of the nation's exploits, is designed to prevent the comparative analysis becoming

96   *Imperialisms*

trapped in a national ethnocentrism with its correlative censorship. For example, I wrote a criticism of American cultural anthropology (in the book *À la recherche de la France*):[5] that research produced some very interesting documents on ethnocentrism.

Secondly, with this history, we should overcome the rather mechanical comparison of demographic, social and economic statistical data, and all the difficulties associated with the comparison of data constructed in terms of national categories. As soon as we engage in true comparison, the nation itself is one of the instruments that we use to study the nation; the categories are national and they are often linked to histories of the nation or histories of the national subfield in question. For instance, to understand the socio-professional categories of INSEE (National Institute for Statistics and Economic Studies), you have to know your history of France, but you also have to know the specific history of the body of social engineers, etc. We need to draw up a history oriented towards the explanation of the present, questioning the different national traditions, using an explicative problematic, that is, starting out from a present that is a problem and needs explaining. This is still too general a definition. We need to question the past, starting out from a system of pertinent differences or socially significant variations between nations. In other words, the comparatist programme is itself comparative: looking for the system of pertinent differences means that we need to construct the space of the nations and the space of the differences that differentiate them. Obviously this system of pertinent differences is the opposite of the adversarial questioning that condemns us to lapse into the retrospective illusion (as we tend to do for the French Revolution[6]). We need to transform social problems – which are problems of the present, being fought over in the present, in struggles involving the intellectual, historical or political fields – into sociological problems.

One of the ways of making the break with the prefabricated problems that historians often allow themselves to be caught up in is to undertake a historical sociology of the genesis of these historical problems. There are obviously so many preliminary measures that you would have to take for the research to be viable that they would be never-ending, and the research would never get done, but we still mustn't forget that it is possible. It would be interesting to take as an object of research the research programmes of the people who do comparative history or comparative sociology, and relate the objects that they find important to their general and specific national traditions. Dutch sociology, whose traditions are very different from those of French sociology, must give rise in retrospect to problems very different from

The Specifics of National Histories   97

those of French sociology, besides the fact that it must be much less interested in history because it is much more synchronist, etc. This questioning of standard, spontaneous problematics must also imply a questioning of historic stereotypes and presumptions.

We are still only at a preliminary stage, and I think that the great difficulty facing this comparative history of the differences liable to explain the pertinent divergences between nations lies in the effect of obviousness or naturalization: their national history has become naturalized in the minds of historians, sociologists and ethnologists, and this naturalized version of history appears obvious and beyond discussion. This is a fundamental precept of the methodology that has been triggered to some extent by ethnomethodology, which has followed Schütz in warning us to beware of the taken-for-granted: ethnologists have always been much more alert than sociologists to the fact that the chief impact of exoticism and disorientation is to make ordinary things seem extraordinary. And in fact one of the main functions of ethnological research is to have an impact, in principle, on the ethnologist. But we must not be satisfied with merely saying 'take care, you must defamiliarize, you must unpick the obvious, etc.' We need to provide the practical means to operate this defamiliarization, to encourage what the Russian Formalists called 'estrangement', making yourself a stranger to your own tradition. It is historical reflexivity that can enable us to become ethnologists of our own society, to become historians of our own historical experience, to become socio-analysts of our own social unconscious. It is important to raise this question in advance.

Imagine a German, a Frenchman and an Italian sitting round a table together. Their nationality is the first thing they forget, because in general they understand each other (or get the impression that they do). What they want to do is draw up a sociological questionnaire that will direct their enquiry into the historical facts that are pertinent for a proper understanding of what is happening today in the French or the German educational system. How to design a historical questionnaire that helps me understand why, when a German tells me about a student revolt, I don't really understand? (It's difficult enough already, without the fact that you need to understand that you don't understand. . .). Unless you want to go in for a UNESCO-type sociology, based on mistranslation and misunderstanding, you have to ask the Germans to stop pretending to understand what the French are saying, which they are all the more prone to do, since if they are discussing things with the French, it means that they are already familiar with France (they are not very German Germans). What is more, there are hosts of

98   *Imperialisms*

false similarities, or 'equivalences', as they are called: 'the *Abitur* is the equivalent of the baccalaureate'. There are problems of translation. When we have to translate 'middle class', we know that we shouldn't write 'classe moyenne', but 'bourgeoisie'. But is this enough? There are official committees that look for equivalences between diplomas. We need to understand. And to understand *Abitur*, we need to know the whole educational structure. The *Abitur* is equivalent to the baccalaureate, *except for the systems* within which each is embroiled and which make all the difference. The false familiarity based on superficial phenomenal similarities prevents us from understanding that we don't understand.

How do we become an ethnologist of our own milieu? How do we become capable of transforming social problems into sociological problems? How, for example, do we approach the sociology of journalism without writing sociological journalism about journalism? How do we approach the sociology of women if we are women? The danger is believing that we understand it all, and feeling smart. There are relations with the object of study that are very difficult to manage. So we need many techniques to help us make the break, including statistical methods and intensive enquiries, but not everyone can handle these. Otherwise we are just going to be indulging in 'Cultural Studies', like those people who believe, pardon the caricature, that if they watch a baseball match on telly in the afternoon, they have done something sociological. It's not that I am a diehard ascetic (saying 'you have to suffer if you want to succeed in research'). You need to enjoy your research, there is nothing more fun than research. But you have to go out onto the pitch, engage in interviews, do the difficult things that the profession demands of you, not only to guarantee your knowledge but also to guarantee your knowledge of the knowing subject, your control and transformation of the knowing subject. Statistics have their virtues. We can also do fine research without statistics, but it is true that it is often the crude positivist statistics that have the virtue of transforming the researcher's vision.

(There is a sort of eulogy of laxism today, led by people like Maffesoli.[7] Rigour is not a sin. At the same time, however, we need to be wary of punctilious bogeymen and strict methodologists. When I was just starting out in the milieu I had to fight against bogeymen who could quote nobody but Lazarsfeld, who never did any research themselves but tried to stop other people doing it by imposing demands that even Lazarsfeld had never insisted on. Just a passing remark. . .).

The problem is understanding that we don't understand one another. How do we avoid forgetting that we don't understand, how do we

The Specifics of National Histories 99

understand that we don't understand, or rather, how can we be immediately called to order the moment we forget that we don't understand? Because it is not enough to have an epistemological principle: 'pay attention, stay on the watch'. It doesn't work. You need to create a situation where as soon as you forget, someone will call you to order. We need to adopt an outsider's viewpoint over our own practices, we need to make our own practices feel foreign to us by using our knowledge of foreign practices. That sounds abstract, but it's already better than nothing. For example, we can find out about things in books; if we are working on the French educational system, we can look up how things function in Germany. That is already better than nothing. But the ideal, and this is the whole sense of the enterprise that we are hoping to set in motion, is to establish social relations between foreign bodies in such a way that each one sees with foreign eyes the practices and traditions of the others, and therefore of their own practice. We need to create a social organization, a group, a multinational collective which should be alert to this question of the danger of the obvious, alert to this point of view, and determined not to pretend to understand, to be ready to ask silly questions and not be satisfied with fake comprehension.

What I am saying for international relations is also valid for the interdisciplinary. I think that just as there are national historical unconsciouses, there are disciplinary historical unconsciouses. When a French historian discusses something with a German sociologist, there are two layers of unconscious screening. There is on the one hand the national unconscious and on the other hand the disciplinary unconscious. The position of history in the space of disciplines in the two countries is not at all the same. I refer you to the dialogue, published in *Actes*, that I had with a German historian specializing in the *Annales* school, on the relationship between the social sciences in France and in Germany.[8] This arrangement is not an epistemological arrangement, it is a *social arrangement with an epistemological function*. It is a group of epistemologically savvy people who are alert to the question of the historical unconscious and the danger of treating the obvious as obvious, and who have adopted the aim of elaborating the collective means of exploring this historical unconscious methodically. Obviously enough, this means of collective exploration of the historical unconscious can only be a historical method, which brings us back to the starting point, comparative history. What should be the aim of this special kind of history capable of responding to this problem? It is a history that aims to unveil the historical unconscious and historical transcendentals. Of course this is bound to antagonize the historians, even the most

100   *Imperialisms*

open and willing. Behind everything that goes without saying and is
self-evident, there is complicity between historical unconsciouses. It is
because the systems of categories of thought of the producer and the
receiver of the message overlap that there is this illusion of obviousness. Whence the urgency of observing a double historicization, which
we need to translate into something practical. We need to operate a
double historicization, of both the knowing subject and the object
known. We need to turn this abstract demand into something practicable. If I were a positivist, I would say: I call this the *lexical fallacy*,
the *fallacy* of believing in the superficial evidence of the lexicon. And I
warn you to beware the *lexical fallacy*. And you must pay attention to
every word, in particular the most banal and obvious, such as the word
'originality' in a text on aesthetics or art criticism. These researchers, then, must come to an agreement on a common programme of
scientific struggle: working to objectify the historical unconscious that
prevents us from really objectifying our object of study. That is the
programme. Once we come to an agreement about this, then we need
the mechanisms. We can say that for the *lexical fallacy* we have the
Begriffsgeschichte [conceptual history].[9] It is described in the article
in *Actes de la recherche* that I mentioned just now. It is a history of
concepts. You take the concept of civilization, which is very important
in Elias,[10] and you draw up its historical genealogy, etc. So far so good,
but I have admitted the limitations of this analysis.

What I have proposed as a collective tool for researchers engaged
in this collective research is what I have called the vocabulary of
European institutions. I highlight the title of Benveniste's splendid
book (*Le vocabulaire des institutions indo-européennes*[11]). This is a
model that should help us record the effects on the thinker exercised by
the instruments of thought that he is obliged to use because he is thinking through language, and a historical language at that. Benveniste
takes a word's root and then follows it through all the Indo-European
languages; he is guided in this exploration by two principles of association: his philological culture (he scents affinities between roots where
the layman would not see that there is the same word in Greek and in
Aramaic) and his anthropological culture (he is situated in the great
tradition of Durkheimian sociologists and linguists), with his sense of
mythico-ritual roots. When he encounters a word that means East, he
thinks 'East–West, orientation, structure of the space, etc.' And letting
himself be guided by one or other of these roots, he conjures up an
unconscious which is a social unconscious and something we all have
parts of in our minds. He unwraps that kind of historical unconscious
which is deposited in words and which is very powerful because it is a

The Specifics of National Histories 101

social philosophy. For instance, the text that Benveniste wrote on the performative,[12] and which was commented on everywhere in the period of rampant structuralism, is less interesting, I find, than what he wrote on the power of language when he comments on the words that refer to law in the Indo-European languages. This is because there is in fact more philosophy in language than there is in the minds of the linguists who study languages. Philosophers have always amused themselves with roots and with puns, and we have contemporaries who enjoy playing these games, following Heidegger's example. It is the perfect antithesis of what Benveniste is doing. Benveniste traces the articulations of words to try to extract the social philosophy and the theory they contain, which has been elaborated and tested by generations.

One of the collective aims of our organization is to create a vocabulary of analogous European institutions. We won't choose words like delinquency, but more banal words: wretchedness, *Armut*; we shall take words that are difficult to translate, which are of the order of national idiolects, which are laden with history and which translation destroys, annihilates. When you interview foreigners, are you conscious enough of this? If for instance the interview is to be in English, what do people lose when they move into English, in terms of saying profound things that concern their national structure? Is the essential not lost? There would be much to develop here.

That would be the first approach, in the area of vocabulary. The second is this comparative history of pertinent characteristics. This is what we are going to investigate with Christophe Charle next time, and then with Nikos Panayotopolos, a Greek researcher who initiated this reflection, because he was rather indignant at the incomprehension that we showed in the face of certain particularities of Greek tradition. He raised the problem. He said to us: I must tell you a story about Greece, not the whole history of Greece from its origins to the present day, but the history of Greece that you need to know to understand that you don't understand. You say to an American: this is what you need to know about France to understand the reactions of French intellectuals to the problem of the PACS (*pacte civil de solidarité* [civil partnership][13]). It's the whole Catholic Church, the review *Esprit*, all that. It's a very rich subject. What do you need to know about French history? We shall see that each of the participants in this sort of scientific collective has to be able to transform the others into enlightened informants (and not simply into interviewees replying to questions asking whether they are for or against), the ideal being that the group itself becomes an agency of systematic interrogation, so that nobody can forget that they are obliged to act as an informant and

102 *Imperialisms*

not be satisfied with telling trivial anecdotes drawn from their own encounters with delinquency.

The second difficulty for this comparative history (it's rather like the problem of fitting together a set of Russian dolls) is that these histories that we are trying to tease out and objectify are themselves the product of comparison or rather of confrontation. A comparative history must not forget that the history it is studying comparatively is the product of real comparisons between nations. For example, in one of the recent issues of *Liber* I reviewed an article taken from a very fine book entitled *The Britons*.[14] It is a splendid piece of work by an Englishwoman, Linda Colley, showing how the English have composed themselves since the French Revolution in opposition to the French in a systematic way, in their manner of being, their manner of speaking, etc. She uses a whole lot of ethnographic techniques. There is also a book by a German that's just been translated into French (in the Maison des sciences de l'homme series) following the same logic, showing how the Germans have composed themselves in an almost systematic manner in opposition to the French.[15] We can also find this in Elias.[16]

THE CRISIS OF BRITISHNESS

The British nation, an artificial construction, ethnically and culturally diverse, which has been superimposed on much more ancient partnerships and alliances, has been forged principally in war, and through war. In the work of construction in opposition to a hostile, 'tyrannical' and Catholic France, the principal resource is Protestantism, which authorizes the 'Britons' to feel different, and to see themselves as a sort of chosen people (a sentiment that contact with the peoples of the colonial empire could only corroborate), distinguished in particular by the superiority of their constitutional liberties. The 'making of the British ruling class' also owes a lot to the public schools, fox hunting, the cult of military heroism and a particular form of 'manliness', to the love of uniforms, without forgetting, obviously, the magical majesty of a hereditary royalty which gradually adopted a consciously patriotic and even populist style (with royal visits around the kingdom, or carefully choreographed royal ceremonies). It was once more against France, 'effeminate' and dominated by women and 'feminine' preoccupations – cuisine, etiquette and sexuality – that a 'masculine' culture took shape, intentionally rational and realist to the point of philistinism. And the struggle against revolutionary France obliged the British to imitate the revolutionary methods of the French, such as mass mobilization for the war effort, in an expression of popular nationalism that would have to be compensated for by a broadening of political rights, in particular by universal suffrage and an increase in economic advantages, with the Welfare State. The present crisis of Britishness is easy to explain if we see that the majority of the factors that helped forge the nation have ceased to be effective.

This note by Bourdieu appeared in Liber, *32, September 1997, p. 2.*

104 *Imperialisms*

It is important to realize that comparison lies in the object, because we are going to compare people who are comparing one another and whose makeup is partly the product of these comparisons. It is more complicated still: We should not speak of the Germans as a whole and say that the Germans will be constructing themselves in opposition to the French, or the English in opposition to the French. We would be forgetting that left-wing Germans will be constructing themselves alongside the French in opposition to the right-wing Germans, which makes things more complicated, by inverting our imagery. If we don't realize that comparison lies in the object that we submit to comparison, we risk taking for comparative science what are in fact comparative stereotypes produced by the struggle between the nations being compared. The different nations measure up to one another, compare themselves to one another, and construct themselves in opposition to one another; and this work of comparison, even when it is fantastical and confined to the realm of representation, helps to make up the historical reality of the nations. The nations are a historical fabrication. In other words, we can't simply say that the image of Paris in the eighteenth century is a myth. It is a myth that has an impact on Parisians, but also on those who visit Paris, who come looking for Paris. In the real life of Germany and England there are things that have been introduced by the concern to be different from France, and vice versa.

In conclusion I would like to tell you briefly about E. P. Thompson and Norbert Elias. E. P. Thompson's 'The Peculiarities of the English' is an article that has been republished in a collection entitled *The Poverty of Theory*.[17] It is a very long paper which takes as its starting point an article in the *New Left Review* co-authored by Perry Anderson and Tom Nairn that Thompson describes as ultra-francophile.[18] They are doing something very banal for the world's left-wing movements, above all Marxist ones: they are taking the French Revolution as the measure of all revolutions. It's the same thing in Japan: everyone asks whether the Japanese revolution is a real revolution. Is the American revolution a real revolution? No, there is something missing – of course, since the model has been imposed by Marxism. Thompson's two opponents have a French vision of England and describe England in terms of lack, through an inverse ethnocentrism. Thompson sketches a sociology of his two opponents and says that they transform an impulse of very legitimate rebellion against the neoliberals, Popper and Hayek, etc., into a universal interpretation of history. So the first question: Why did England not have a real revolution, meaning a French one? 'The English revolution in the 17th century is impure, premature, unfulfilled, and driven by a religious logic.' Already Engels saw the same problem with the seventeenth-century peasant revolts in Germany. It was a revolution driven by a religious logic. Consequently, it was not a revolution and the bourgeoisie that emerged from it was not a real bourgeoisie, whence the English exceptionalism.[19] The prime error in this kind of comparison is ethnocentrism. One nation is taken as the measure of all the others. 'It is impossible to understand even the beginnings of English capitalism if one peers out, through Parisian eyes, at the backward "provinces", seeing in the landowners only a feudal aristocracy "with bourgeois traits".'[20] The idea is that they are not real bourgeois capitalists, and in passing Thompson remarks that this agrarian bourgeoisie, described as archaic, did nonetheless invent political economics. Or that political economics was at least inspired by a vision linked to a naturalistic political economics, which, with Adam Smith and the theory of laissez-faire, etc., expressed this not-so-archaic category. Thompson asks why this agrarian and mercantile capitalism continued to dominate the industrial bourgeoisie in the nineteenth century. He does not completely refute the analysis by the others, who do not detect the characteristic traits of a bourgeoisie, he does try to understand them on their own terms. Why did the industrial capitalism of the nineteenth century maintain an alliance with this eighteenth-century agrarian, mercantile capitalism? Why did the two remain interwoven?

Two explanations. I schematize somewhat. Firstly, because the fear of the French Revolution bonded the two social strata together all the more since the burgeoning national proletariat threatened their privileges and they feared contagion from the French Revolution. Secondly, because in this symbiosis of an aristocracy and a bourgeoisie, the aristocracy dominated, because it had control of the State (which is very important for understanding the particularities of the State: an apparently very archaic State, bound by tradition – royalty, pomp and circumstance, etc.) and on the other hand because, through its aristocratic lifestyle, it continued to set the cultural tone.

Another question raised by Thompson: Why does England not have 'French-style' (my adjective) intellectuals. (These are issues that, in intellectual discussions, either you don't mention, or, if you do, you regress to the level of local café gossip. Whence the need to explicate, elaborate and bring them up to a conscious level, otherwise the national unconscious and all its prejudices will crowd back in and flood the conceptual void.) So, why does England not have intellectuals? Because, given the role of Protestantism, England did not need Enlightenment intellectuals and their struggles against obscurantism. (I am simplifying somewhat.) The intelligentsia is not centralized.

106 *Imperialisms*

Thompson describes a tradition of dissidence, of rebellion.[21] He shows that in Glasgow and Edinburgh there have always been intellectuals, who, because of the national opposition [to England], were close to the French; and there were Irishmen, etc. On the other hand, there was no conflict with a central authority, since academic power was not concentrated. This is one of the factors explaining the difference, which I mentioned last year in my lectures on Manet.[22] As there was no academic concentration, there was no cause to revolt and make a revolution against a central agency, for in a paradoxical sense the Academy in France produced the conditions favourable to the existence of Manet, through the extreme concentration of power that it attained. Among other prejudices, people say that the English working class is passive, positivist, uncritical and generally un-Marxist. Thompson says: not at all. This tradition has produced Darwin, but neither Voltaire nor Marx. Here Thompson has a very fine, long development on the experimental method as opposed to intellectual struggle. The experimental method diminishes the part that transcendence can play, making a break between the ultimate, 'last analysis', which we should leave to theology, and what is of the order of science. Science moves onward, and accomplishes its task.

Last question: Why are there no revolutionary trade unions and intellectuals?[23] Meaning Marxists, once again. Thompson shows that to a large extent this is linked with external politics, that every time there have been national movements of strong political protest, they have been stifled: the movement of the 1890s came up against the Boer War,[24] the syndicalist insurrection of 1911–14[25] was weakened or came to nothing in the First World War, and the potential revolt of the years 1945–7 was cancelled out by the Cold War. After that, there is a whole debate on the notion of class.

Elias is particularly interested in the Germans.[26] Of course (it is important) Elias is an immigrant Jewish intellectual. He holds an inverse ethnocentric viewpoint. He adopts on Germany the viewpoint of France, which gives him liberty in relation to German nationalism (Christophe Charle tries to construct a totally decentred space where we no longer know if we are speaking from a French, English or German viewpoint; he attempts to create a polycentric viewpoint[27]). Germany's first characteristic is that it did not experience the period of precocious national construction (rapid centralization of State functions, monopoly of legitimate violence, fiscal monopoly, etc.) that occurred in France: it did not experience the transmission of the code of *savoir vivre* from the nobility to the bourgeoisie, the process of civilization. This explains the underdevelopment, the historical delay,

The Specifics of National Histories   107

it is the *Sonderweg*: that theme of the original (or eccentric) way of the Germans, which is almost a stereotype of German history. Historical delay, historical reform, etc. In fact, Elias uses France in two ways. He uses it as a theoretical reference for the historian, but without forgetting that France has in reality been a historical reference for the Germans. Collective representations of France have played an effective role in German history since the eighteenth century. For instance, in what he calls self-thematization, the representation of self that is made by the Germans, he shows that Germany constructs itself in opposition to the model of civilization. It is the culture–civilization antithesis, that appears in the writings you know:[28] *culture*, depth, Goethe and the tradition of Rousseau, sincerity and truth. Depth and morality is German, and *civilization* is French, superficial, worldly, etc. According to Elias, this opposition has created some of the structure, at least, of the self-image that German intellectuals have developed. It is a pattern of thinking developed by German intellectuals, a pattern for the construction of the German image of the French and France.

This pattern of construction was composed in the relations between the German bourgeois and the aristocrats, the princelings who spoke French, played French music, lived in mini-Versailles chateaux and rabbited on about *civilization*. Against them the bourgeois constructed culture and bourgeois seriousness, and then served it up again against the French. This was obviously easy enough to do, because that civilization came from France in the first place. This collective resentment is that of a petit bourgeoisie excluded from polite society and resentful of a nobility which was not only mediocre and uneducated but also exclusive and arrogant. This national resentment was reinforced at the time of the occupation of Germany by Napoleon's army, something we see crystallized in Herder's works. This resentment, this long-standing habitus of resentment, is attributed by Elias to the loss of real power linked to the collapse of the (Germanic) Holy Roman Empire. That is his argument, but fair enough: the different Germanic ethnic groups that held a dominant role saw themselves demoted, and definitively lost their dominance at the time of the Thirty Years War [1618–48], which made incredible ravages on all the German territories (wiping out 30 per cent of the population). According to Elias, the German cultural habitus is characterized by a certain 'brutality': the habitus of 'heavy drinking' and *Gemütlichkeit* behaviour would find its roots in the rapid and lasting 'impoverishment' of a cultural code based on courtliness, courtesy.[29] This code collapsed. Elias also analyses the German tradition of duels, which were practised up until quite recent times (cf. *Liber*[30]). The students had to have virile virtues and fight with

108 *Imperialisms*

sabre or sword. There were selected corporations of students, which was a way of eliminating Jews, etc. Elias detects a sort of 'barracks' habitus among the Germans – the Prussian man of the barracks. After the defeat of 1914–18, this archaic, ancestral habitus was particularly revolted by the humiliation of Germany – which helps explain the present. So, on to the genesis of Nazism, the resentment and trauma of post-Nazi Germany, etc. It is a very weighty tome, but I have given you the main lines.

I think that I should also have picked out Durkheim's *L'Évolution pédagogique en France* [1938] as a very important contribution. It is a formidable aid to comprehension. It is another way of making a structural history of unconsciouses. Here it is not a national historical unconscious but a regional historical unconscious, linked to education.

FINAL DISCUSSION

Frédéric Lebaron: You have not made much mention of the importance of educational habits and habitus in the construction of pre-fabricated national problematics and even comparative problematics. Moreover, we may perhaps need to study how comparative history is practised in different countries; it would be a very interesting comparative study, and a strategically important one. You have just mentioned it in speaking of Durkheim. Perhaps it is a point that you could . . .

Pierre Bourdieu: If this seminar works out, the actual contents of the seminar should be defined as we proceed. I said this very briefly at the start: there would normally be a nucleus of active people responsible for organizing things, but all the participants should bring in some of their national experience, etc. I think that we might imagine a seminar where we would present the results of a working party that I organized two months ago at Neuchâtel which was called 'The Scholarly Unconscious'.[31] It is a subset of everything that I have been saying. I could perhaps try to present it or ask one of the participants to present our first findings on the national educational unconsciouses as they emerge from a comparative history of educational systems, or rather of pedagogical practices or even more of the automatisms of pedagogical practices. The things that go without saying: the three-point plan, the discussion, a whole lot of things. That makes up a major part of the project.

Gérard Mauger: . . . What topics should we choose to study, what are the pertinent topics? It seems to me that we could sum up the programme by saying that we are trying to recognize the identical beneath the apparently different and the different beneath the apparently identical. The whole problem then is to know where we are going to start looking. . . . Could we reflect on a rational way of organizing the programme? In particular I have in mind the question of the scale of the observation. For instance, you referred to a possible macro-scale in a comparative analysis that would use a certain number of indicators, with the difficulty that you mentioned in passing, but which in my opinion is serious: At what scale do we construct the statistics? National? Regional? Whatever? On a more fundamental level, are we looking to seek out the identical where we don't think of looking for it . . . perhaps it is situated on a scale that we never consider? That is, in objects that are not worthy of attention or considered not worthy of attention. [*He explains that in the domain of the study of transformations of the space of delinquent practices, you first of all have to bring the background up to date by studying objects that nobody is interested in (here, street culture) in order to perceive the differences and transformations*]. The question then is the scale of the observation. Will there be privileged levels . . . My second question has to do with what you rapidly dismissed, no doubt for good reasons, but in my opinion not entirely. You bin the sites of memory, but I want to retrieve them; in the same way that you put the misunderstandings and the mistakes in the bin, I want to retrieve them from the bin. I understand all your reasons for binning them, but I think that they are also modes of inculcation that can be effective: I don't think that they can be dismissed. [*He gives examples of bad translations, of meetings of the Council of Europe where nobody understands a word and which function according to mutual misunderstandings; similarly, for ceremonies and monuments.*]

Pierre Bourdieu: I agree with you entirely. What I said about the sites of memory was rather superficial. The historical unconsciouses are the product of a whole historical work of reconstruction. And the sites of memory are places of commemoration, etc. I wanted to say that we should not stop at that. But I am absolutely in agreement with what you are saying. What you say about comparison makes me think of another example: violence in school. You only have to have been a boarder at school thirty years ago to know that everything that is described as being without precedent . . . Perhaps there is a difference in degree, but the greatest difference is that it has become identified as a problem, by the media, etc. So the fact of accomplishing the work of disaggregation that comparison would make possible would be a very important way of putting the question: What has changed in the perception of these things? Has it changed in reality or in the perception of it? And I think that many phenomena that are described as unprecedented are in large part phenomena whose socially constructed perception has changed. That is why we keep coming across journalism. Journalism is an interesting object of analysis in that it contributes more and more to the construction of the objects of our analysis, and is itself something that we must take as an object of analysis because it is one of the objects of analysis that it helps to construct, and that are imposed upon us as objects of analysis. The programmes of research are made by journalists to a considerable extent. In the critical work that has to be done to liberate us from imposed, circumstantial problematics, journalism is not at all secondary. If we have been led to take journalism more and more often as an object of study, it is partly for epistemological reasons. We have a sociology of knowledge, a sociology of imposed problematics. There is the whole process: the journalists, the opinion polls, the questioning of opinion, the imposition of problematics. And these problems invented and imposed can then become real: we can find them in enquiries and even in people's minds. And we may have to fight to reject these problems. For instance, for some time now when I speak with researchers, I tell them to be on their guard against the temptation to take at face value things that are the result of the populations interviewed re-echoing the dominant discourse on these populations. We have known this for some time now; we know that since the Third Republic, farmers make speeches in the language they have learned from books in primary school, that is, from nineteenth-century Goncourt prize novels.[32] And then people say that this is popular or populist literature . . . Finally, I am saying things that are simplistic, but I am aware that it is more complicated than that. It is rather a call for awareness. I think that today many of the things that we record on tape are the result of the interviewees re-echoing comments concerning them. I think for example that all these comments on delinquency at school, etc., will have very profound effects on the schools.

Frédéric Lebaron: A remark on the question of relations of domination between nations, which you have not really tackled and which can be a means of studying certain nations and States comparatively, through their reactions to transnational domination, which is itself a product of the national. Here I am thinking of employment policies, and the economic vocabulary of 'flexibility' and 'employability', of discourses on 'workfare',[33] which are today quite central issues imported at a European level, and which pose problems of comparison. What is more, 'workfare' is not translated into French. And we can tell that it is not merely a question of words but also a question of organization and practice: there is strong reticence and resistance, coming from certain poles of the trade union field, from certain social forces and forces of the social movement. And so finally I wonder if this axis of transnational domination isn't pretty central to comparative analysis today. Which is to say: thinking of comparison without bearing in mind the pivotal role of international domination is perhaps dangerous, especially in the economic domain.

Pierre Bourdieu: On this point, there is a book that might serve as a theoretical model. It is the book by Pascale Casanova on *La République mondiale des lettres*,[34] which focuses on the very special domain of literature to study the effects of domination, and proposes a model of the effects of domination on international exchanges. The literary world, which is commonly described as a peaceful world, in which there are no power relations, but a circulation and communion of minds (it is almost Kant's 'kingdom of ends'[35]), is in fact a world in which there are specific relations of domination and power, which means that the writers of small nations . . . There are some splendid examples: a writer from an African country who wants to write like Joyce in his particular language is very soon obliged to resort to English.[36] These power relations are very important, and I think that it would be important to bear this model in mind in addressing the phenomena you mention: the circulation of economic models. There is also Wacquant's book, *Les Prisons de la misère*,[37] which gives an idea of how certain dominant models become universal in the logics of power relations, which are complex and symbolic relations of domination. I think that you are right and that we should take it into account in the model. The relations between the three imperial nations – which is a special case – are more or less those between equals, although there are some relations of domination.[38] It is a special case. But as soon as we pass from the relations between these three imperial nations and their empires, we can easily see that there is dissymmetry. The intra-European relations are such that we tend to forget the relations of domination. It is easier to forget them. That doesn't mean that there aren't any.

Frédéric Lebaron: The problem of the Greeks will be interesting in this case.

Pierre Bourdieu: Indeed. It is no accident that this problem has arisen in Greece. The problem came from the Greeks being in a dominated position within Europe.

Yves Dezalay: I would like to return to the question of the inter-echoing effect. I understand very well that to escape the domination of the institutions that fund the research programme you want to look as far ahead as possible, but in fact isn't it a very long road that supposes a whole effort of constructing research teams, training researchers, etc.? And are there not also routes that are perhaps more risky and dangerous, but which would allow us precisely to see what happens in this inter-echoing effect between disciplines or nations that you mentioned, on the subject of these comparisons where everyone situates themselves in relation to the others and where the comparison is itself produced by comparison. So isn't that what we should look at first? Look first, not simply by taking a sort of textual viewpoint, but by observing the tools, the places and the institutions. And that is where we find the researchers and the university world . . . And try to analyse a little what happens in the circuits of exchange, whether between powers of equivalent imperial rank, or whether in fact in the countries of the immediate European periphery or further out. Might that not be a route too – a fairly treacherous one, because it is also one where we most risk falling into journalism, but one which must be taken nonetheless.

Pierre Bourdieu: I am really grateful to you for saying that. Because I realize that I always tend to go for what is furthest away and most difficult, most impossible. What I am describing is a programme on a twenty-year scale, the vocabulary of European institutions for example . . . It's true. But I maintain that it is important to have such a programme, even if we know that it is impossible. It has the virtue of a certain form of scientific utopianism: as long as we have not done this, we still risk falling back into the *doxa* . . . At the same time, this programme can have something terrifying, crushing about it. If that is what should be done, everything that we are doing is absolutely derisory . . . That said, it is also a kind of reminder of the practice of a sociology reflecting on the very universe that we are caught up in. The vocabulary of European institutions. I think that will be granted to us. But taking Eurostat as an object of study – as we plan to do – taking all the research programmes funded by Europe, studying the genesis of all of these projects, how they are debated, etc., what the sums allocated are, what the relations are, is going to be a pain in the arse, and socially dangerous. And very useful as a wake-up call. But at the same time, I hear where you are coming from. You are right. We must take the plunge . . .

· ·

ANNEX: PREPARATORY NOTES[39]

We need to break with national histories of national traditions and with the simple juxtaposition of national histories of national traditions (cf. various histories claiming to be 'European'); that is, with the obsession with events from the national past (the logic of anniversaries) and with national viewpoints over these events (which condemn the comparative analysis to remain confined within a national ethnocentrism despite itself, with all its correlative censorship – cf. American cultural anthropology of France or Japan v. the freedom of Norbert Elias as a German Jewish émigré writing on Germany).

To move beyond the simple, rather mechanical comparison of statistical data (demographic, social and economic) – with all the difficulties associated with the comparison of data constructed according to the same national categories that are going to be compared – which neither explain nor provide any means of interpreting the variations, we need to create a comparative history oriented towards the explanation of the present, and question the different national traditions using an explicative problematic, that is, one starting out from the present, from present data that formulate a problem that needs explaining, or more precisely, from a *pertinent present difference, from a socially significant variation*. (All the while taking care not to start out from a present problem facing our national and international society and towards which we would have to take up a defensive or adversarial position, *as in a trial – which would condemn us to eternally rewrite the same national history*: e.g. French Revolution; a simple reminder of the basic imperative: transform social problems into sociological problems, to which we may add Bergson's warning: avoid lapsing into the 'retrospective illusion'.)

The main problem comes from the fact that their national history is naturalized in the minds of the historians, sociologists and ethnologists, so that the historically naturalized seems obvious and beyond question to them. And it is not sufficient to warn them against the temptation of taking literally the certainties of 'common knowledge', the 'taken for granted'. We need to provide practical means to operate defamiliarization, which is what serves as the starting point for a historical enquiry.

Historical reflexivity

How can we become ethnologists of our own society, of our own historical experience, socio-analysts of our own social unconscious? How can we draft an ethnological questionnaire capable of orienting an enquiry into the pertinent historical facts that we need to know to really understand what is happening today in the French and German educational systems?

When we ask the Germans to tell us what they don't understand in the French educational system, and vice versa (but the problem is that, as with the national system, we find the same sort of false familiarity based on apparently similar phenomena, preventing people from understanding that they don't really understand).

Really fundamental problem: How to be an ethnologist of our own milieu, how to manage to transform social problems into sociological problems, how to practise a sociology of journalism rather than sociological journalism on journalism (the same for sport, or women, etc., etc.). Danger: we think we are smart, and that we have understood everything. Subjects seen as fashionable are falsely facile; in fact they are the most difficult (formerly not advised for beginners). We need many different systems to achieve the break: otherwise we lapse into 'Cultural Studies'. We think we are practising sociology by watching football matches on telly or chatting with journalists. Just as in former times some people might have thought they were practising sociology of the media when they were hanging out with starlets on the Croisette at the Cannes film festival and writing books on the stars (we still see the equivalent today). It is here that statistics, even weighty, positivistic statistics, are indispensable; as an instrument for the break as much as an instrument of knowledge. Ethical and scientific danger created by those who encourage a 'return to the real thing' and denounce the break and reliance on statistics as being aristocratic and scientistic.

How do we understand that we do not understand? By taking a truly foreign and alien view of our own practices ('making strange', *ostranenie* in the Russian Formalists[40]). By making ourselves foreigners to our own practices, using our knowledge of foreign practices (but this remains abstract); by striving to set up social relations with foreigners, between foreigners, so that each person adopts a foreign view of their own practices.

Inventing a social system

We need not only to put people from different nations, preferably sociologists, ethnologists and historians, round the table for discussion. (*Idem* for the interdisciplinary: there is a historical unconsciousness in each discipline which raises the same problems: false semi-comprehensions, etc.) We should on the one hand define an aim (the object of study is the historical unconscious) and on the other hand elaborate the practical means of attaining this aim, the methodical exploration of the historical unconscious.

We immediately see that the means, instrument or method can only be historical; but using what kind of history? We are back where we started. Not ordinary history, but a history that assumes the aim of uncovering and unveiling historical unconsciousness and historical transcendentals. This is not for positivist historians . . . Lurking behind what goes without saying are the harmonics of the different historical unconsciouses, of the national historical habitus, as well as the coincidence of the systems of categories of thought, perception and action involved in the historical data considered and the categories used by the scholar.

Double historicization

But how do we put this double historicization into practice, how make it really *practicable*?

A more precise system: group together researchers from different nations working on the same topics and armed with the same research programme, that we might call epistemological or even *meta-practical*.

The vocabulary of the European institutions: cf. Benveniste. To explore the social unconscious invested in ordinary words that name things social in the different European countries. *Begriffsgeschichte* [history of concepts] (not an analysis of content: but open-ended, neutral accounting).

The history of the pertinent historical data that a sociologist should master to truly understand what a sociologist from another country is telling him, and to truly understand what he is telling a sociologist from another country on delinquency, drug abuse or social workers in the housing estates. Questionnaire, i.e. programme for a true comparative history: what do you need to know about France (*cathos* [true Catholic believers], *Esprit* [Catholic journal], etc.) to understand reactions to the PACS, or Greece (the colonels, etc.) to understand Greek policies towards delinquency. Each of the participants in the scientific debate should be capable of transforming each of the others into an ethnographic informant and transforming themselves into an ethnographic informant to reply to questions from the others.

Second important theme: our comparative history should not forget that the history it is studying comparatively is the product of real, permanent comparisons between the nations: on the one hand because it is in danger of taking for comparative science what are comparative stereotypes resulting from the conflict between nations (or in danger of being perceived and read as such: cf. Pascale Casanova: role given to Paris which could be perceived as an effect of gallocentrism in a book entirely constructed against gallocentrism[41]). The different nations measure up against each other, comparing and constructing themselves in relation to each other; on the other hand, because real comparison, even if it is more or less fantasized, plays a part in making up the historical reality of nations. There is in the real life of Germany and England a host of things that have been introduced by the concern to be different from France, and vice versa. A certain idea of revolutionary France, whether true or not, has affected the Germans and the English, for most as a repellent (but also for others as a model).

Some models

- Durkheim, *L'Évolution pédagogique en France*
- E. P. Thompson, 'The Peculiarities of the English', *The Poverty of Theory and Other Essays* (London: Merlin Press, 1978), pp. 35–91.

Starting point: a current debate with Perry Anderson and Tom Nairn (and the *New Left Review*). From the start, reference to France and more particularly to the French Revolution posited as paradigm for all possible revolutions (true everywhere from England to Japan, especially for Marxists): E. P. Thompson's two opponents are given as francophile left-bank coffee-bar intellectuals (great fans of Althusser). So they describe England in terms of lack and absence:

- (E. P. Thompson sketches a sociology of these two adversaries: transforming a spontaneous impulse of rebellion – against the neo-liberals, Popper, Hayek, etc. – into an interpretation of history, p. 65.)

First question: Why did England not have a true (French) revolution? The English revolution of the seventeenth century (1688) is 'impure', premature and unfulfilled, driven by a religious logic; the English bourgeoisie is not a true bourgeoisie (p. 37); the same thing, consequently, for the proletariat. 'English exceptionalism'.

(First mistake: ethnocentrism: they take a nation – and more precisely the model of the French Revolution, as a measure of all the others; here it is not *nationalism*, but *inverse nationalism*: a chic refusal of the national: 'It is impossible to understand even the beginnings of English capitalism if one peers out, through Parisian eyes, at the backward "provinces", seeing in the landowners only a feudal aristocracy "with bourgeois traits"' (p. 42). In fact the eighteenth-century gentry 'made up a superbly successful and self-confident capitalist class' (p. 253). It is they who inspire a 'naturalistic political economy', 'most notably with Adam Smith', the theory of laissez-faire. In the nineteenth century the agrarian and mercantile capitalism (of the eighteenth century) and the industrial capitalism (of the nineteenth) are brought together by the fear of the French Revolution and the challenge from the national proletariat. In this symbiosis, the aristocracy is dominant because it controls the State and because it imposes its style of life through symbolic domination. Whence the perpetuation of a certain aristocratic lifestyle.

Second question: why does England not have (French-style) intellectuals? Because of the role that Protestantism has played, she has not needed the intellectuals of the Enlightenment and their fight against obscurantism (p. 58). There exists a 'tradition of dissent'. No centralization of the intelligentsia (example: role of the Scots and Edinburgh or Glasgow). No conflict with an authority: whence less inclination to produce systematic criticism (same phenomenon as for the Academy and the Impressionists). Produces science and Darwin, but not Voltaire or Marx. Greatness of English political economy (pp. 62–3).

Third question: why no (Marxist) revolutionary trade unions and intellectuals? (p. 66) In fact, role of external politics which refers us to nationalism (p. 67). The article finishes with a debate on Marxism and on the notion of class.

Annotated bibliography

Difficult to define, because there is no agreement on what we mean by *comparative* or *comparatist history*, in the sense of a comparison of national historical unconsciouses (historical transcendentals), very little.

To compare comparatisms

Immense biblio. Basis: Tilly, Zolberg, David Brion, Davis, people I think are good (with a few exceptions: but useful = opposite Lipset). *Charles Tilly, Louise Tilly, Richard Tilly, *The Rebellious Century, 1850–1930*, Cambridge, 1975.

Comparisons of the historical dynamics of global societies. Great ambitions:

- Cyril E. Black, *The Dynamics of Modernization: A Study in Comparative History*, New York, 1966.
- Cyril Black (ed.) et al., *Comparative Modernization: A Reader*, New York, 1976.

[theory] of 'modernization' – seven '*patterns*' of 'political modernization' *comparative modernization studies*
interrelation of state formation, culture, tradition, and technological development
critical: evolutionist model; implicit hierarchization

- Barrington Moore, *Social Origins of Dictatorship and Democracy: Lord and Peasant in the Making of the Modern World*, Boston, 1966.
- Role of the social classes, especially the peasantry: comparison of the agrarian sources of modernity in England, France, United States, China, Japan, India.
- Three paths: one leads
  - to capitalist democracy through bourgeois revolution
  - to fascism, revolution from above
  - to communism, revolutionary mobilization of the peasantry

Two contradictory 'paradigms'
Critical: refuses to take the nation-state as unit of analysis and comparison

Comparison *pro domo* or American exceptionalism

- Compare with another history to add something to one's own history

- Much practised by USA: a central trait of American history has an equivalent elsewhere
  - Cf. black slavery: comparative research / slavery and race relations
  - Women: comparative history of women and 'sex roles'
  - 'frontier': *settler societies* (Hartz)
  - development of *welfare states*.

Means of exploring the national (or local) specifics of a problem by examining an analogous phenomenon elsewhere – better to understand something American

American exceptionalism

Tocquevillian tradition

American exceptionalism because of absence of (1) feudal tradition (2) anti-feudal revolution so they don't have the ideological and social cleavages of Europe.

- Seymour Martin Lipset, *Continental Divide: The Values and Institutions of USA and Canada*, New York, 1990.
- (Maybe isolate the critical factors or the independent variables that account for national differences.)
- Lipset doesn't really look into history for the origins of the differences noted by contemporary observation and opinion surveys.
- Typical exceptionalism: the American revolution has bequeathed to the United States a lasting 'pattern' of liberal individualism that still today opposes the Canadian tradition, which retains traces of collectivism and Tory conservatism.

Aristide Zolberg. Each nation is the unique product of a unique history.

- [cf. national historical habitus as habitus produced by past history which is the basis of the selection and perception of historical events. Cumulative effect: tends to perpetuate differences – what is more, national societies construct themselves in opposition to one another.]
- But this does not mean that they diverge from a general pattern composed by all the others. No reason to consider one nation as the rule and the others as exceptions [cf. 'the French exception']

Breaking with exceptionalism

- A. Zolberg, 'How Many Exceptionalisms?', in *Working-Class Formation: Nineteenth-Century Patterns in West Europe and the United States*, Ira Katznelson and A. R. Zolberg, Princeton, 1986.

- David Brion Davis, *The Problem of Slavery in Western Culture*, New York, 1967.

Comparison: Isolate the effects of history on a particular point; isolate factors, criteria or variables that explain national differences.
- G. M. Fredrickson, *Black Liberation: A Comparative History of Black Ideologies in the United States and South Africa*, New York, 1995.
Postulate that each case is equally distinctive.

Initial traumatism

A historical particularity may give rise to a lasting difference: lasting consequences of the civil war on the ideological and constitutional plane: slavery was abolished through massive bloodshed not comparable to any other case.

Structural analysis. Explain the emergence of modern social insurance and welfare in Europe and the United States.
- Theda Skocpol and Anne Skola Orloff, comparisons of the policies of social assistance in the United States and England at the beginning of the twentieth century.
- Theda Skocpol, *Protecting Soldiers and Mothers: The Political Origins of Social Policy in the United States*, Cambridge, MA, 1992.
- Major variable: United States, absence of a 'normal' State organization.
- Failure of a publicly administrated policy of retirement pensions which succeeded in England.
- Cause: the American experience of the pension system of the civil war casting suspicion on government action in this domain – based on the fact that the United States has neither the body of specialized civil servants nor the administrative resources that exist in England.

Daniel Levine, *Poverty and Society: The Growth of the American Welfare State in International Comparison*, New Brunswick, 1988.
- The fundamental attitude towards poverty engendered by the historical experience of a particular nation explains the differences in their social policies. Cf. Europe.

Problematic comparatisms
Comparisons in the areas of work and the class struggle
Katznelson and Zolberg, *Working-Class Formation*.

- • <u>Why do American strikes tend to be more violent than English ones?</u> Why are American and French but not German and English workers attracted by anarcho-syndicalist ideologies and organizations?
- • *Comparison that explains a singularity: Gerschenkron*[42]
  - – against global comparisons; comparisons by strata
    rejection of aggregated indicators: averages (ignore class and region)
    different grids: linked to national history
  - – Appearance of convergence
  - – Fine comparisons

• •

3.4

The Scholarly Unconscious[1]

The system of cognitive patterns which underlie the construction of reality, and which are common to the whole of a society at a given moment, constitutes the cultural unconscious, or rather, the 'historical transcendental' that founds common sense (or the *doxa*), which is everything that is 'taken for granted', self-evident and goes without saying. Of all the aspects of historical reality, this 'historical transcendental' is no doubt the one that historians are most likely to miss, and not only because there is no trace of it in the historical documents, which by definition do not register it (these historians act as those whom Hegel calls the 'original historians',[2] who, because they live in the very period they describe, discuss everything but the essential, which is too obvious).

The scholarly (or transcendental) unconscious is the whole set of cognitive structures, in this historical transcendental, that are imputable to specifically scholarly experiences, and which are therefore largely common to all the pupils produced by the same – national – school system or, in a specified form, to all the members of the same discipline. It is a fact that, beyond the differences, depending in particular on the disciplines and the competition, pupils produced by the same national school system present a collection of common dispositions, often imputed to a 'national character', which means that they can often understand one another implicitly; many things, and not the least important, go without saying, such as what subject at a given moment needs or doesn't need to be discussed, what is important and interesting (what is a 'good topic' or, on the contrary, a 'banal' or 'trivial' idea or argument).

The scholarly unconscious is historically arbitrary, but, due to the fact that it has been incorporated and thereby naturalized, it escapes the grasp of the conscious mind – in particular because it leads us to

124 *Imperialisms*

apprehend as natural the structures which have produced it. Having gradually become consubstantial with intellectual activity, it can only be grasped in its manifestations or its objective effects, that is, by empirical, historical or sociological enquiry, functioning as epistemological experience. The *doxa*, a belief which does not recognize itself as such, is more difficult to uproot than any dogma, and when academic struggles disturb the bedrock of unconscious truths and presuppositions which constitute it, they can attain an extreme pitch of violence. Thus, for example, spelling (like grammar) is an orthodoxy which, in becoming naturalized, has become converted into *doxa*, and some writers may be ready to die for the circumflex accent or the right way to spell some word or other, such as *nénuphar* or *nénufar*, whose correct spelling they have been fighting over only recently.[3]

These cognitive structures are produced by the explicit work of inculcation that accompanies the educational system, but also and above all by a structural absorption without intent or subject, which operates through immersion in a structured environment: we may suppose that the main academic divisions (and hierarchies) of the disciplines and the forms of exercise (the *ex cathedra* lecture as opposed to the seminar, for instance) tend to reproduce themselves in *specific principles of vision and division*, themselves enveloped in more general principles which support them (the opposition between two disciplines – literature v. grammar or philology, history v. geography – or between two specialisms – metaphysics v. the history of philosophy or science – may for instance be hiding an opposition between the brilliant and the worthy).

This means that the analysis of this unconscious must be applied firstly to the relation, until now hardly explored, between the institutional structures (the history of the disciplines, for instance) and the cognitive structures, or more precisely their objectification in bodies and systems of knowledge. The history of institutionalized forms of production, communication or evaluation of knowledge, and also of the technical differences in recording and storing knowledge or the techniques of organizing data, is not in itself its end. No doubt nothing would be more precious than a (comparative) genealogy of institutions such as dialogue, *disputatio*, dispute of the Jesuit colleges, *ex cathedra* lecture, inaugural lecture, seminar, colloquium, oral examination (including defence of a thesis) and today, video conference or the internet. But such research would only properly fulfil its function if it set itself the specific goal of determining if and how these conventions structure cognitive forms, particularly by analysing the situations where a change in forms of communication provokes transformations in the forms of thought.

The Scholarly Unconscious   125

In this work of objectification of the historical unconscious, the researchers (historians, ethnologists or sociologists) are faced with two unconsciouses: the unconscious that they take as object, and their own academic unconscious (linked to national and disciplinary traditions), which they should also take as object, to avoid the risk of unwittingly investing it in their analysis of the historical unconscious of others. This work of double objectification is accomplished through a methodical comparison between the social and more precisely the academic environment of the object studied and the universe enclosing the analysts, who, if they omit to bring themselves into play, are always vulnerable to being caught in the trap of false truths of the over-familiar academic world. History (like ethnology) only fully accomplishes its mission when it also functions as an instrument of objectification of the subject of objectification, that is, as an especially powerful means of objectifying – by historicizing them – the historically (and academically) constituted cognitive structures that the historian engages in their historical work. This work of objectification of the unconscious of the researcher is accomplished not in the sudden illumination of a blinding flash of insight, but rather through the progressive accumulation of everything that is learnt in the prolonged give-and-take between observation of the object and observation of the observer, of everything that observing the object reveals about the observer and everything that observing the observer reveals about the object.

In this work of reflexive objectification, the comparative method [*see below*] is quite clearly indispensable, because its primary effect is to 'defamiliarize' the 'familiar' and make the obvious strange. And the interdisciplinary, international colloquium absolutely fulfils its remit in this case by enabling us to gain the greatest benefit from the defamiliarization effect produced by the confrontation of unconscious minds from different disciplines and nations.[4] Rather like the formation of ancient cities, which by uniting separate tribes and traditions forced them to discover that so many things they thought were what they were by nature (*phusei*) were in fact only thus 'by law' (*nomô*), that is, by virtue of the arbitrariness of one tradition among many, so the confrontation of specialists from different nations, and even more from alien disciplines, necessarily produces (as does, no doubt to a lesser degree, the assembly of their contributions in the same issue of a journal) the 'estrangement' effect described by the Russian Formalists,[5] which is one of the conditions, if not of the discovery of the unconscious, at least of the discovery of its existence and its power. This confrontation does in fact oblige us to realize that, through our absorption of instruction in arbitrary, contingent, historical cognitive patterns, our schooling has infiltrated the most superficial reflexes of our thoughts, but also their apparently most creative improvisations, with a whole opaque body of the unthought, the fossilized and the naturalized, which, paradoxically, only historicization can revitalize, only historicization can liberate.

Our cognitive structures embrace above all everything that concerns classification, and a study of the academic unconscious must turn back against itself the instruments of knowledge that it has elaborated for and through the knowledge of the 'primitive forms of classification', as described by Durkheim and Mauss;[6] that is, classificatory systems such as those that ethnobotany and ethnoscience have elaborated, thanks in particular to techniques like componential analysis. It thus reveals the cognitive schemas that all those who have been subjected to an implicit or explicit scholarly indoctrination bring into play in their explicit operations of classification,[7] and, more generally, in their practical 'choices', and also the social conditions of production and reproduction of these patterns. These classifications, these principles of division, which are inscribed both in reality (in the very structure of the space, on the notices of lectures, on school reports, in lesson plans and timetables, etc.) and in people's minds, are constantly both the instruments and the goals of struggles for classification, cognitive struggles that are always in part struggles for power. In fact, in a universe where the struggles for knowledge are also struggles for recognition, they aim to legitimize hierarchies, or question or overthrow them; their goal is the conservation or transformation of the established cognitive order, the order which, thinking of Spinoza, I shall call *gnoseologico-political.* To achieve recognition of a new manner of creating literature, painting or science, to have a new discipline accredited, to impress people with the interest and importance of a new object, is to transform both symbolic and also material power relations by installing a new distribution of the material and symbolic profits procured by the corresponding practices.

Even if our cognitive structures are relatively well protected from change by the fact that, like linguistic structures, they partly escape the grasp of consciousness, they do change under the impact of the struggles of which they are the object, but also as a function of the transformation of the arrangement of cognitive techniques and instruments available. I am thinking for instance of what Vygotsky calls *stimuli-instruments* (as opposed to *stimuli-objects*),[8] that is, objects like the knot in a handkerchief or the notch in a stick, but also the diary, the timetable, the calendar, the family tree or lecture notes – tools of knowledge which change the structure of knowledge (as Goody has shown for writing, a simple instrument of transcription which has

The Scholarly Unconscious 127

completely changed the modalities of knowledge,[9] as people now make the case for the computer), which transform the user and their psychological functions, such as memory and attention.

This analysis of the cognitive unconscious leads to the source of certain of the structural misunderstandings that affect international communication, even in its scientific dimension. The ethnocentrism (or chronocentrism) that we must be wary of when we are dealing with societies that are far removed in time and space appears much less credible and much less dangerous when we are dealing with the Middle Ages or the nineteenth century, or, a fortiori, with the contemporary world. The illusion of obviousness separates us from ourselves, from our own historical unconscious, thus from all those, contemporary or not, near or far, who do not share it with us. This is why we need to historicize our modes of thinking, not in order to relativize them, but, paradoxically, to tear them away from history.

THE COMPARATIVE METHOD

The comparative method is one of the highroads to generalization. Taking the comparative method explicitly as object can at least have the virtue of heightening vigilance against all the forms of wild comparatism to which we so often succumb: this is the case for example when we apply to strange worlds terms borrowed from our universe (democracy, politics, etc.), or when, to be understood, or create a modern effect, we invoke contemporary institutions or events in discussing events from the past. A critical examination of the use that historians make of language (in particular through metaphorical references to the present) would discover numerous anachronisms: this is the case in particular with all the classificatory concepts such as the names of professions, or age groups, which are very closely linked to very specific historical contexts, so that, in the absence of a preliminary critique of taxonomies, the commentaries concerning long statistical series risk comparing things that are not comparable. The illusion of the constancy of the nominal, which leads us to forget that the same name (of a profession for example) can designate quite different realities, cannot resist a methodical reflection on the conditions and limits of comparability. This kind of reflection has the virtue of putting us on our guard against the inclination to universalize the individual case.

In fact, before entering into a description of the legitimate usage of the comparative method, we should, in order to submit them to a critical examination, record all the scientific practices that derive from this method: in ethnology, with Murdoch, who has the merit of showing up the absurdity of the positivist comparison of preconstructed objects;[10] or with Lévi-Strauss, who looks for formal invariants;[11] in history, with more or less thoughtful attempts to compare theoretical models of succession, without considering the logic of the actual practices.[12] In sociology we should compare the very different presumptions of the major usages of the comparative method which are associated with the names of Durkheim and Weber: on the one hand, the search for elementary forms associated with the use of ethnological comparison; on the other hand, the search for the specificity of European societies, based on a comparison of the great religious traditions.

Finally, we need to question the conditions of validity of comparison, and its limits. Here we must introduce something that forms one of the prime characteristics of the evolution of societies, that is, the process of differentiation at the end of which separate universes, endowed with their own specific laws of functioning, are established (universes that I call fields). This process of differentiation is what separates what we call undifferentiated societies, those studied by ethnologists, from societies like our own, in which universes governed by specific laws, those of economics *qua* economics ('business is business'), those of art for art's sake, etc., have gradually evolved. As a result, we must take all due precautions before attempting to transfer to our societies the concepts constructed to understand undifferentiated societies. It is as dangerous and naive to speak of ritual or magic when discussing bureaucratic practices (for instance the children's Christmas tree), which certain contemporary currents of the study of organizations do,[13] as to speak of aesthetics or economics in the modern sense of those terms when discussing undifferentiated societies. As long as we are fully conscious of these limits, and avoid lapsing into ethnologism, we can investigate the anthropological invariants (for example, in relation to our own body and the body of the other, and everything that flows from the fact that social agents are both subjects that perceive and objects of perception, etc.). And we may thus propose to establish a programme for a comparative historical science of anthropological invariants.

But the core of the work assigned to a comparative science would be an attempt to disentangle the invariant properties from a single field (the religious field, the literary field, etc.) considered at different moments of their history, or the properties common to the different fields of the same universe; that is, more precisely, the structural and functional homologies that are established between different fields – for example between the religious field and the political or the intellectual field.

> *This text has been established on the basis of Bourdieu's intervention in an EHEE seminar organized at Montrouge, 12–13 June 1987, on the initiative of Françoise Héritier (archives of Éditions Raisons d'agir).*

4

Sketch of Analyses of International Fields

4.1

The Olympics
An Agenda for Analysis[1]

What exactly do we mean when we talk about the Olympics? The apparent referent is what "really" happens. That is to say, the gigantic spectacle of sport in which athletes from all over the world compete under the sign of universalistic ideals; as well as the markedly national, even patriotic ritual of the parades by various national teams, and the award ceremonies replete with flying flags and blaring anthems. But the hidden reference is the television show, the ensemble of representations of the first spectacle, as it is filmed and broadcast by television in selections which, since the competition is international, appear unmarked by national bias. The Olympics, then, are doubly hidden: no one sees all of it, and no one sees that they don't see it. Every television viewer can have the illusion of seeing *the* (real) Olympics.

It may seem simply to record events as they take place, but in fact, given that each national television network gives more airplay to athletes or events that satisfy national pride, television transforms a sports competition between athletes from all over into a confrontation between champions, that is, officially selected competitors from different countries.

To understand this process of symbolic transformation, we would first have to analyze the social construction of the entire Olympic spectacle. We'd have to look at the individual events and at everything that takes places around them, such as the opening and closing parades. Then we'd have to look at the production of the televised image of this spectacle. Inasmuch as it is a prop for advertising, the televised event is a commercial, marketable product that must be designed to reach the largest audience and hold on to it the longest. Aside from the fact that these events must be timed to be shown on prime time in economically dominant countries, these programs must be tailored to meet audience demand. The expectations of different national publics and their preferences for one or another sport have to be taken into account. The sports given prominence and the individual games or meets shown must be carefully selected to showcase the national teams most likely to win events and thereby gratify national pride. It follows that the relative importance of the different sports within the international sports organizations increasingly depends on their television popularity and the correlated financial return they promise. More and more, as well, the constraints of television broadcasting influence the choice of sports included in Olympic competition, the site and time slot awarded to each sport, and even the ways in which matches and ceremonies take place. This is why (after negotiations structured by tremendous financial considerations) the key final events at the Seoul Olympics were scheduled to coincide with prime time in the United States.

All of which means that to understand the games, we would have to look at the whole field of production of the Olympics as a *televised show* or, in marketing terms, as a "means of communication." This is to say, we would have to assess all the objective relations between the agents and institutions competing to produce and sell the images of, and commentary about, the Olympics. These would include first the International Olympic Committee (IOC), which has gradually become a vast commercial enterprise with an annual budget of $20 million, dominated by a small, closed group of sports executives and representatives from major companies (Adidas, Coca-Cola, and so on). The IOC controls transmission rights (which were estimated, for Barcelona, at $1.635 billion), sponsorship rights, and the Olympic city selection. Second, we would need to turn our attention to the big (especially American) television networks competing for transmission rights (divided up by country or by language). Third would be the large multinational corporations (Coca-Cola, Kodak, Ricoh, Philips, and so on) competing for exclusive world rights to promote their products in connection with the Games (as "official sponsors").[2] Finally, we cannot forget the producers of images and commentary for television, radio, and newspapers (some ten thousand at Barcelona), since it is their competition that conditions the construction of the representation of the Olympics by influencing how these images are selected, framed, and edited, and how the commentary is elaborated. Another important consideration is the intensified competition between countries that is produced by the globalization of the Olympic spectacle. The effects of this competition can be seen in official *sports policies* to promote international sports success, maximizing the symbolic and financial rewards of victory and resulting in the *industrialization of the production of sports* that implies the use of drugs and authoritarian forms of training.[3]

A parallel can be seen in artistic production. The individual artist's directly visible actions obscure the activity of the other actors – critics, gallery owners, museum curators, and so on – who, in and through their competition, collaborate to produce the meaning and the value of both the artwork and the artist. Even more important, they produce the very belief in the value of art and the artist that is the basis of the whole art game.[4] Likewise, in sports, the champion runner or javelin thrower is only the obvious subject of a spectacle that in some sense is produced twice.[5] The first production is the actual event in the stadium, which is put together by a whole array of actors, including athletes, trainers, doctors, organizers, judges, timekeepers, and masters of the ceremonies. The second show reproduces the first in images and commentary. Usually laboring under enormous pressure, those who produce on the second show are caught up in a whole network of objective relationships that weighs heavily on each of them.

As a collectivity, the participants in the event we call "the Olympics" might conceivably come to control the mechanisms that affect them all. But they would be able to do so only by undertaking a serious investigation to bring to light the mechanisms behind this *two-step social construction*, first of the sports event, then of the media event. Only with the conscious control of these mechanisms that can be gained from such a process of research and reflection would this collectivity be able to maximize the potential for universalism – today in danger of extinction – that is contained within the Olympic Games.[6]

Translated by Priscilla Parkhurst Ferguson

4.2

The Global Legal Field[1]

There is no epistemological obstacle worse than the declarations that are not entirely true but not completely false made by journalists, essayists and semi-scientists, all doxosophers who, feigning a break with appearances and a revelation of hidden mysteries, do no more than announce and reinforce the most obvious truisms, those that Aristotle would have called 'endoxic'. This is the case with discourses on the theme of 'globalization' ('global culture', 'global economy', 'global city', etc.) which we see proliferating everywhere today, and which, like the invocations of 'planetary' and 'planetization' by French essay writers in the 1960s, are based on a series of common-sense observations such as, in no particular order, the diffusion of electronic media and the commercial entertainment they transmit (with sports matches as their paradigm); transcontinental humanitarian solidarity; the global circulation of goods and services; the intensification and acceleration of information and migration flows, linked to improvements in means of transport and communication, etc. You would in fact seem to have a warped mind or a perverse character if you were to wonder whether the globalization proclaimed were not another name for Westernization or Americanization, for instance, and more precisely whether a new world order were not gradually being established, dominated by a few great industrial powers capable of exporting and imposing on a universal scale not only their products but also their lifestyle. But adopting that standpoint is only a knee-jerk reaction, and, finally, nearly as superficial as the naively ecumenical representation it opposes. And we must break with both of these views if we want to truly construct the genuine object of a scientific analysis of the phenomenon that an endoxic discourse only disguises in disclosing it: the global field in the process of construction in the different domains of practice, or, to put it another way, the process leading to the composition of specific global fields (economic, literary, legal, etc.) at the heart of which the national fields are caught, but with a greater or lesser degree of autonomy. In this perspective, analysis of the emergence of an international field of law can, through its exemplary character, determine a genuine shift of paradigm in a domain that seemed given over to the verbose and random half-truths of the essay writers.

The notion of a global, or better, *international* legal field immediately allows us to escape the alternative of harmonious unification or conflictual division, and take note of the fact that it is precisely unification through competition and struggle that characterizes the field (as opposed in particular to the 'profession', a preconstructed notion that the Anglo-American sociological tradition has borrowed straight from its historical doxa). It will suffice to make the essential break, implied in the notion of field, with common sense and the academic alternative between consensus and conflict to understand that, paradoxically, it is the struggles between jurists of different countries for the imposition of legal forms, or rather, of modes of production of the law, that have contributed to the unification of the global legal field and the global market for legal expertise (or, in a very similar logic, economic expertise).

In *Dealing in Virtue*, Yves Dezalay and Bryant Garth have thus been able to combine their own experience (linked to their national origins and disciplinary training, involving two of the great legal traditions confronting each other) with their learned knowledge of a great number of national legal spaces (including their own). What is shown by the study of the emergence of the domain of international commercial arbitration is the fact that 'the international' is constructed largely from competition among national approaches. Since lawyers are trained, and largely pursue their careers, at a national level, it is not surprising that they seek as a matter of course to import their ways of thinking and practising when it comes to the construction of international institutions. This process makes the international the site of a statutory competition between essentially national approaches.

In the fight for new markets for their legal services, the large law firms rely on the fact that legal capital plays a determining role in the regulation not only of commercial but also of human rights organizations, which, along with the great international institutions like the IMF and the World Bank, often act as a Trojan horse for the 'Chicago Boys'[2] with their juridico-economic import/export strategies that associate ethical idealism with economic realism. But these *new bourgeois* conquerors have to contend with the resistance of the national legal fields threatened by the new world legal order, or rather, with the

138 *Imperialisms*

balance of power and the struggles that actually become established at the heart of these fields between the modernists who side with the international and the traditionalists who opt for protectionist closure and maintaining the national tradition (echoing the alternative that we have seen manifested in the political stances adopted in many countries towards supranational institutions).

Thus thinking in terms of fields also grants us the means of grasping the global logic of the new world legal order, while still avoiding those geopolitical considerations, as vague and vast as their object, to which supporters of the 'global' and 'globalization' often pay homage, and enabling us to return to the more concrete strategies of the agents, who are themselves defined by their dispositions (linked to social positions and trajectories), their properties and their interests. It also enables us to discover for example that, at the heart of each national field, the partisans of the 'global' or the 'local' are not distributed at random, because the international strategies are only really accessible to those who owe to their (very) privileged social origins the dispositions and competences (in particular, linguistic) which are not readily acquired in the classroom. If in addition we know that the prohibitive cost of training in the great North American universities, which open up access to the market of international law, reserves them in fact for the students best endowed with social and financial capital, we can understand why the educated, cosmopolitan inheritors of the national bourgeoisies whose privileges are threatened, on the national market, by the effects of the intensification of educational competition are the first to find paths to salvation in careers opened up for them by the new international space of expertise. And it is perhaps because they have this quite particular interest in a particular form of the universal that the members of this new international *noblesse de robe*, when they exercise their talents in the transnational organizations, whether humanitarian organizations or even large multinational legal firms, can help to raise their local universes to a superior level of universalization by joining in the struggles of the world legal field, taking as their weapon and their goal the law (whether the rights of business, the rights of man or the rights of businessmen), with its – piously hypocritical – reference to the universal.

4.3

The Internationalization of the Economic Field[1]

Historically, the economic field has been constructed within the framework of the national state, with which it is intrinsically linked. Indeed, the state contributes in many respects to unifying the economic space (which contributes in return to the emergence of the state). As Karl Polanyi shows in *The Great Transformation*, the emergence of national markets in Europe was not the mechanical product of the gradual extension of economic exchanges, but the product of a deliberately mercantilist state policy aimed at increasing domestic and foreign trade (especially by fostering the commercialization of land, money, and labor).[2] But, far from leading to a process of homogenization, as one might believe, unification and integration are accompanied by a concentration of power, which can go all the way to monopolization, and, at the same time, by the dispossession of part of the population thus integrated. This is to say that integration into the state and the territory it controls is in fact the precondition for domination (as can be readily seen in all situations of colonization). As I was able to observe in Algeria, unification of the economic field tends, in particular through monetary unification and the generalization of monetary exchanges that ensue, to pitch all social agents into an economic game for which they are not equally prepared and equipped, culturally and economically.[3] It tends, by the same token, to subject them to the norm objectively imposed by competition from more efficient productive forces and modes of production, as can clearly be seen with small producers from the countryside, who are increasingly wrenched from a state of autarky. In short, *unification benefits the dominant*, whose difference is turned into capital by the mere fact of their being brought into relation. (To take a recent example, in the 1930s Franklin D. Roosevelt had to establish common social rules in matters of employment such as the minimum wage, the limitation of working hours,

140 *Imperialisms*

pensions, etc. to avoid the deterioration in wages and working conditions attendant upon the integration of unequally developed regions into a single national entity.)

But in other respects, the process of unification and concentration remained confined within national borders; it was limited by all the barriers, especially juridical ones, to the free movement of goods and persons (customs duties, exchange controls, etc.). And it was limited also by the fact that production and particularly the circulation of goods remained closely bound to geographical place (owing in part to transport costs). It is these limits on the extension of economic fields that tend today to weaken or disappear under the impact of various factors: on the one hand, purely technical factors, such as the development of new means of communication (air transport and the internet); on the other, more properly political or juridical-political factors, such as policies of liberalization and deregulation. Together they foster the formation of *a global economic field*, particularly in the financial realm (where computerized means of communication tend to eliminate the time gaps that traditionally separated the various national markets).

The double meaning of "globalization"

We must return here to the word "globalization." We have seen that, in a rigorous sense, it could refer to the unification of the global economic field or to the expansion of that field to the entire world. But it is also made to mean something quite different, in a surreptitious slide from the descriptive meaning of the concept, such as I just formulated, to a normative or, better yet, *performative* meaning. In this second sense, "globalization" refers to an *economic policy* aimed at unifying the economic field by means of a whole set of juridical-political measures designed to tear down all the obstacles to that unification – obstacles that are mostly linked to the nation-state. And this very precisely defines the neoliberal policy inseparable from the veritable economic propaganda that lends it part of its symbolic force by playing on the ambiguity of the notion.

Economic globalization is not a mechanical effect of the laws of technology or the economy but the product of a policy implemented by a set of agents and institutions, and the result of the application of rules deliberately created for specific ends, namely, trade liberalization (that is, the elimination of all national regulations restricting companies and their investments). In other words, the "global market" is *a political creation*, just as the national market had been, the product of

The Internationalization of the Economic Field 141

a more or less consciously concerted policy. And, as was the case with the policy that led to the emergence of national markets, this policy has as an effect (and perhaps also as an end, at least among the most lucid and the most cynical of the advocates of neoliberalism) the creation of the conditions for domination by brutally confronting agents and firms hitherto confined within national boundaries with competition from more efficient and more powerful forces and modes of production. Thus in the emerging economies the disappearance of protection spells ruin for national enterprises. In countries such as South Korea, Thailand, Indonesia, or Brazil, the elimination of all obstacles to foreign investment leads to the collapse of local enterprises, which are then bought up, often at ridiculously low prices, by the multinationals. For these countries, public procurement contracts remain one of the only methods that enable local companies to compete with the big Northern concerns. Whereas they are presented as necessary for the creation of a "global field of action," the directives of the World Trade Organization on competition and public procurement policies would, by establishing competition "on an equal footing" between the big multinationals and small national producers, cause the mass destruction of the latter. For we know that, as a general rule, formal equality in a situation of real inequality favors the dominant.

The word "globalization" is, as we can see, a *pseudo-concept, at once descriptive and prescriptive*, that has supplanted the term "modernization," long ago used by American social scientists in a euphemistic manner to impose a naively ethnocentric evolutionary model according to which the different societies of the world are classified in terms of their distance from the most economically advanced society, that is, US society, instituted as the endpoint and end goal of all human history. (This is the case, for instance, when the criterion used to measure the degree of evolution is one of the distinctive, but apparently neutral and undisputable, properties of that society, such as energy consumption per capita, as criticized by Claude Lévi-Strauss in *Race and History*.[4]) This word embodies the most accomplished form of the *imperialism of the universal*, which consists in universalizing for a society its own particularity by tacitly instituting it as a universal yardstick (as French society did for a long time when, as the supposed historical incarnation of human rights and of the legacy of the French Revolution, it was posited – especially by the Marxist tradition – as the model of all possible revolutions).

Through this word, then, it is the process of unification of the global economic and financial field, that is, the integration of hitherto compartmentalized national economic universes, that is now organized

142 *Imperialisms*

along the lines of an economy rooted in the historical particularities of a particular social tradition, that of American society, which is instituted both as an inevitable destiny and as a political project of universal liberation, as the endpoint of a *natural evolution* and as the civic and ethical ideal that promises political emancipation for the peoples of all countries, in the name of a postulated connection between democracy and the market. The most fully accomplished form of this *utopian capitalism* is no doubt the myth of the "stockholders' democracy," that is, a universe of wage earners who, being paid in the form of shares, would collectively become "owners of their companies," thereby bringing about the perfect association between capital and labor. And the triumphant ethnocentrism of "modernization" theories reaches sublime heights with the most inspired prophets of the new economic religion who see the United States as the new homeland of "realized socialism" (we see here in passing that a certain scientistic madness triumphant today in Chicago concedes nothing to the most exalted ravings about "scientific socialism" that flourished in another age and place, with consequences that are well known).

We would need to pause here to demonstrate, firstly, that what is universally proposed and imposed as the norm of all rational economic practice is in reality the universalization of the particular characteristics of an economy embedded in a particular history and social structure, that of the United States; and that by the same token the United States is, by definition, the fully realized form of a political and economic ideal that for the most part is the product of the idealization of its own economic and social organization, characterized among other things by the weakness of the social state. But we would also have to demonstrate, secondly, that the United States occupies a dominant position in the global economic field which it owes to the fact that it cumulates a set of exceptional competitive advantages: *financial advantages*, including the exceptional position of the dollar, which enables Washington to drain off from all over the world (that is, from countries with a strong savings rate, such as Japan, but also from the ruling oligarchies of poor countries and from global networks of trafficking and money laundering) the capital it needs to finance its enormous public and trade deficits and to compensate for an exceedingly low rate of savings, and which enables it to implement the monetary policy of its choice without worrying about its repercussions for other countries, especially the poorest of them, which are objectively chained to American economic decisions and which have contributed to American growth not only by virtue of the low cost in dollars of their labor and products (particularly raw materials) but also with the levies they have paid into

The Internationalization of the Economic Field

the coffers of American banks; *economic advantages*, with the strength and competitiveness of the sector of capital goods and investment and, in particular, of industrial microelectronics, or the role of banking in the private financing of innovation; *political and military advantages*, its diplomatic weight allowing the United States to impose economic and commercial norms favorable to its interests; *cultural and linguistic advantages*, with the exceptional quality of the public and private system of scientific research (as measured by the number of Nobel laureates), the power of lawyers and of the big law firms, not to forget the practical universality of English, which dominates telecommunications and the whole of commercial cultural production; *symbolic advantages*, with the imposition of a lifestyle quasi-universally recognized, at least by adolescents, especially through the production and diffusion of representations of the world (as in movies) to which an image of modernity is attached. (We see in passing that the superiority of the American economy, which in reality is moving further and further away from the model of pure and perfect competition in the name of which it is being thrust onto the rest of the world, *is due to effects of structure and not to the particular efficacy of a given economic policy*, even as it has benefited from the intensification of work and the unprecedented lengthening of hours worked combined with very low wages for the least skilled, and also from the emergence of new economic sectors driven by science and information technology.)

One of the most unquestionable expressions of the relations of force being established within the global economic field is the asymmetry and "double standard" that allows, for example, the dominant powers and particularly the United States to resort to the very protectionist measures and public subsidies they deny to developing countries (which are prohibited from limiting imports of a product inflicting serious damage on their industry or from regulating flows of foreign investment). And it takes a great deal of goodwill to believe that concern for social standards and economic rights in the countries of the South (as with the prevention of child labor) is shorn of protectionist designs when we see that concern coming from countries, such as the United States, engaged in the wholesale deregulation of their own labor market and in sharply curtailing trade union rights. The policy of "globalization" is no doubt in itself the best illustration of this asymmetry since it aims at extending to the entire world, but *without reciprocity*, on a one-way basis (that is, in combination with redoubled isolationism and particularism), the organization most favorable to the dominant.

The unification of the global economic field through the imposition of the absolute rule of free exchange, the free movement of capital,

144   *Imperialisms*

and export-led growth is marked by the same ambiguity as integration into the national economic field was in another age. While featuring all the outward signs of a boundless universalism, a kind of ecumenism justified by the universal diffusion of the "cheap" lifestyles of the "civilization" of McDonald's, jeans, and Coca-Cola, or by "juridical harmonization," often regarded as an indicator of positive "globalization," this "societal project" serves the dominant, that is, the big investors who, while standing above states, can count on the major states and in particular on the most powerful of them politically and militarily, the United States, and on the major international institutions – the World Bank, the International Monetary Fund, and the World Trade Organization – which those states control, to ensure conditions favorable to the conduct of their economic activities. *The effect of domination linked to integration within inequality* can be clearly seen in the fate of Canada (which could well be the fate of Europe if the latter moves toward a kind of customs union with the United States): due to the lowering of its traditional protective barriers, which has left it defenseless particularly in matters of culture, this country is undergoing virtual economic and cultural integration into the American empire.

Like the old national states, the dominant economic forces are in effect capable of making (international) law and the great international organizations, which are exposed to the influence of lobbyists, operate to their advantage. The lobbies work to clothe the economic interests of powerful firms or nations with juridical justifications (for example, by guaranteeing industrial investors maximum rights and prerogatives); and they devote a very substantial part of their intellectual energies to dismantling national laws, such as legislation and regulations that ensure the protection of consumers. Without fulfilling all the functions ordinarily assigned to national states (such as those pertaining to social welfare), the international institutions invisibly govern the national governments which, seeing their role increasingly reduced to managing secondary matters, form a political smoke screen that effectively masks the true sites of decision making. They reinforce at the symbolic level the quasi-mechanical action of economic competition which compels national states to vie with each other in terms of both taxation (by lowering rates and granting special breaks) and competitive advantage (by providing free infrastructures).

The state of the global economic field

The global economic field presents itself as a set of global subfields, each of which corresponds to an "industry," understood as a set of firms competing to produce and commercialize a homogeneous category of products. The almost always oligopolistic structure of each of these subfields corresponds to the structure of the distribution of capital (in its different forms) between the different firms capable of acquiring and maintaining the status of efficient competitor at the global level, the position of a firm in each country being dependent on the position occupied by that firm in all the other countries. The global field is highly polarized. Owing to their mere weight within the structure (which functions as a barrier to entry), the dominant national economies tend to concentrate the assets of companies and to appropriate the profits they produce, as well as to orient the tendencies immanent in the functioning of the field. The position of each firm in the national and international field depends not only on its own specific assets but also on the economic, political, cultural, and linguistic resources that flow from its membership in a particular nation, with this kind of "national capital" exerting a positive or negative multiplier effect on the structural competitiveness of the different firms.

Today these different fields are structurally subordinated to the global financial field. That field was abruptly released (through measures such as the French financial deregulation law of 1985–6) from all the regulations that had been imposed on it for almost two centuries and which had been strengthened after the great string of banking collapses of the 1930s. Having thus achieved almost complete autonomy and integration, the global field of finance has become one among many sites within which to generate returns on capital. The large concentrations of money effected by the big investors (pension funds, insurance companies, investment funds) have become an autonomous force, controlled solely by bankers who increasingly favor speculation, financial operations with no end other than financial, at the cost of productive investment. The international economy of speculation thereby finds itself freed from the control of the national institutions, such as central banks, which used to regulate financial operations, and long-term interest rates tend henceforth to be determined not by national bodies but by a small number of international operators who set the trends on the financial markets.

The concentration of finance capital in the pension funds and mutual funds that attract and manage collective savings enables the trans-state managers of those savings to impose on firms, in the name

146   *Imperialisms*

of shareholder interests, demands for financial profitability that gradually divert and direct their strategies. This is effected in particular by restricting their opportunities for diversification and by requiring them to engage in "downsizing" or in mergers and acquisitions in which all the risks are borne by the employees (who are sometimes fictitiously associated with profits, at least the higher-ranking among them, through remuneration in the form of shares). The increased freedom to invest and, perhaps more crucially, to divest capital so as to obtain the highest financial profitability promotes the mobility of capital and the generalized delocalization of industrial or banking enterprises. Direct investment abroad makes it possible to exploit the differences between nations or regions in terms of capital and labor costs and to move closer to the most favorable markets. Just as nascent nations transformed autonomous fiefs into provinces subordinated to the central power, "network firms" find in a market that is both internal and international the means for "internalizing" transactions, as Oliver Williamson puts it, that is, for organizing them within production units that incorporate the firms absorbed and thereby reduce them to the status of "subsidiary" of a "parent company," while others look to outsourcing as another way of establishing relations of subordination within relative independence.[5]

Integration into the global economic field thus tends to weaken all regional or national powers. By discrediting the other paths of development, and particularly national models condemned from the outset as nationalistic, the formal cosmopolitanism in which that integration is draped leaves citizens powerless in the face of the transnational economic and financial powers. The so-called policies of structural adjustment aim at ensuring the incorporation through subordination of the dominated economies by reducing the role of all the so-called artificial or arbitrary mechanisms of political regulation of the economy associated with the social welfare state (the only body capable of opposing the transnational firms and the international financial institutions) in favor of the so-called free market through a series of converging measures of deregulation and privatization, such as abolishing all protection for the domestic market and relaxing controls on foreign investment, in the name of the Darwinian tenet that exposure to competition will make firms more efficient. In so doing, they tend to grant concentrated capital almost total freedom and allow free rein to the big multinationals that more or less directly inspire these policies. (Conversely, they contribute to neutralizing the attempts of the so-called emerging nations, that is to say, those nations capable of mounting effective competition, to rely on the national state in order to construct an

The Internationalization of the Economic Field 147

economic infrastructure and to create a national market by protecting national production and fostering the development of a real demand linked to the access of peasants and workers to consumption by way of increased purchasing power, itself promoted by state policies such as agrarian reform or the introduction of progressive income taxation.)

The relations of force of which these policies are a thinly euphemized expression, and which tend more and more to reduce the most dispossessed nations to an economy relying almost exclusively on the extensive or intensive exploitation of natural resources, are also manifested in the asymmetrical treatment granted by the global institutions to various nations depending on the position they occupy within the structure of the distribution of capital. The most striking example of this is no doubt the fact that requests by the International Monetary Fund that the United States reduce its persistent public deficit have long fallen on deaf ears, whereas the same body has forced many an African economy, already greatly at risk, to reduce its deficit at the cost of increasing levels of unemployment and poverty. And we know also that the same countries that preach the opening of borders and the dismantling of the welfare state to the whole world can practice more or less subtle forms of protectionism through import quotas, voluntary export restrictions, the imposition of quality or safety standards, and enforced currency revaluations, not to mention certain self-righteous calls for the universal enforcement of labor rights, or through state assistance via what are called "mixed oligopolies" (based on state intervention aimed at dividing up markets through VRAs, voluntary restraint agreements), or through production quotas for foreign subsidiaries.

Unlike the unification that took place in centuries past at the national state level in Europe, present-day unification at the global level is carried out without the state – counter to the wish of John Maynard Keynes to see the creation of a world central bank issuing a neutral reserve currency liable to guarantee trade on an equal footing between all countries – and at the exclusive service of the interests of the dominant, who, contrary to the jurists who presided over the origins of the European states, do not really need to wrap the policies that suit their interests in the trappings of universalism. It is the naked logic of the field and the intrinsic force of concentrated capital that impose relations of force favorable to the interests of the dominant. The latter have the means to transform these relations of force into apparently universal rules of the game through the falsely neutral interventions of the great international bodies (IMF, WTO) they dominate, or under cover of the representations of the economy and politics that they

148 *Imperialisms*

are able to inspire and disseminate. These representations have found their most thorough formulation in the draft Multilateral Agreement on Investment (MAI); this quasi-utopia of a world freed of all state restraints and turned over to the arbitrary whim of investors alone allows us to gain a realistic idea of the truly "globalized" world that the conservative International of heads and executives of the industrial and financial multinationals of all nations intends to impose by relying on the political, diplomatic, and military power of an imperial state gradually reduced to its function of law enforcement in domestic and foreign theaters.[6] It is therefore vain to hope that this unification produced by the "harmonization" of national legal provisions will, by its own logic, lead to a genuine universalization, embodied by a universal state. But it is not unreasonable to expect that the effects of the policy of a small oligarchy looking only after its own short-term economic interest will foster the gradual emergence of political forces, themselves also global, capable of demanding the creation of transnational bodies entrusted with controlling the dominant economic forces so as to subordinate them to truly universal ends.

Translated by Loïc Wacquant

Guide
To a Flourishing Research Programme

In a climate which has seen the rise of transnational approaches since the 1990s, Bourdieu's reflections on the international, which accompanied and responded to this expansion, have inspired a number of research projects after his demise which share a common origin in his theory of fields and types of capital. We will limit ourselves here to signalling the research which makes explicit reference to the research programme that he elaborated.

In the domain of cultural production, the theory of fields has been used to study on the one hand international exchanges and the circulation of works, and on the other hand the formation of international or transnational fields. This has generated quantitative and qualitative studies of translation, which led in 2002 to an issue of *Actes de la recherche en sciences sociales*[1] and later to collective surveys of the translations of literature and works in the social sciences, carried out at the Centre for European Sociology in partnership with Argentinian and Brazilian teams.[2] In federating individual research projects[3] and establishing a methodology, they helped to constitute the sociology of translation as a domain in its own right.

Also developed in the line of research mapped out by Bourdieu[4] were methodological reflections on international or transnational circulation[5] as well as empirical enquiries articulating comparatism and cultural transfer, which were extended later to other domains such as the cinema, television series, music, publishing for young people and theatrical studies.[6] The social history of the human and social sciences has also been revitalized in this perspective by research into the reception in France of Russian Formalism, the work of Norbert Elias and theories of justice.[7]

These reflections were prolonged and expanded in the framework of European projects. The European network ESSE (Pour un espace

150 *Imperialisms*

des sciences sociales en Europe [For a European Social Sciences Space]) set up a pluri-disciplinary research programme articulating the comparatist approach with the study of cultural transfers, while at the same time relocating them in the system of the balance of power (rivalry, hegemony and dependence, etc.) between national intellectual fields.[8] This programme developed later around the history of the human and social sciences in the framework of the European project INTERCO-SSH (International Cooperation in the Social Sciences and Humanities),[9] which once again combined comparatism, circulation and transnational perspectives.[10]

The problematics of the international or transnational fields were inaugurated by Pascale Casanova's book *The World Republic of Letters*,[11] based on a thesis supervised by Bourdieu, which served as reference and model, not only in comparative literature, where it is one of the works that established the domain of 'world literature', but also in sociology, where research has started to look into the formation of transnational or global fields[12] and the role of cultural intermediaries in the domains of literature,[13] art[14] and cinema.[15] The review *Actes* has devoted an issue to 'Transnational Intellectual Fields',[16] proposing a terminological and conceptual clarification, distinguishing between diverse notions often used without distinction: the *international* ought to be reserved for spaces comprising international politics and organizations, where the nations are represented as such;[17] the *supranational* qualifies regional spaces like the European Union which are formed on the basis of nation-states on which they remain largely dependent (see below, on the research into the construction of the European Union); the *transnational* designates the spaces transcending national logics, such as the linguistic areas and spaces that are relatively autonomous from the nation-states and from these international organizations; the *world*, born of the term *Welt-Literatur* forged by Goethe, refers to spaces more or less autonomous and hierarchized, in which national or regional adherence is denied; finally, the *global* is linked to the slogan of globalization which aimed to overthrow the obstacles to free circulation, allowing it to expand and spread over the whole globe, and which must for this reason be deconstructed so that it can be employed with good sense, by asking which regions for example are disadvantaged or excluded by their globalization.[18] Moreover, in an echo of Bourdieu's questioning of Belgian literature, theses articulated around postcolonial problematics have focused on the literatures of the old French colonies of Africa and the Maghreb and their reliance on the French literary field.[19]

In parallel with this research into cultural heritage and bodies of knowledge, the construction of Europe has been the object of empirical

To a Flourishing Research Programme

research and theoretical and methodological reflections, also stimulating an issue of *Actes* dealing with the dynamics of the institutionalization of a supranational space (that of the European Union) at the crossroads of the national fields of power, alert to the emergence of the 'new professionals of Europe' as well as the permanence of struggles within the states themselves.[20] Although the political field remains strongly national, the construction of Europe encourages the appearance of a European administrative field and the emergence of a European legal field (although both are still strongly dependent on the nation-states).[21]

This research follows some of the furrows ploughed by Dezalay, which have also opened the way for research into the formation of an international legal field.[22] Moreover, some American researchers have directed studies into the field of international penal justice, situated at the intersection of three transnational fields, those of inter-state relations, the defence of human rights and, still in the process of internationalization, penal justice.[23] In addition, the concept of field has been introduced into the domain of international relations, where it is utilized in particular to think about diplomatic relations as a metafield.[24]

Dezalay's reflections on globalization and the way in which it transforms the modes of reproduction of both the marginal elites and bodies of State-sponsored knowledge[25] have moreover been subsumed by a new generation of researchers under the notion of a 'sociology of the international'.[26] We should also mention the research into the elites of globalization[27] and the European elites,[28] as well as the international circulation of students.[29] Issues of *Actes* have also focused on 'Social Capital in Migration', and certain topics such as beaches, rethought in a transnational perspective.[30]

Finally, enquiries into the historical sociology of colonialism, which *Actes* reported on in 2008 and 2010 with issues entitled 'Imperialist Politics' and 'Representing Colonialism',[31] have been conducted in the United States in a perspective that explicitly claimed affiliation to the theory of fields.[32] The global transformations of the twentieth century have also been rethought with the help of the concept of the field,[33] and theories of imperialism have been revisited in this perspective by a new generation of political scientists who reject 'the idea of an open transnational society that would be the carbon copy, on the world stage, of American pluralism', and refute the thesis of 'the emergence of a transnational capitalist class' intending to pursue 'the enrolment and support of local communities sharing American values and modes of thinking'.[34]

This guide, by no means exhaustive, indicates the vitality of the research programme and the type of problematics and innovative studies that it continues to stimulate in France and the United States, but also in Italy, Brazil, Argentina, Scandinavia and elsewhere.[35]

F. P. and G. S.

Notes

Introduction

1 P. Bourdieu, *Microcosmes* (Paris: Raisons d'agir, 2022), p. 659.

2 On this last point, see P. Bourdieu, J.-C. Passeron, 'Sociology and Philosophy in France since 1945: Death and Resurrection of a Philosophy without Subject', *Social Research*, 34/1, 1967, pp. 162–212; P. Bourdieu, 'Structuralism and Theory of Knowledge', *Social Research*, 35/4, 1968, pp. 681–706, and 'Sur le pouvoir symbolique', *Annales. Économies, Sociétés, Civilizations*, 32/3, 1977, pp. 405–11.

3 See in particular P. Bourdieu, 'Pour une sociologie des sociologues', in *Questions de sociologie* (Paris: Minuit, 1980), pp. 79–85; F. Poupeau, 'The Invention of the State: Bourdieu between Béarn and Kabylia', *Berkeley Journal of Sociology*, 59, 2015.

4 P. Bourdieu, *Sketch for a Self-Analysis*, trans. R. Nice (Cambridge: Polity, 2007); L. Wacquant, 'Following Pierre Bourdieu into the Field', *Ethnography*, 5/4, 2004, pp. 387–414.

5 See P. Bourdieu and A. Sayad, *Le Déracinement. La crise de l'agriculture traditionnelle en Algérie* (Paris: Minuit, 1964); P. Bourdieu, *Travail et travailleurs en Algérie* (Paris: Mouton, 1963; new edition: Raisons d'agir, 2021).

6 P. Bourdieu, J.-C. Chamboredon and J.-C. Passeron, *The Craft of Sociology* (New York and Berlin: De Gruyter, 1991 [1968]), p. 51.

7 Ibid.

8 P. Bourdieu and J.-C. Passeron, 'La comparabilité des systèmes d'enseignement', in R. Castel and J.-C. Passeron (eds.), *Éducation, démocratie et développement* (Paris/La Haye: Mouton), 'Cahiers du Centre de sociologie européenne', 4, 1967, pp. 21–58.

9 P. Bourdieu and A. Darbel (with D. Schnapper), *The Love of Art: European Art Museums and Their Public*, trans. C. Beattie and N. Merriman (Cambridge: Polity, 1997 [1966]).

10 See J. Heilbron, 'Comparatisme', in G. Sapiro (ed.), *Dictionnaire international Bourdieu* (Paris: CNRS Éditions, 2020), pp. 185–7. On the enquiries organized by the CSE, and then the CSEC, see also J. Duval, J. Heilbron and P. Issenhuth (eds.), *Pierre Bourdieu et l'art de l'invention scientifique* (Paris: Classiques Garnier, coll. 'Bibliothèque des sciences sociales', 2022). On the European

154   *Notes to pp. 5–7*

vocation of the CSE, see M. Joly, *Pour Bourdieu* (Paris: CNRS Éditions, 2018), pp. 25–38.

11 Bourdieu, *Sketch for a Self-Analysis*, p. 72.

12 On the relations between the CSE/CSEC and the sociology of the United States, see P. Pasquali, 'Une "école de Chicago" en banlieue parisienne?', in G.Laferté, P. Pasquali and N. Rénahy, *Le Laboratoire des sciences sociales* (Paris: Raisons d'agir, 2018), pp. 235–91.

13 M. Pollak, 'La planification des sciences sociales', *Actes de la recherche en sciences sociales*, 2, 1976, pp. 105–21; 'Paul F. Lazarsfeld, fondateur d'une multinationale scientifique', *Actes de la recherche en sciences sociales*, 25, 1979, pp. 45–59.

14 G. Sapiro, 'Une consécration paradoxale: les conditions sociales de la circulation de la sociologie bourdieusienne et de son appropriation comme programme de recherche aux États-Unis', in A. Garcia, M.-F. Garcia Parpet, A. Perez, F. Poupeau and M. E. Rocha (eds.), *Bourdieu et les Amériques* (Paris: Éditions de l'IHEAL, 2023).

15 P. Bourdieu, 'Secouez un peu vos structures', in Y. Winkin, J. Dubois and P. Durand (eds.), *Le Symbolique et le social. La réception internationale du travail de Pierre Bourdieu* (Liège: Éditions de l'Université de Liège, coll. 'Sociopolis', 2005), p. 350.

16 G. Sapiro, 'Sens commun (le)', in Sapiro (ed.), *Dictionnaire international Bourdieu*, pp. 782–4.

17 G. Sapiro and M. Bustamante, 'Translation as a Measure of International Consecration: Mapping the World's Distribution of Bourdieu's Books in Translation', *Sociologica*, 2–3, 2009.

18 On the importance and the difficulties of the relations with Brazil, see the witness and analyses of Sergio Leite Lopes, Sergio Miceli, Francine Muel-Dreyfus, Maria Eduarda Rocha and Monique de Saint-Martin, in Garcia et al. (eds.), *Bourdieu et les Amériques*. One of the stalwarts of the network, Afrânio Garcia, later joined the CSEC, where he developed his studies on Brazil in the 1990s.

19 P. Bourdieu, *The Political Ontology of Martin Heidegger*, trans. P. Collier (Cambridge: Polity, 1991).

20 A. Sayad, 'Les trois "âges" de l'émigration algérienne en France', *Actes de la recherche en sciences sociales*, 15, 1977, pp. 59–79.

21 F. Muel-Dreyfus and A. Martins Rodrigues, 'Réincarnations. Note de recherche sur une secte spirite de Brasilia', *Actes de la recherche en sciences sociales*, 62–63, 1986, pp. 118–34.

22 See for example, V. Karady, 'Les juifs et le "placement pierre" en Hongrie autour de 1930', *Actes de la recherche en sciences sociales*, 85, 1990, pp. 81–93. We can also cite, among the long-standing collaborators with the CSEC/CSEC, Jean-Claude Combessie, who published his enquiries into the rural workers of Andalusia in *Actes* in 1982, and who was later codirector of the centre from 1984 to 1996 with Monique de Saint-Martin.

23 In the sense given to this notion by A. Wimmer and N. G. Schiller, 'Methodological Nationalism, the Social Sciences and the Study of Migration: An Essay in Historical Epistemology', *International Migration Review*, 37/3, 2003, pp. 576–610.

24 See M. Lamont and A. Lareau, 'Cultural Capital: Allusions, Gaps and Glissandos in Recent Theoretical Developments', *Sociological Theory*, 6/2, 1988, pp. 153–68; G. Sapiro, 'La carrière internationale de *La Distinction*', in

Notes to pp. 8–13 155

Ph. Coulangeon and J. Duval (eds.), *Trente ans après* La Distinction *de Pierre Bourdieu* (Paris: La Découverte, 2013), pp. 45–58.

25 See the literature review and the reply by D. B. Holt, 'Distinction in America? Recovering Bourdieu's Theory of Tastes from His Critics', *Poetics*, 25, 1997, pp. 93–120; R. Harker, C. Mahar and C. Wilkes, *An Introduction to the Work of Pierre Bourdieu: The Practice of Theory* (London: Palgrave Macmillan, 1990); D. Swartz, *Culture and Power: The Sociology of Pierre Bourdieu* (Chicago: University of Chicago Press, 1997), pp. 288–9. In Germany, see the critique by Jörg Blasius and Jürgen Winkler, 'Gibt es *die feinen Unterschiede*? Eine empirische Überprüfung der Bourdieuschen Theorie', *Kölner Zeitschrift für Soziologie und Sozialpsychologie*, 41, 1989, pp. 72–93.

26 The translation into French appeared the following year: P. Bourdieu and L. Wacquant, *Réponses* (Paris: Seuil: 1992), and was republished under the title *Invitation à la sociologie réflexive* (Seuil, coll. 'Liber', 2014). See also L. Wacquant, '*Bourdieu in America*: Notes on the Transatlantic Importation of Social Theory', in C. Calhoun, E. Lipuma and M. Postone (eds.), *Bourdieu: Critical Perspectives* (Chicago: University of Chicago Press, 1993), pp. 263–75; L. Wacquant, 'Bourdieu aux États-Unis: notes éparses et personnelles', in Garcia et al. (eds.), *Bourdieu et les Amériques*.

27 In the following paragraphs we reproduce a large part of the presentation of the comparative approach in these lectures by G. Sapiro: 'Du théoricien du social à l'intellectuel global: la réception internationale de l'œuvre de Pierre Bourdieu et ses effets en retour', in F. Lebaron and G. Mauger (eds.), *Lectures de Bourdieu* (Paris: Ellipses, 2012), pp. 373–89.

28 P. Bourdieu, 'Social Space and Symbolic Space', in *Practical Reason* (Cambridge: Polity, 1998 [1994]), p. 2. These lectures first appeared in English in the journal *Poetics Today* (12/4, 1991, pp. 625–70), which was at the time edited by Itamar Even-Zohar (to whom Bourdieu had sent them), in a translation done by G. Sapiro and revised by B. McHale.

29 Ibid., p. 3.

30 Ibid., p. 6.

31 Ibid., p. 13.

32 'The New Capital', in *Practical Reason*, p. 22 (Bourdieu's emphasis).

33 Ibid., p. 23.

34 Ibid., p. 28 (Bourdieu's emphasis).

35 Ibid., pp. 29–30.

36 'The "Soviet" Variant and Political Capital', in *Practical Reason*, p. 16.

37 The Centre for the Sociology of Education and Culture, founded by Bourdieu in 1968, merged in 1998 with the Centre for European Sociology, which Bourdieu had taken over on his arrival at the Collège de France in 1981. This merger expressed both the continuity of the history of the laboratory and the will to fit into a European perspective.

38 Among the publications of the projects JEUNPREC (Jeunesse et Précarité) and PENSOC (État pénal/État social), see these issues of *Actes de la recherche en sciences sociales*: 'De l'État social à l'État pénal' (124, 1998) and 'Nouvelles formes d'encadrement' (136–7, 2001).

39 L. Colley, *Britons: Forging the Nation 1707–1837* (New Haven: Yale University Press, 1994).

40 N. Elias, *The Civilizing Process*, trans. E. Jephcott (Oxford: Blackwell, 1994 [1939]).

156   *Notes to pp. 13–18*

41 The article appeared in *The Socialist Register* (1965, pp. 311–62) and was republished in E. P. Thompson, *The Poverty of Theory* (New York: Monthly Review Press, 1978), pp. 35–91. This book was translated as *Misère de la théorie. Contre Althusser et le marxisme anti-humaniste* (Paris: L'échappée), 2015.

42 See N. Elias, *Studien über die Deutschen: Machtkämpfe und Habitusentwicklung im 19. und 20. Jahrhundert* (Frankfurt: Suhrkamp, 1989); English translation: *The Germans: Power Struggles and the Development of Habitus in the Nineteenth and Twentieth Centuries*, trans. S. Mennell and E. Dunning (Cambridge: Polity, 1996); French translation by R. Chartier: *Les Allemands. Luttes de pouvoir et développement de l'habitus aux XIXe et XXe siècles, précédé de 'Barbarie et "décivilisation"'* (Paris: Seuil, 2017).

43 P. Bourdieu, 'L'inconscient d'école', *Actes de la recherche en sciences sociales*, 135, 2000, pp. 3–5.

44 See P. Bourdieu, 'L'objectivation du sujet de l'objectivation', in J. Heilbron, R. Lenoir and G. Sapiro (eds.), *Pour une histoire des sciences sociales* (Paris: Fayard, 2004), pp. 19–23.

45 P. Bourdieu, *General Sociology*, vol. 1, *Classification Struggles*, trans. P. Collier (Cambridge: Polity, 2018 [2015]).

46 On the project of this review, see P. Casanova, 'La revue *Liber*: réflexions sur quelques usages pratiques de la notion d'autonomie relative', in L. Pinto, G. Sapiro and P. Champagne, *Pierre Bourdieu, sociologue* (Paris: Fayard, 2004), pp. 413–30.

47 P. Bourdieu, 'Les conditions sociales de la circulation internationale des idées', *Romanistische Zeitschrift für Literaturgeschichte/Cahiers d'histoire des littératures romanes*, 14/1–2, 1990, pp. 1–10; reprinted in *Actes de la recherche en sciences sociales* (145, 2002, pp. 3–8) and in P. Bourdieu, *Forschen und Handeln. Recherche et action. Conférences prononcées au Frankreich-Zentrum de l'Université de Fribourg*, ed. J. Jurt (Freiburg: Rombach, 2004), pp. 21–33.

48 Thus Bourdieu shows how heretical imports are often the work of marginals in the field, who import a message or a position that has strength in a different field, resulting in strategies that subvert the legitimate principles of hierarchization of the field concerned.

49 J. Jurt, 'L'"intraduction" de la littérature française en Allemagne', *Actes de la recherche en sciences sociales*, 130, 1999, pp. 86–9. There is also an interest in translation in Bourdieu's enquiry into publishing: 'Une révolution conservatrice. Le champ éditorial', *Actes de la recherche en sciences sociales*, 130, 1999, pp. 3–28, republished in *Microcosmes*, pp. 455–89.

50 See Bourdieu and Darbel, *The Love of Art.*

51 Bourdieu, 'Une révolution conservatrice'.

52 As part of a cycle of lectures entitled 'Pierre Bourdieu: Fieldwork in Culture', held from 21 to 23 April 1995. The text appeared under the title 'Passport to Duke' in *Metaphilosophy*, 28/4, 2003, pp. 449–55.

53 See P. Bourdieu, 'La cause de la science. Comment l'histoire sociale des sciences sociales peut servir le progrès de ces sciences', *Actes de la recherche en sciences sociales*, 106–107, 1995, pp. 3–10. An English version was published under the title 'Epilogue. On the Possibility of a Field of World Sociology', trans. L. Wacquant, in P. Bourdieu and J. S. Coleman (eds.), *Social Theory for a Changing Society* (London: Routledge, 1991), pp. 373–87. The English

Notes to pp. 19–23   157

translation of the *Actes de la recherche en sciences sociales* article, 'The Cause of Science', by Peter Collier, is to be found in *Return to Reflexivity* (Cambridge: Polity, 2024), pp. 72–93 (abbreviated as RR in the text).

54 See the introduction by the editors ('Le travail de l'œuvre et l'œuvre au travail') in Garcia et al. (eds.), *Bourdieu et les Amériques*.

55 In May 1989, he gave a lecture in Turin titled 'For an International of Intellectuals', reproduced in *Politis*, 1, 1992, pp. 9–15, and republished in P. Bourdieu, *Interventions (1961–2001). Science sociale et action politique*, ed. F. Poupeau and T. Discepolo. English translation in *Political Interventions: Social Science and Political Action*, trans. D. Fernbach (London: Verso, 2008 [2002]), pp. 209–17. In October, the third lecture delivered in Japan was entitled 'Pour un corporatisme de l'universel'. It appeared in English as 'For a Corporatism of the Universal', post-scriptum to *The Rules of Art: Genesis and Structure of the Literary Field*, trans. S. Emanuel (Cambridge: Polity, 1996), pp. 337–48.

56 P. Bourdieu, 'L'histoire se lève à l'Est. Pour une politique de la vérité. Ni Staline ni Thatcher', *Liber*, 2, 1989, p. 3, and 'Responsabilités intellectuelles. Les mots de la guerre en Yougoslavie', *Liber*, 14, 1993, p. 2. Translated in Bourdieu, *Political Interventions*, as 'History Rises in the East', pp. 218–20, and 'Intellectual Responsibilities', pp. 228–9.

57 P. Bourdieu, 'Against the Destruction of a Civilization', in *Acts of Resistance*, trans. R. Nice (Cambridge: Polity, 1998), pp. 24–8; and J. Duval, C. Gaubert, F. Lebaron, D. Marchetti and F. Pavis, *Le 'décembre' des intellectuels français* (Paris: Raisons d'agir, 1998).

58 As in his interview with the anthropologists Pierre and Micheline Centlivres on Afghanistan in September 1980 in no. 34 of *Actes de la recherche en sciences sociales*, 'And if we actually spoke about Afghanistan' (see *Political Interventions*, p. 113), or his participation in the conferences in support of Solidarność in December 1981 (see *Political Interventions*, pp. 118, 121, 126–32).

59 P. Bourdieu, 'Abuse of Power by the Advocates of Reason', in *Acts of Resistance*, p. 19.

60 P. Bourdieu, 'The Myth of "Globalization" and the European Welfare State', in *Acts of Resistance*, pp. 29–44 (cit. p. 41).

61 Ibid., pp. 41–2.

62 Broadcast online: http://www.dailymotion.com/video/xx6kd_pierre-bourdieu -davos-26-janv-2001_news. The record of his public positions taken during this period is collected in Bourdieu, *Political Interventions*, pp. 271–388 (1995–2001).

63 P. Bourdieu, 'De la maison du roi à la raison d'État: le champ bureaucratique', in *Microcosmes*, pp. 369–93.

64 P. Bourdieu, 'Unite and Rule', in *Firing Back: Against the Tyranny of the Market 2*, trans. L. Wacquant (London: Verso, 2003), pp. 82–3.

65 Bourdieu points out that: 'To the mythology of the extraordinary differentiation and diversification of products one can counterpose the trend toward uniform supply at both the national and international levels. Far from promoting diversity, competition breeds homogeneity.' P. Bourdieu, 'Culture is in Danger', in *Firing Back*, p. 77. Reprinted in P. Bourdieu, *Sociology is a Martial Art*, ed. G. Sapiro (New York: The New Press, 2010), p. 224.

66 Bourdieu, *Firing Back*, p. 86.

67 Ibid., p. 90.

158   *Notes to pp. 23–29*

68 Y. Dezalay and B. Garth, *Dealing in Virtue: International Commercial Arbitration and the Construction of a Transnational Legal Order* (Chicago: University of Chicago Press, 1996).

1.1 Two Imperialisms of the Universal

1 [Ed. note] This text first appeared as 'Deux impérialismes de l'universel', in C. Fauré and T. Bishop (eds.), *L'Amérique des Français* (Paris: Bourin, 1992), pp. 149–56.

2 [Ed. note] The French Revolution is mentioned in many of Marx's writings, in particular the *Manifesto of the Communist Party* (1848), co-written with Engels, *The Class Struggle in France* (1850) and *The 18th Brumaire of Louis Bonaparte* (1869). Although he most often treats it as a bourgeois revolution, it did enable proletarian interests to be brought to the front of the movement, unlike the 1848 revolution. Moreover the (French) bourgeoisie appeared to Marx to be a veritable revolutionary force. See the anthology *Sur la Révolution française. Écrits de Marx et Engels*, ed. C. Mainfroy (Paris: Messidor-Éditions sociales, 1985). Among the Marxists who have held the French Revolution up as a model, there are of course Lenin, Karl Kautsky, Clara Zetkin, Rosa Luxemburg and Antonio Gramsci. Here Bourdieu is alluding more precisely to the article by Perry Anderson, 'Origins of the Present Crisis', *New Left Review*, 23, 1964. In Japan, the Revolution served as reference for the leaders of the movement of the rights of the people (Minken) who called for a democratic constitution in the years 1870–80, then for the school of Koza which in the 1930s compared Japan to revolutionary France in a controversy with the school of Rono, to define the stage of capitalism in the Meiji era and the revolutionary strategies to put in place. This reflection was then developed by Kohachirō Takahashi, a specialist in the economic history of France. Bourdieu, who visited Japan in 1989, might have read the contribution by Tadami Chizuka and Michio Shibata, 'L'image de la Révolution française dans l'historiographie japonaise', in M. Vovelle (ed.), *L'Image de la Révolution française*, vol. 2 (Paris: Pergamon Press, 1989).

3 [Ed. note] According to Kant, the Revolution demonstrates the tendency of humanity to make moral progress. Those who supported it (more than those who made it) took part in the universal, in a disinterested manner. See I. Kant, 'The Conflict of the Faculties' (1798), trans. A. W. Wood, in *Religion and Rational Theology* (Cambridge: Cambridge University Press, 1996), pp. 301–2: 'It is simply the mode of thinking of the spectators which reveals itself publicly in this game of great revolutions, and manifests such a universal yet disinterested sympathy for the players on one side against those on the other, even at the risk that this partiality could become very disadvantageous for them if discovered. Owing to its universality, this mode of thinking demonstrates a character of the human race at large and all at once; owing to its disinterestedness, a moral character of humanity, at least in its predisposition, a character which not only permits people to hope for progress toward the better, but is already itself progress insofar as its capacity is sufficient for the present.'

4 [Ed. note] See P. Valéry, 'Fonction de Paris' (1937) and 'Présence de Paris' (1937), in *Regards sur le monde actuel* (Paris: Gallimard, 1945), republished

Notes to pp. 29–31 159

in *Oeuvres*, vol. 2 (Paris: Gallimard, 'Bibliothèque de la Pléiade', 1960), pp. 1007–10.

5 [Ed. note] This refers to Philippe Sollers, on whom Bourdieu wrote a scathing critique: 'Sollers *tel quel*', *Libération*, 27 January 1995 (there was also a version in *Liber*, 21–2, 1995, p. 40), republished in P. Bourdieu, 'Sollers *tel quel*', *Acts of Resistance*, trans. R. Nice (Cambridge: Polity, 1998), pp. 11–14.

6 [Ed. note] In 1782, in a context of hegemony of the French language, spoken at the court of Friedrich II, the Academy of Berlin ran a competition on the following theme: 'What is it that makes the French language the universal language of Europe? Why does it merit this prerogative? May we presume that it will preserve it?' The first prize was awarded to Rivarol (1753–1801), author of the *Discours sur l'universalité de la langue française* (1784).

7 [Ed. note] A. de Tocqueville, *Democracy in America* (London: Penguin, 2003).

8 [Ed. note] In the article that he devoted to Paris in 1937, 'Fonction de Paris', the writer Paul Valéry sees it as a 'political, literary, scientific, financial, commercial, voluptuary and sumptuary capital of a great country', of which it represents 'the whole history'. The city of Paris concentrates 'its entire thinking substance'. See note 4 above.

9 [Ed. note] Here Bourdieu is alluding in particular to the Chicago School of Economics, a laboratory of neoclassical liberal thought, with figures like Milton Friedman (Nobel Prize winner in economics in 1976), George Stigler (winner in 1982), Frank Knight, Richard Posner and Ronald Coase (prize winners in 1991), Gary Becker (winner in 1992), or again Robert Lucas (winner in 1995). The Chicago School influenced the American monetary politicians from the arrival of Paul Volcker at the presidency of the FED in 1979, as well as the economic policies of the World Bank from the middle of the 1980s. These theories served as a 'scientific' justification for the imposition of policies of austerity and *new public management*, that is, the management of State institutions as well as private enterprise. The School was also a centre for the theories of rational choice, political realism and decisionism (inspired by the pro-Nazi German jurist Carl Schmitt, and opposed to the normativism of Hans Kelsen) that were imposed in American political science at the time. On the economic Nobel Prize of the period, see F. Lebaron, 'Le "Nobel" d'économie. Une politique', *Actes de la recherche en sciences sociales*, 141–142, 2002, pp. 62–6.

10 [Ed. note] This war was launched in January 1991 by a coalition of thirty-four countries led by the United States, under its then president George Bush, following the invasion of Kuwait in August 1990 by the Iraqi Army. Under cover of moralizing discourses which presented the coalition as the camp of the good facing the dictatorship of Saddam Hussein, this offensive enabled the United States to safeguard its economic interests in the region and reinforce its position as the leading world power.

11 [Ed. note] S. Guilbaut, *How New York Stole the Idea of Modern Art: Abstract Impressionism, Freedom, and the Cold War* (Chicago: Chicago University Press, 1983).

12 [Ed. note] Here Bourdieu is alluding in particular to the fight to be recognized as a cultural exception, waged by France against the extension, from 1986, of the General Agreement on Tariffs and Trade (GATT) on the circulation of immaterial (therefore cultural) goods and services (an accord that was to be absorbed in 1994 into the World Trade Organization). In 1993, at the instigation of France, the European Parliament voted for a special status to be

160   *Notes to pp. 31–33*

granted to audiovisual works to protect them from the rules of free exchange, for the reason that culture is not a commodity like any other. In fact this argument is linked to the desire of European countries to protect their national production – through assistance and quota policies, considered as 'monopolies' breaking with the equality of competition according to the doctrine of free exchange – faced with the flood arriving from the United States. Criticized as too elitist, in particular from the viewpoint of the countries of the South, the notion of *cultural exception* was replaced by that of *cultural diversity* at the instigation of UNESCO, who adopted it officially in 2001.

13 [Ed. note] Here Bourdieu picks up the expression used by Edmund Husserl to designate the philosophers and their responsibility for 'the true being of humankind', in *The Crisis of European Sciences and Transcendental Phenomenology*, trans. D. Carr (Evanston: Northwestern University Press, 1970 [1954]). This enables him to underline the tension between the aspiration of the cultural producers to represent the universal interest in a disinterested way, and their inclination to universalize their individual interests.

1.2 The Cunning of Imperialist Reason

1 [Ed. note] This is a revised and expanded translation of Pierre Bourdieu and Loïc Wacquant, "Sur les ruses de la raison impérialiste," written as an afterword to the issue of *Actes de la recherche en sciences sociales* devoted to "The Cunning of Imperialist Reason," 121/2 (March 1998): 109–18. It is reprinted here by kind permission of Jérome Bourdieu and the journal. The English text was published in *Theory, Culture & Society* 16, no. 1 (1999): 41–58.

2 It bears stressing at the outset to avoid any misunderstanding – and to ward off the predictable accusation of "anti-Americanism" – that nothing is more universal than the pretension to the universal or, more accurately, to the universalization of a particular vision of the world; and that the demonstration sketched here would hold, *mutatis mutandis*, for other domains and other countries, notably for France, as argued in Pierre Bourdieu, "Deux impérialismes de l'universel," in *L'Amérique des Français*, ed. Christiane Fauré and Tom Bishop (Paris: Éditions François Bourin, 1992), pp. 149–56 [reproduced here as Chapter 1.1].

3 Fritz Ringer, *The Decline of the Mandarins: The German Academic Community, 1890–1933* (Cambridge: Cambridge University Press, 1969).

4 Among the books that attest to this rampant McDonaldization of thought, one may cite the elitist jeremiad of Alan Bloom, *The Closing of the American Mind* (New York: Simon & Schuster, 1987), immediately translated into French by Éditions Julliard under the spiritualist title *L'Âme désarmée* ("The Disarmed Soul," 1987), and the angry pamphlet by the neo-conservative Indian immigrant (and biographer of Reagan) based at the Manhattan Institute, Dinesh D'Souza, *Illiberal Education: The Politics of Race and Sex on Campus* (New York: The Free Press, 1991), translated into French as *L'Éducation contre les libertés* ("Education against Freedom") (Paris: Gallimard, Collection "Le Messager," 1993). One of the best indicators for spotting works partaking of this new intellectual doxa with planetary pretensions is the quite unusual *speed* with which they are translated and published abroad (especially in comparison with scientific works). For a comprehensive native vision of the joys and sorrows of

Notes to pp. 34–36 161

contemporary American academics, see the issue of *Daedalus* devoted to "The American Academic Profession" (126, Fall 1997), especially Burton R. Clark, "Small Worlds, Different Worlds: The Uniqueness and Troubles of American Academic Professions," pp. 21–42, and Philip G. Altbach, "An International Academic Crisis? The American Professoriate in Comparative Perspective," pp. 315–38.

5 Douglas Massey and Nancy Denton, *American Apartheid: Segregation and the Making of the Underclass* (Cambridge, MA: Harvard University Press, 1993); Mary Waters, *Ethnic Options: Choosing Ethnic Identities in America* (Berkeley: University of California Press, 1990); David A. Hollinger, *Postethnic America: Beyond Multiculturalism* (New York: Basic Books, 1995); and Jennifer Hochschild, *Facing Up to the American Dream: Race, Class, and the Soul of the Nation* (Princeton: Princeton University Press, 1996); for an analysis of all these questions that rightfully spotlights their historical roots and recurrence, see Denis Lacorne, *La Crise de l'identité américaine. Du melting pot au multiculturalisme* (Paris: Fayard, 1997).

6 On the imperative of cultural recognition, see Charles Taylor, *Multiculturalism: Examining the Politics of Recognition* (Princeton: Princeton University Press, 1994), and the texts collected and presented by Theo Goldberg, ed., *Multiculturalism: A Critical Reader* (Cambridge, MA: Blackwell, 1994); on the floundering of the strategies of perpetuation of the US middle class, see Loïc Wacquant, "La généralisation de l'insécurité salariale en Amérique: restructurations d'entreprises et crise de reproduction sociale," *Actes de la recherche en sciences sociales* 115 (December 1996): 65–79; the deep malaise of the American middle class is well depicted by Katherine Newman, *Declining Fortunes: The Withering of the American Dream* (New York: Basic Books, 1993).

7 Pierre Grémion, *Preuves. Une revue européenne à Paris* (Paris: Julliard, 1989), and *Intelligence de l'anticommunisme. Le Congrès pour la liberté de la culture à Paris* (Paris: Fayard, 1995); James A. Smith, *The Idea Brokers: Think Tanks and the Rise of the New Policy Elite* (New York: The Free Press, 1991); and David M. Ricci, *The Transformation of American Politics: The New Washington and the Rise of Think Tanks* (New Haven: Yale University Press, 1993).

8 On "globalization" as an "American project," read Neil Fligstein, "Rhétorique et réalités de la 'mondialisation,'" *Actes de la recherche en sciences sociales* 119 (September 1997): 36–47; on the ambivalent fascination with America in the postwar period, Luc Boltanski, "America, America . . . Le Plan Marshall et l'importation du 'management,'" *Actes de la recherche en sciences sociales* 38 (June 1981): 19–41; and Richard Kuisel, *Seducing the French: The Dilemma of Americanization* (Berkeley: University of California Press, 1993).

9 This is not the only case where, by a paradox that displays one of the most typical effects of symbolic domination, a number of topics that the United States exports and imposes across the whole universe, beginning with Europe, have been borrowed from those who now receive them as the most advanced forms of theory.

10 For a bibliography on this sprawling debate, see *Philosophy & Social Criticism* 14, nos 3–4 (1988), special issue on "Universalism vs. Communitarianism: Contemporary Debates in Ethics."

11 H. L. A. Hart, "Rawls on Liberty and Its Priority," in Norman Daniels, ed., *Reading Rawls: Critical Studies on Rawls' "A Theory of Justice"* (New York: Basic Books, 1975), pp. 238–59.

162   *Notes to pp. 36–38*

12 From this point of view, crudely sociological, the dialogue between Rawls and Habermas – about whom it is no exaggeration to say that they are structural similes, each within his own philosophical tradition – is highly significant. Cf., for example, Jürgen Habermas, "Reconciliation through the Public Use of Reason: Remarks on Political Liberalism," *Journal of Philosophy* 3 (1995): 109–31.

13 According to the classic study by Carl N. Degler, *Neither Black nor White: Slavery and Race Relations in Brazil and the United States* (Madison: University of Wisconsin Press, 1995 [1974]).

14 Michael Hanchard, *Orpheus and Power: The Movimento Negro of Rio de Janeiro and São Paulo, 1945–1988* (Princeton: Princeton University Press, 1994). One could find a powerful antidote to ethnocentric poison on this subject in the comparative history of racial domination, which demonstrates that ethno-racial divisions are closely linked to the social and political history of each country (and particularly to the history of symbolic struggles over official classification), with each state producing and reproducing the conception of "race" that fits the formation of its national compact. Alas, even studious efforts in this direction often end up projecting raw Americano-centric categories and thus effacing the very historical differences they are intended to highlight. For a paradigmatic example, see Anthony Marx, *Making Race and Nation: A Comparison of the United States, South Africa and Brazil* (Cambridge: Cambridge University Press, 1998).

15 Edmund S. Morgan, *American Slavery, American Freedom: The Ordeal of Colonial Virginia* (New York: W. W. Norton, 1975).

16 Gilberto Freyre, *The Masters and the Slaves: A Study in the Development of Brazilian Civilization* (New York: Knopf, 1964 [1943]).

17 How long will it be before we get a book entitled "Racist Brazil" patterned after the book with a scientifically scandalous title, "Racist France," by a French sociologist more attentive to the expectations of the journalistic field than to the complexities of social reality? Michel Wieviorka et al., *La France raciste* (Paris: Seuil, 1993).

18 Charles Wagley, "On the Concept of Social Race in the Americas," in Dwight B. Heath and Richard N. Adams, eds., *Contemporary Cultures and Societies in Latin America* (New York: Random House, 1965), pp. 531–45; also Richard Graham, ed., *The Idea of Race in Latin America, 1870–1940* (Austin: University of Texas Press, 1980), and Peter Wade, *Race and Ethnicity in Latin America* (London: Pluto Press, 1997).

19 The anthropologist Marvin Harris famously elicited 492 "race-color terms" from 100 respondents by presenting to them two decks of thirty-six cards of drawings of men and women featuring permutations of three skin tones, three hair forms, and two lip sizes and nose widths. Marvin Harris, "Referential Ambiguity in the Calculus of Brazilian Racial Identity," *Southwestern Journal of Anthropology* 26 (1970): 1–14.

20 Edward E. Telles, "Race, Class, and Space in Brazilian Cities," *International Journal of Urban and Regional Research* 19, no. 3 (September 1995): 395–406, and *idem*, "Residential Segregation by Skin Color in Brazil," *American Sociological Review* 57, no. 2 (April 1992): 186–97; for a century-long overview, see George Andrews Reid, *Blacks and Whites in São Paulo, 1888–1988* (Madison: University of Wisconsin Press, 1992).

21 F. James Davis, *Who is Black? One Nation's Definition* (University Park, PA: Pennsylvania State University Press, 1991), and Joel Williamson, *New People:*

Miscegenation and Mulattoes in the United States (New York: New York University Press, 1980).

22 Reynolds Farley, *The New American Reality: Who We Are, How We Got There, Where We Are Going* (New York: Russell Sage Foundation, 1996), pp. 264–5.

23 James McKee shows in his masterwork, *Sociology and the Race Problem: The Failure of a Perspective* (Urbana and Chicago: University of Illinois Press, 1993), first, that these allegedly scientific theories borrow the stereotype of the cultural inferiority of blacks and, second, that they proved singularly incapable of predicting and then explaining the wide mobilization of the African-American community in the postwar decades culminating in the nationwide race riots of the 1960s.

24 This status of a universal standard, a "Greenwich meridian" in relation to which all advances and lags, all "archaisms" and "modernisms" (the avant-garde), come to be evaluated, is one of the universal properties of those who symbolically dominate a given universe. Cf. Pascale Casanova, *La République mondiale des lettres* (Paris: Seuil, 1999).

25 Thomas Bender, "Politics, Intellect, and the American University, 1945–1995," *Daedalus* 126 (Winter 1997): 1–38; on the importation of the theme of the ghetto in the recent French debate about the city and its ills, see Loïc Wacquant, "Pour en finir avec le mythe des 'cités-ghettos': les différences entre la France et les États-Unis," *Annales de la recherche urbaine* 52 (September 1992): 20–30.

26 One will find an exemplary description of the process of transfer of the power of consecration in avant-garde art from Paris to New York in the classic book by Serge Guilbaut, *How New York Stole the Idea of Modern Art: Abstract Impressionism, Freedom and the Cold War* (Chicago: University of Chicago Press, 1983).

27 Yves Dezalay and Bryant Garth, "Droits de l'homme et philanthropie hégémonique," *Actes de la recherche en sciences sociales* 121/2 (March 1998): 23–41.

28 Enzo Mingione, ed., *Urban Poverty and the Underclass: A Reader* (Cambridge, MA: Blackwell, 1996). This is not an isolated incident: as this article was going to press, the same publishing house was embroiled in a row with the urbanologists Ronald van Kempen and Peter Marcuse to try and get them to change the title of their joint work, *The Partitioned City*, into the more glitzy *Globalizing Cities* (they ended up publishing two volumes by these two titles but with two different publishers).

29 Maria P. Root, ed., *The Multiracial Experience: Racial Borders as the New Frontier* (Newbury Park: Sage Publications, 1995); Jon Michael Spencer, *The New Colored People: The Mixed-Race Movement in America* (New York: New York University Press, 1997); and Kimberley DaCosta, "Remaking 'Race': Social Bases and Implications of the Multiracial Movement in America," Doctoral thesis, University of California, Berkeley, 2000.

30 Howard Winant, "Racial Formation and Hegemony: Global and Local Developments," in *Racism, Modernity, and Difference: On the Western Front*, ed. Ali Rattansi and Sallie Westwood (Cambridge, MA: Blackwell, 1994), and *idem, Racial Conditions: Politics, Theory, Comparisons* (Minneapolis: University of Minnesota Press, 1995).

31 As John Westergaard already noted a few years back in his presidential address to the British Sociological Association: "About and Beyond the Underclass:

164 *Notes to pp. 42–46*

Some Notes on the Influence of the Social Climate on British Sociology Today," *Sociology* 26, no. 4 (July–September 1992): 575–87.

32 Christopher Jencks and Paul E. Peterson, eds., *The Urban Underclass* (Washington: The Brookings Institution, 1991), p. 3. Peterson closes this opening paragraph of the book by noting that Richard Wagner's *The Ring of the Nibelung* best evokes the "underclass" as a "vile and debased subhuman population."

33 Just three examples among many: Theo Roeland and Justus Veenman, "An Emerging Ethnic Underclass in the Netherlands? Some Empirical Evidence," *New Community* 19, no. 1 (October 1992): 129–41; Jens Dangschat, "Concentration of Poverty in the Landscapes of 'Boomtown' Hamburg: The Creation of a New Urban Underclass?," *Urban Studies* 77 (August 1994): 1133–47; Christopher T. Whelm, "Marginalization, Deprivation, and Fatalism in the Republic of Ireland: Class and Underclass Perpectives," *European Sociological Review* 12, no. 1 (May 1996): 33–51; and, for a ringing note of dissent, Enrico Pugliese, "La disoccupazione di massa e la questione dell'*underclass*," *La Critica Sociologica* 117/18 (April–September 1996): 89–98.

34 In taking considerable trouble to argue the obvious – viz., that the concept of "underclass" does not apply to French cities – Cyprien Avenel accepts and reinforces the preconceived notion that it has purchase on urban reality in the United States in the first place. "La Question de l'*underclass*' des deux côtés de l'Atlantique," *Sociologie du travail* 39, no. 2 (April 1997): 211–37.

35 As proposed by Nicolas Herpin, "L'*underclass* dans la sociologie américaine: exclusion sociale et pauvreté," *Revue française de sociologie* 34, no. 3 (July–September 1993): 421–39.

36 Loïc Wacquant, "L'*underclass* urbaine' dans l'imaginaire social et scientifique américain," in *L'Exclusion. L'état des savoirs*, ed. Serge Paugam (Paris: La Découverte, 1996), pp. 248–62.

37 These differences have deep historical roots, as attested by a comparative reading of the works of Giovanna Procacci and Michael Katz: Giovanna Procacci, *Gouverner la misère. La question sociale en France, 1789–1848* (Paris: Seuil, 1993), and Michael B. Katz, *In the Shadow of the Poorhouse: A History of Welfare in America* (New York: Basic Books, new edition 1997).

38 Gunnar Myrdal, *Challenge to Affluence* (New York: Pantheon, 1963).

39 Rick Fantasia, "Everything and Nothing: The Meaning of Fast-Food and Other American Cultural Goods in France," *The Tocqueville Review* 15, no. 7 (1994): 57–88.

40 "Embattled Minorities around the Globe: Rights, Hopes, Threats," *Dissent*, Summer 1996.

41 The problem of language, invoked here in passing, is at once crucial and thorny. Knowing the precautions that ethnologists take in introducing indigenous words, one cannot but be surprised – although one is also well aware of all the symbolic profits that this veneer of "modernity" provides – that social scientists should stock their technical language with so many theoretical "faux amis" based on a mere lexicological facsimile (with *minority* becoming "minorité," "profession," etc.), without seeing that these morphologically twinned words are separated by the whole set of differences between the social and symbolic system in which they were produced and the new system in which they are inserted. Those most exposed to the "faux ami" fallacy are obviously the British, because they apparently speak the same language, but also because they have

Notes to p. 46   165

often learnt their sociology in American textbooks, "readers," and books, and thus do not have much to oppose to such conceptual invasion, save extreme epistemological vigilance. (Of course, there exist strong centers of resistance to American hegemony, such as, for example in the case of ethnic studies, around the review *Ethnic and Racial Studies*, directed by Martin Bulmer, and around Robert Miles's research group on racism and migration at the University of Glasgow. But these alternative paradigms, concerned with taking the specificities of the British ethno-racial order into full account, are of necessity no less defined by their opposition to American concepts and their British derivatives.) It follows that Great Britain is structurally predisposed to act as the Trojan horse by which the notions of American scholarly common sense penetrate the European intellectual field (it is with intellectual matters as with matters of economic and social policy, and lately of penal policy as well). It is in England that the activity of conservative foundations and mercenary intellectuals has been established the longest and is the most sustained and the most effective. Proof is the diffusion there of the scholarly myth of the "underclass" as a result of the high-profile media interventions of Charles Murray, expert of the Manhattan Institute and intellectual guru of the libertarian right in the United States, and of its counterpart, the theme of the "dependency" of the dispossessed upon public aid, brought in by Murray's ideological sidekick, Lawrence Mead, which Tony Blair has proposed to reduce drastically in order to "free" the poor from the "yoke" of assistance, as Clinton did before for their American cousins in the summer of 1996.

42 Cf. notably Robert Erikson and John Goldthorpe, *The Constant Flux: A Study of Class Mobility in Industrial Societies* (Oxford: Clarendon Press, 1992); Erik Olin Wright arrives at much the same result with a notably different conceptualization and methodology in *Class Counts: Comparative Studies in Class Inequality* (Cambridge: Cambridge University Press, 1997). On the political determinants of the scale of inequalities in the United States and their increase over the past two decades, see Claude Fischer et al., *Inequality by Design: Cracking the Bell Curve Myth* (Princeton: Princeton University Press, 1996).

43 In a work essential for taking the full measure of the weight of the historical unconscious that survives, in a more or less misrecognizable and repressed form, in the scholarly problematics of a country and the historical gravity that gives American academic imperialism much of its extraordinary force of imposition, Dorothy Ross reveals how the American social sciences (economics, sociology, political science, and psychology) were erected from the outset upon two complementary dogmas constitutive of the national doxa: "metaphysical individualism" and the idea of a diametrical opposition between the dynamism and elasticity of the "new" American order, on the one side, and the stagnation and rigidity of "old" European social formations, on the other. Dorothy Ross, *The Origins of American Social Science* (Cambridge: Cambridge University Press, 1991). One finds direct retranslations of these two founding dogmas in the ostensibly purified idiom of "grand" sociological theory: of the first, in the canonical attempt by Talcott Parsons to elaborate a "voluntaristic theory of action" and, more recently, in the resurgent popularity of so-called rational-choice theory; and, of the second, in the "theory of modernization" that reigned supreme over the study of societal change in the three decades after World War II and that has recently made an unexpected return in post-Soviet studies.

166   *Notes to pp. 49–52*

2.1 The International Circulation of Ideas

1 [Ed. note] Bourdieu delivered this lecture at the University of Freiburg, Germany, on 30 October 1989, to commemorate the inauguration of the Frankreich-Zentrum (directed by Joseph Jurt). It appeared in the *Romanistische Zeitschrift für Literaturgeschichte/Cahiers d'histoire des littératures romanes*, 14/1–2, 1990, pp. 1–10, and was republished in *Actes de la recherche en sciences sociales*, 145, 2002, pp. 3–8. The text appeared in English in *Bourdieu: A Critical Reader*, ed. Richard Shusterman (Oxford: Blackwell, 1999).

2 [Ed. note] The German writer Ernst Jünger (1895–1989), an ultra-nationalist who identified as a 'conservative anarchist' but who had refused the National Socialist Party's advances, was promoted to the rank of captain and sent to serve in France during the Occupation. Before the war, translations of his work had started to be published by Gallimard, and this continued during and after the war. His equivocal attitude provoked controversy. Bourdieu is probably referring to the honorary citizenship of the city of Montpellier bestowed on him by the socialist mayor Georges Frêche at the Maison de Heidelberg in 1983 (Montpellier was twinned with Heidelberg, Jünger's birthplace). In 1984, Chancellor Helmut Kohl and Jünger jointly attended a Verdun commemoration ceremony. During a visit to Germany the year after, President François Mitterrand visited Jünger, accompanied by Kohl, in his home in the village of Wiflingen. On the occasion of his hundredth birthday in 1995, the Maison de Heidelberg organized a large conference attended by Jünger, and the latter was invited to have lunch with Mitterrand at the Élysée Palace.

3 [Ed. note] Bourdieu refers to the heterodox Marxists Henri Lefebvre, François Châtelet and Kostas Axelos, mentioned by him in *The Political Ontology of Martin Heidegger* (Cambridge: Polity, 1991): 'We only have to reread the often astonishing arguments whereby Jean Beaufret, Henri Lefebvre, François Châtelet and Kostas Axelos justify the parallels they draw between Marx and Heidegger, to be convinced that this unexpected philosophical combination owes little to strictly "internal" argument' (p. 94).

4 [Ed. note] B. Pascal, *Discours sur la condition des grands*, 'Les grandeurs d'établissement et les grandeurs naturelles', 1660. B. Pascal, *Three Discourses on the Condition of the Great* ('The Greatness of Establishment and Natural Greatness'), trans. S. Webb, Marxists Internet Archive.

5 [Ed. note] In *The Sociology of Science: Theoretical and Empirical Investigations* (Chicago and London: University of Chicago Press, 1973 [1942]), Robert Merton defines 'gate-keeping' as one of the four functions of the scientist role, its three other functions consisting of researcher, teacher and administrator. This notion was adopted by Diana Crane, in 'The Gatekeepers of Science: Some Factors Affecting the Selection of Articles for Scientific Journals', *The American Sociologist*, 11/4, 1967, pp. 195–201, and theorized by Rita James Simon and James F. James in the specific case of publishing: *Editors as Gatekeepers: Getting Published in the Social Sciences* (Lanham, MD: Rowman & Littlefield, 1994).

6 [Ed. note] J. Benet, *Tu reviendras à Région*, trans. C. Murcia (Paris: Minuit, 1989). Other translations of Benet's work were published by Les Éditions de Minuit, who were also Samuel Beckett's publisher. Benet adapted four pieces by Beckett in his 'Beckettiana' (1991). Bourdieu was still the editor of the 'Le sens commun' series at Minuit at the time of this conference.

Notes to pp. 52–53 167

7 [Ed. note] B. Pascal, *Pensées*, fragment 332 of Brunschvicg's edition. This passage was notably cited by Bourdieu in *Pascalian Meditations* (Cambridge: Polity, 2000), pp. 103–4.

8 [Ed. note] A. Boschetti, *The Intellectual Enterprise: Sartre and Les Temps Modernes* (Evanston, IL: Northwestern University Press, 1988).

9 [Ed. note] Jean Beaufret (1907–82), who became a student at the ENS in 1928 (four years later than Sartre) and obtained his *agrégation* in philosophy in 1933, was one of Heidegger's importers in postwar France. In 1947 Heidegger published his *Lettre sur l'humanisme* in response to a letter by Beaufret which asked of him, 'How to restore meaning to the word "humanism"?' In it, Heidegger recommended a way forward which would open discussion with Marxists around the concept of alienation, which, for him, would be an essential dimension of history once it had been distanced from materialism and reinterpreted under the mantle of technique.

10 [Ed. note] The critic Maurice Blanchot (1907–2003) notably applied Heidegger's reflections on the constitutive character of poetic language in his work on Hölderlin, which had been of interest to him since 1951, in order to explore the creative potential of madness, as outlined in his article 'La Folie par excellence', *Critique*, 45, 1951, pp. 99–118. Blanchot mentions Heidegger in 'L'itinéraire de Hölderlin', in an appendix to *L'Espace littéraire* (Paris: Gallimard, 1955), p. 283. In it he refers to Beda Allemann's thesis *Hölderlin und Heidegger* (Freiburg: Atlantis, 1954), translated into French as *Hölderlin et Heidegger*, prefaced and translated by F. Fédier (Paris: PUF, 1959), in the Épiméthée series.

11 [Ed. note] The heterodox Marxist review *Arguments* was launched in late 1956 by Edgar Morin, Roland Barthes, Jean Duvignaud and Colette Audry and published by Les Éditions de Minuit, before ceasing to operate in late 1962. It drew on Georg Lukács and Herbert Marcuse, among others, and introduced the social sciences (sociology and anthropology) into the intellectual field. Henri Lefebvre and François Châtelet were also contributors and aimed to develop a synthesis of Marx and Heidegger, similarly to Kostas Axelos (who became director-in-chief of the review in 1958). In *The Political Ontology of Martin Heidegger* (p. 94), Bourdieu refers to two works by Axelos in which the latter cites Marx and Heidegger: *Arguments d'une recherche* (Paris: Éditions de Minuit, 1969), pp. 93ff., and *Einführung in ein künftiges Denken über Marx und Heidegger* (*Introduction à une pensée future sur Marx et Heidegger*) (Tübingen: Marx Niemeyer Verlag, 1966). The latter volume, which contains in an epigraph a verse by Hölderlin, was translated into English: *Introduction to a Future Way of Thought: On Marx and Heidegger*, ed. S. Elden, trans. K. Mills (Milton Keynes: Lightning Source, 2015).

12 [Ed. note] Apart from a volume of collected writings published in 1912, the work of German sociologist Georg Simmel was not translated into French until the 1980s, at the initiative of Raymond Boudon and François Bourricaud. Bourdieu is no doubt alluding to Julien Freund's (who, in turn, was the controversial translator and commentator of Max Weber) long introduction to *Sociologie et épistémologie*, trans. L. Gasparini (Paris: PUF, 1981).

13 [Ed. note] In 1957, the writer and member of the Académie française François Mauriac, launched the young Philippe Sollers, then aged 21, by mentioning his short story *Le Défi* in one of his *Bloc-Notes*, vol. 1, *1952–1957* (Paris: Seuil 'Points essais', 1993), p. 554. Sollers had written to Mauriac the year before and the latter had invited him to pay a visit. A mentoring relationship thus

168   *Notes to pp. 54–56*

developed between the old member of the Académie française and the literary newcomer. Mauriac would also mention Sollers's first novel, *Une curieuse solitude*, in his *Bloc-Notes* of 22 November 1958, contributing to his recognition and success.

14 [Ed. note] See C. Lévi-Strauss, 'Introduction à l'oeuvre de Marcel Mauss', in Mauss's *Sociologie et anthropologie* (Paris: PUF, 1950), pp. ix–lii.

15 [Ed. note] The German publisher Suhrkamp, founded in 1950 in Frankfurt, has accumulated significant symbolic capital by publishing writers such as Brecht, philosophers such as Adorno and Habermas, and authors in the social sciences and humanities such as the sociologist Axel Honneth.

16 [Ed. note] This refers to the 'L'ordre philosophique' series. After the translation of his first book (*L'Analyse formelle des langues naturelles*, in collaboration with A. Miller, published by Mouton in 1968), Noam Chomsky's linguistic research, from *La Linguistique cartésienne* followed by *La Nature formelle du language* (1969) to *Théories du langage – Théories d'apprentissage* (1979, not in a series), has been published by Seuil; when it comes to his political work, Seuil has only published one volume: *L'Amérique et ses nouveaux mandarins* in 1969.

17 [Ed. note] Phenomenologist and hermeneutist, trained in the Christian existentialist tradition and specialist on Husserl, Paul Ricoeur (1913–2005) developed an anti-structuralist approach, notably in *Temps et récit* (1983–5) and *Du texte à l'action* (1986).

18 [Ed. note] Research on this theme was carried out by Louis Pinto, in *Les Neveux de Zarathoustra. La reception de Nietzsche en France* (Paris: Seuil, 1995).

19 [Ed. note] The Enlightenment.

20 [Ed. note] Bourdieu is referring here to Luc Ferry and Alain Renault's virulent essay against the May 68 movement, *La Pensée 68. Essai sur l'anti-humanisme contemporain* (Paris: Gallimard, 'Folio essais' series, 1985).

21 [Ed. note] Antoine Fouquier-Tinville (1746–95) was a magistrate who served as public prosecutor for the French Revolutionary Court.

22 [Ed. note] A member of the USSR's political bureau since 1939, Andrei Zhdanov (1896–1948) was in charge of controlling cultural production and, by means of condemnations and exclusions, promoted 'socialist realism' as a creative method, reigning terror in the art world – what came to be known as 'Zhdanovism'. By setting up the Cominform in 1947, he also laid the foundations for the Cold War 'doctrine' that divided the world into two camps.

23 [Ed. note] What has been called the 'Heidegger affair' in France, questioning his allegiance to the National Socialist regime and, more broadly, the relationship between his political ideas and his philosophy, has gone through several phases. It began at the end of the Second World War, with articles by Alexandre Koyré ('L'évolution philosophique de Martin Heidegger', *Critique*, 1946) and Karl Löwith ('Les implications politiques de la philosophie de l'existence chez Heidegger', *Les Temps Modernes*, 14, 1946, pp. 343–60). In 1969, the issue resurfaced in Marxist circles, with Jean-Pierre Faye's attack on the magazine *Tel Quel* and Jacques Derrida, who were accused of drawing inspiration from the sources of Nazi thought by relying on Heidegger (on this point, see F. Matonti, *Intellectuels communistes. Essai sur l'obéissance politique* (Paris: La Découverte, 2005)). A new 'affair' was triggered by Victor Farias's book *Heidegger et le nazisme* (Paris: Verdier, 1987), to which Bourdieu refers here. He himself shifts and reformulates the stakes of this polemic with his *Political*

Notes to pp. 56–59 169

Ontology of Martin Heidegger, in which he takes up and develops an analysis published in 1975 in an article of the same name in *Actes de la recherche en sciences sociales*, 5–6, 1975, pp. 109–56.

24 [Ed. note] P. Bourdieu, 'Pour une *Realpolitik* de la raison' (interview with W. Hiromatsu and H. Imamura), *Gendaï Shiso*, March 1990, pp. 181–203. This theme is later developed in *Invitation à la sociologie réflexive* (with Loïc Wacquant) (Paris: Seuil, 2014 [1992], updated and expanded 2nd edition), pp. 229–59, before notably being discussed again in the second chapter of *Pascalian Meditations* (Cambridge: Polity, 2000).

25 [Ed. note] This quotation, which is likely apocryphal, is said by Francine Muel to refer to the following passage: 'in each one of us, in differing degrees, is contained the person we were yesterday . . . It is just that we don't directly feel the influence of these past selves precisely because they are so deeply rooted within us. They constitute the unconscious part of ourselves.' É. Durkheim, *The Evolution of Educational Thought: Lectures on the Formation and Development of Secondary Education in France*, vol. 2, trans. P. Collins (Abingdon: Routledge, 2006 [1902]), p. 11.

26 I. Chiva and U. Jeggle (eds.), *Ethnologies en miroir. La France et les pays de langue allemande* (Paris: Éditions de la Maison des sciences de l'homme, 1987).

27 [Ed. note] 'People' and 'popular' in German, with connotations of community of language and culture, and of rootedness, due to their association with the ideology of the Conservative Revolution in interwar Germany. See Bourdieu, *The Political Ontology of Martin Heidegger*, pp. 9–13.

28 [Ed. note] A mining engineer, Frédéric Le Play (1806–82) was a pioneer of sociological research in working-class environments, with a paternalistic, conservative approach to social reform.

29 [Ed. note] A German term for homeland or home that is rich in connotations.

30 [Ed. note] 'Community' in German. Community is a concept theorized by the German sociologist F. Tönnies, *Communauté et société. Catégories fondamentales de la sociologie pure* (Paris: Presses Universitaires de France, 2010).

31 [Ed. note] See P. Bourdieu, 'Systèmes d'enseignement et systèmes de pensée', *Revue internationale des sciences sociales*, 19/3, 1968, pp. 367–88.

32 [Ed. note] É. Durkheim and M. Mauss, 'De quelques formes de classification. Contribution à l'étude des représentations collectives', *L'Année sociologique*, 6, 1901–2, pp. 1–72.

33 [Ed. note] Ringer, *The Decline of the German Mandarins*.

34 [Ed. note] See N. Elias, 'Culture et civilisation', first part of *La Civilisation des mœurs* (Paris: Calmann-Lévy, 1973, republished by Pocket, 'Agora' series, 2002).

35 [Ed. note] *La Nouvelle Revue française*, launched in 1909 by André Gide and Jean Schlumberger at Éditions de la NRF (renamed Gallimard after the Second World War), had become a symbolically dominant authority in the French intellectual field between the wars. Among its favourite authors were the radical-socialist philosopher and pacifist Alain (pseudonym of Émile Chartier, 1868–1951), who taught philosophy at the Lycée Henri IV, and the poet and thinker Paul Valéry (1871–1945), member of the Académie française and professor at the Collège de France from 1937, two leading figures of the Third Republic, embodying rationalism and individualism.

36 [Ed. note] E. Cassirer, *The Myth of the State* (New Haven and London: Yale University Press, 1974).

170 *Notes to pp. 59–68*

37 [Ed. note] 'Philosophy of life' in German. On the objective relations between Martin Heidegger and the Neo-Kantian, rationalist and humanist philosopher Ernst Cassirer, as well as on their confrontation around the Kantian philosophical heritage in the Davos encounters, see Bourdieu, *The Political Ontology of Martin Heidegger*, pp. 59–60, 64–5 and 123–4 note 13. The debate has been translated into French: E. Cassirer and M. Heidegger, *Débat sur le kantisme et la philosophie, Davos, mars 1929*, trans. P. Aubenque, J.-M. Fataud and P. Quillet (Paris: Beauchesne, 1972). On this debate, see P. Gordon, *Continental Divide: Heidegger, Cassirer, Davos* (Cambridge MA: Harvard UP, 2010), and S. Truwant, *Cassirer and Heidegger in Davos: The Philosophical Arguments* (Cambridge: Cambridge University Press, 2022).

2.2 Programme for a Sociology of the International Circulation of Cultural Works

1 [Ed. note] Colloquium on 'The International Circulation of Ideas', 7 February 1991 at the Hugot foundation. An issue of *Actes de la recherche en sciences sociales*, 'Des empires aux nations' (98, 1993) was composed around some of the participants' contributions.
2 [Ed. note] The Frankreich-Zentrum [France Centre] was founded by Joseph Jurt, professor of Romance literature, and one of the principal introducers of Bourdieu to Germany, at the University of Freiburg.
3 [Ed. note] For the case of sociology, see P. Bourdieu, 'The Cause of Science', trans. P. Collier, in *Return to Reflexivity* (Cambridge: Polity, 2024), pp. 72–93.
4 [Ed. note] See P. Bourdieu and A. Darbel (with D. Schnapper), *The Love of Art: European Art Museums and Their Public*, trans. C. Beattie and N. Merriman (Cambridge: Polity, 1997 [1966]).
5 [Ed. note] D. Crane, *Invisible Colleges: Diffusion of Knowledge in Scientific Communities* (Chicago: University of Chicago Press, 1972).
6 [Ed. note] S. Guilbaut, *How New York Stole the Idea of Modern Art: Abstract Impressionism, Freedom, and the Cold War* (Chicago: Chicago University Press, 1983).
7 [Ed. note] M. Pollak, 'La planification des sciences sociales', *Actes de la recherche en sciences sociales*, 2, 1976, pp. 105–21.
8 [Ed. note] This is true for some small publishing houses, but not for the larger ones, which reinforces the point made by Bourdieu on the differential logics of export and import.
9 [Ed. note] The DAAD (Deutscher Akademischer Austauschdienst) [German Academic Exchange Service] is the German office for university exchanges.
10 [Ed. note] This was the paper given at the conference on 30 October 1989 at the University of Freiburg, reproduced in the present volume as Chapter 2.1.
11 [Ed. note] See P. Bourdieu, 'Une révolution conservatrice: le champ éditorial', in particular the analysis of axis 3 of the field devoted to small avant-garde publishers whose position incites them to invest in the translation of foreign works. *Microcosmes* (Paris: Raisons d'agir, 2022), pp. 482–4.
12 [Ed. note] In 1972 the sociologist Robert Picht (1937–2008) completed a third-cycle doctoral thesis supervised by Pierre Bourdieu entitled 'Les étudiants germanistes et l'Allemagne' (Paris: EPHE, 1972).

Notes to pp. 69–71 171

13 [Ed. note] P. Bourdieu, 'For a Corporation of the Universal', in *The Rules of Art: Genesis and Structure of the Literary Field*, trans. S. Emanuel (Cambridge: Polity, 1996 [1992]), pp. 337–48; 'For an International of Intellectuals', in *Political Interventions: Social Science and Political Action*, trans. D. Fernbach (London: Verso, 2008 [2002]), pp. 209–17.

14 [Ed. note] These debates in the years 1988–90 circled around what was called the 'Rocard' reform, which proposed to modernize French spelling, as suggested by linguists. A group presided over by Bernard Cerquiglini made propositions accepted by the Académie française and by the Conseils supérieurs de la langue française in Quebec and Belgium. Published in the *Journal officiel de la République française on* 6 December 1990, under the title 'Les rectifications de l'orthographe. Conseil supérieur de la langue française', the final text, although it had no binding force, unleashed the 'guerre du nénufar' (spelling proposed for 'nénuphar' – the 'water lily'). A first attack by a 'Robespierre Committee', published in *Le Monde* on 30–1 December 1990, calling for 'a moral guillotine of contempt against the soulless and thoughtless technocrats who dare profane our language', was followed by lively reactions from Bernard Pivot, Philippe Sollers, Jean d'Ormesson and Frédéric Vitoux in *Madame Figaro*, 5 January 1991, in particular against the partial suppression of the circumflex accent. Bourdieu mentioned this debate in his lecture at the Collège de France on 10 January 1991, and at the beginning of the next one. See *On the State: Lectures at the Collège de France (1989–1992)*, trans. D. Fernbach (Cambridge: Polity, 2014 [2012]), pp. 119–22.

15 [Ed. note] See P. Valéry, 'Fonction de Paris' (1937) and 'Présence de Paris' (1937), in *Regards sur le monde actuel* (Paris: Gallimard, 1945). See notes 4 and 8 to Chapter 1.1.

16 [Ed. note] Friedrich Gottlieb Klopstock was a German poet of the eighteenth century, who became the emblematic figure of the pre-Romantic *Sturm und Drang* political and literary movement.

17 [Ed. note] The review *Liber* was founded by Pierre Bourdieu in 1989 and initially appeared as a supplement to *Le Monde* and five other papers in Europe (in German, English, Spanish and Italian), before becoming autonomous in 1991 (it was issued as a supplement to *Actes de la recherche en sciences sociales*, the review edited by Bourdieu). At first subtitled *Revue européenne des livres*, it became a *Revue internationale* in 1994 and the number of languages it was translated into increased. See P. Casanova, 'La revue *Liber*: réflexions sur quelques usages pratiques de la notion d'autonomie relative', in L. Pinto, G. Sapiro and P. Champagne, *Pierre Bourdieu, sociologue* (Paris: Fayard, 2004), pp. 413–30.

18 [Ed. note] Among the most widely read and translated abroad: G. Deleuze, *Nietzsche et la philosophie* (Paris: PUF, 1962); P. Klossowksi, *Nietzsche et le cercle vicieux* (Paris: Mercure de France, 1969).

19 [Ed. note] We obviously think of Raymond Aron, with *Les Étapes de la pensée sociologique* (Paris: Gallimard, 1967), which complemented his previous publications on German sociology and philosophies of history. But Bourdieu also proposed a reading of Weber's sociology of religion in two articles: 'Genèse et structure du champ religieux', *Revue française de sociologie*, 12/3, 1971, pp. 295–334; 'Une interprétation de la théorie de la religion selon Max Weber', *Archives européennes de sociologie*, 12/1, 1971, pp. 3–21. A study of the reception of Weber in France (with a bibliography) was published by Michaël Pollak, 'Max Weber en France. L'itinéraire d'une œuvre', *Les Cahiers*

172   *Notes to pp. 71–74*

de l'Institut d'Histoire du Temps Présent, 3, 1986, pp. 1–70, which recalls the readings by Maurice Merleau-Ponty, Julien Freund, Jean-Marie Vincent and the translations by René König.

20 [Ed. note] Research by the economist and sociologist Werner Sombart (1863–1941) was the object in his lifetime of translations and reviews in *L'Année sociologique*, alongside other German sociologists such as Georg Simmel, whereas the Durkheimians were more reluctant to handle the work of Max Weber, which was difficult to classify among the disciplines, and which was not appreciated by the economic historians either, as Michael Pollak explains in his study of 'Max Weber en France. . .', which Bourdieu is no doubt implicitly referring to here (see also M. Pollak, 'La place de Max Weber dans le champ intellectuel français', *Droit et société*, 9, 1988, pp. 189–201). It was Raymond Aron who was Weber's principal importer into France after the war, relayed by Bourdieu himself, who drew on Weber's sociology of religion and law to construct his theory of fields. See G. Sapiro, 'Weber, Max', in G. Sapiro, *Dictionnaire international Bourdieu* (Paris: CNRS Éditions, 2020), pp. 885–8. On the reception of Weber in France, see also M. Gemperle, 'La fabrique d'un classique français. Le cas de "Weber"', *Revue d'histoire des sciences humaines*, 18, 2008, pp. 159–77.

21 [Ed. note] An article by M. Chalmers was published later in one of the issues of *Actes de la recherche en sciences sociales* devoted to publishing. See 'Les écrivains allemands en Grande-Bretagne', *Actes de la recherche en sciences sociales*, 130, 1999, pp. 81–5.

22 [Ed. note] A Hungarian sociologist, Associate Professor at Eötvös Loránd University, Faculty of Social Sciences.

23 [Ed. note] Bourdieu is alluding to Talcott Parsons, Paul Lazarsfeld and Robert Merton, the three US sociologists professionally dominant during the years 1960–70, whom he treated as the 'Capitolian triad'. They recommended a positivist (in the American sense) approach, based on quantification, formalization and ethical neutrality. See P. Bourdieu, 'Le champ scientifique', *Actes de la recherche en sciences sociales*, 2/2–3, 1976, p. 103. He returns on several occasions to these US sociologists, in *Science of Science and Reflexivity*, trans. R. Nice (Cambridge: Polity, 2004 [2001]), pp. 18, 102, and in *Sketch for a Self-Analysis*, trans. R. Nice (Cambridge: Polity, 2007), p. 72.

24 [Ed. note] A. Martinet (1908–99), *agrégé d'anglais* (he had decided not to prepare for the competition for entry to the École normale supérieure, in order to specialize in English). He was Director of Studies at the École pratique des hautes études from 1938 to 1946. He introduced functional linguistics to France, in particular in his books *Éléments de linguistique générale* (1960) and *Langue et Fonction* (1962). In his youth he had met Louis Hjelmslev, leader of the Copenhagen Linguistic Circle, before being invited to participate in the research of the Prague Circle. Roman Jakobson invited him to teach at Columbia University, where he became head of the department of linguistics in 1947, and helped him to launch and edit the review *Word*.

Notes to pp. 76–81 173

2.3 Does Belgian Literature Exist?

1 [Ed. note] Article published in *Études de lettres*, 4, 1985, pp. 3–6. The article was preceded by the following summary: 'Strategies and institutions of consecration, examined in the light of the theory of fields, pose the problem of Belgian cultural identity, caught between the alternatives of identification with the dominant model or with alterity.'

2 [Ed. note] Against the nationalist tendencies of the journal *L'Art moderne*, the Groupe du lundi made a stand in 1937 with a manifesto that condemned Belgian literary regionalism, arguing for the priority of the 'language community' over national identity and regional particularism. It was signed by twenty-one writers including Marie Gevers, Horace Van Offel, Charles Plisnier, Franz Hellens and Michel de Ghelderode.

3 Supposing that they did intend to insist on the strategy of retreat into difference, they could, like most provincials, hardly rely on much more than an *accent*, and one stigmatized. All the contradictions and dramas of a dominated cultural identity are concentrated in their relation to the language and the conflict between the central language and the local language that they all treasure, and which can take on dramatic forms when the two usages (distinguished, Parisian/vulgar, Belgian) are incarnated in the two figures of authority, paternal and maternal.

4 [Ed. note] Émile Verhaeren (1855–1916) was a Flemish Belgian poet and art critic of symbolist inspiration, writing in French. He was connected with the journal *L'Art moderne*.

5 [Ed. note] Charles de Coster (1827–79) was a French-speaking Belgian writer, author of *La Légende et les aventures héroïques, joyeuses et glorieuses d'Ulenspiegel et de Lamme Goedzak au pays de Flandres et ailleurs*, written in a Rabelaisian style, which earned him international recognition, but saw him rejected in his own country.

6 [Ed. note] Camille Lemonnier (1844–1913) published a realistic account of the 1870 war, *Les Charniers*, and sealed his reputation with *Un mâle* (1881), which scandalized conservative circles.

7 See for instance 'La Belgique malgré tout', *Revue de l'Université de Bruxelles*, 1980, pp. 502–6.

8 The same analysis would be viable for French-speaking Switzerland and Canada, with differences such as the absence of a tradition predisposed to be constituted as a 'temperament', or the situation of double dependence, concerning Germany or the United States in relation to France, which can empower strategies of defence through using one dominant power to counterattack the other.

3.1 Passport to Duke

1 This chapter was prepared as a paper for the conference "Bourdieu: Fieldwork in Literature, Art, Philosophy," Duke University, Durham, NC, USA, April 1995, and read in absentia. It was first published in the *International Journal of Contemporary Sociology*, vol. 33, no. 2 (October 1996). It is reprinted by permission of the *International Journal of Contemporary Sociology*.

174 *Notes to pp. 87–94*

3.2 Social Structures and Structures of Perception of the Social World

1 [Ed. note] Text written by Bourdieu in 1974, after his return from Princeton, and originally published under the same title in *Actes de la recherche en sciences sociales*, 2, 1975, pp. 18–20

2 [Ed. note] See T. Parsons, *The System of Modern Societies* (Englewood Cliffs, NJ: Prentice Hall, 1971); and 'Comparative Studies and Evolutionary Change', in I. Vallierfed, *Comparative Methods in Sociology* (Berkeley: University of California Press, 1974), pp. 97–139, where Parsons characterizes the United States as the 'new "lead" society'.

3 S. M. Lipset, *Political Man: The Social Bases of Politics* (New York: Doubleday, 1960), pp. 99–100 and 129–30.

4 D. Bell, 'On Meritocracy and Equality', *The Public Interest*, 29, 1972, p. 40.

5 [Ed. note] P. Lazarsfeld, 'Notes on the History of Quantification in Sociology: Trends, Sources and Problems', *Isis*, 52/2, 1961; P. Lazarsfeld, 'Historical Notes on the Empirical Study of Action: An Intellectual Odyssey', in *Qualitative Analysis: Historical and Critical Essays* (Boston: Allyn & Bacon, 1972), pp. 53–106.

6 [Ed. note] Here Bourdieu is no doubt thinking of the books by F. Bourricaud, *Changements à Puno. Étude de sociologie andine* (Paris: Éditions de l'IHEAL, coll. 'Travaux et mémoires', IX, 1962); and by the same author, *Pouvoir et société dans le Pérou contemporain* (Paris: Presses de Sciences Po, 1967).

7 [Ed. note] C. Geertz, 'Ideology as a Cultural System', in D. E. Apter (ed.), *Ideology and Discontent* (Glencoe: The Free Press, 1964), pp. 47–76.

8 D. Lerner, *The Passing of Traditional Society: Modernizing the Middle East* (Glencoe: The Free Press, 1958).

9 Ibid., p. 51.

10 Ibid., p. 412.

11 Ibid., p. 78.

12 Ibid., p. 60.

13 Ibid., p. 96.

14 Ibid., pp. 398–9.

3.3 The Specifics of National Histories

1 [Ed. note] This text has been reconstructed using the transcriptions of a seminar held at EHESS on 1 February 2000 (recorded by B. Dargelos, first part; J. Sedel, second part; P. Rimbert, third part) and from preparatory notes for the seminar. Unpublished lecture and preparatory notes, Raisons d'agir archives.

2 [Ed. note] É. Durkheim, *Textes*, III (Paris: Minuit, 1975 [1888]), chapter 'Introduction à la sociologie de la famille', p. 16.

3 See P. Bourdieu and A. Darbel (with D. Schnapper), *The Love of Art: European Art Museums and Their Public*, trans. C. Beattie and N. Merriman (Cambridge: Polity, 1997 [1966]).

4 [Ed. note] Here Bourdieu is referring to the European project PENSOC (État pénal/État social) run by Rémi Lenoir at the Centre de sociologie européenne from 1998. The results were presented at a conference held in Brussels in October 2001. Among the scientific 'deliverables' provided to the Research Department of the European Commission, we might cite the issues of *Actes de*

Notes to pp. 96–104 175

la recherche en sciences sociales: 'De l'État social à l'État pénal' (124, 1998) and 'Nouvelles formes d'encadrement' (136/137, 2001). Another contract, coordinated by Franz Schultheis, involved the CSEC on the topic of 'Jeunesse et précarité' [Youth and insecurity] (JEUNPREC).

5 [Ed. note] Collectif, *À la recherche de la France* (Paris: Seuil, 1963) (this book was composed by researchers from Harvard and two French researchers: J. B. Duroselle and F. Goguel).

6 [Ed. note] Here Bourdieu is no doubt alluding to F. Furet and M. Ozouf, *Dictionnaire critique de la Révolution française* (Paris: Flammarion, 1988); F. Furet, *Le Passé d'une illusion. Essai sur l'idée communiste au XXe siècle* (Paris: Robert Laffont/Calmann-Lévy, 1995).

7 [Ed. note] Born in 1944, the French sociologist Michel Maffesoli was professor at Paris V. Having held a socially dominant position in the French academic field for many years, and despite a certain notoriety in Latin America in particular, he was looked down on in scientific circles because of the lack of methodology in his various writings on violence, conflict, everyday life and postmodernism, as well as their style, judged more essayistic than scientific.

8 [Ed. note] P. Bourdieu and L. Raphael, 'Sur les rapports entre la sociologie et l'histoire en Allemagne et en France', *Actes de la recherche en sciences sociales* 106–107, 1995, pp. 108–22.

9 [Ed. note] The leading light in the history of concepts was the historian Reinhart Koselleck.

10 [Ed. note] See N. Elias, *The Civilizing Process*, trans. E. Jephcott (Oxford: Blackwell, 2000).

11 [Ed. note] É. Benveniste, *Le vocabulaire des institutions indo-européennes* (Paris: Minuit, 1969); *Dictionary of Indo-European Concepts and Society*, trans. E. Palmer (Chicago: Hau, 2016).

12 [Ed. note] É. Benveniste, *Problems in General Linguistics*, vol. 1, trans. M. E. Meek (Miami: University of Miami Press, 1971 [1966], expanded edition: Chicago: Chicago University Press, 2021).

13 [Ed. note] The *pacte civil de solidarité* is a contract between two adults agreeing to organize their life together. This form of civil union was established in the Civil Code in 1999.

14 [Ed. note] L. Colley, *Britons: Forging the Nation (1707–1837)* (New Haven and London: Yale University Press, 1994).

15 [Ed. note] According to Christophe Charle, this may refer to the book by Michael Jeismann, *La Patrie de l'ennemi. La notion d'ennemi national et la représentation de la nation en Allemagne et en France de 1792 à 1918* (Paris: CNRS Éditions, 1997) (Bourdieu having mistaken the publisher).

16 [Ed. note] N. Elias, 'Culture et civilisation', first part of *La Civilisation des mœurs* (Paris: Calmann-Lévy, 1973; and *Studien über die Deutschen: Machtkämpfe und Habitusentwicklung im 19. und 20. Jahrhundert* (Frankfurt: Suhrkamp, 1989), translated into English as *The Germans: Power Struggles and the Development of Habitus in the Nineteenth and Twentieth Centuries*, trans. E. Dunning and S. Mennell (Cambridge: Polity, 1996). French translation by R. Chartier: *Les Allemands. Luttes de pouvoir et développement de l'habitus aux XIXe et XXe siècles, précédé de 'Barbarie et "dé-civilisation"'* (Paris: Seuil, 2017).

17 [Ed. note] The article was first published in *The Socialist Register*, 1965, pp. 311–62. It was reprinted in E. P. Thompson, *The Poverty of Theory* (New

176   *Notes to pp. 104–112*

York: Monthly Review Press, 1978), pp. 35–91. The book was translated into French in 2015.

18 [Ed. note] E. P. Thompson discusses a group of articles by these two authors published in the *New Left Review* in 1964: P. Anderson, 'Origins of the Present Crisis', *NLR* 23; T. Nairn, 'The British Political Elite', *NLR* 23; 'The English Working Class', *NLR* 24; 'The Anatomy of the Labour Party – 1', *NLR* 27; and 'The Anatomy of the Labour Party – 2', *NLR* 28.

19 Thompson, *The Poverty of Theory*, p. 37.

20 Ibid., p. 42.

21 Ibid., p. 58.

22 [Ed. note] P. Bourdieu, *Manet: A Symbolic Revolution*, trans. P. Collier and M. Rigaud-Drayton (Cambridge: Polity, 2017), pp. 142–59 (Lecture of 4 March 1999).

23 Thompson, *The Poverty of Theory*, p. 66.

24 [Ed. Note] The Boer War was a series of conflicts in South Africa at the end of the nineteenth century between the British and the 'Afrikaner' inhabitants (of Dutch origins) of the two independent Boer republics.

25 [Ed. note] What was called the 'great working-class fever' brought millions of strikers together in the United Kingdom, inspired by a revolutionary syndical-ism that mobilized them on very diverse sites (ports, mines. . .), leading to the promulgation of the Trade Union Act of 1913 and the consolidation of the industrial federations for a while.

26 [Ed. note] Here Bourdieu is referring to Elias's book on *The Germans*. See note 16 above.

27 [Ed. note] C. Charle, *La Crise des sociétés impériales. Allemagne, France, Grande-Bretagne (1900–1940). Essai d'histoire sociale comparée* (Paris: Seuil, 2001).

28 [Ed. note] Elias, *The Civilizing Process*.

29 [Ed. note] Bourdieu is presumably referring to passages from *Studien über die Deutschen* using either the first German edition (Suhrkamp) of 1989, or the English edition, *The Germans* (Polity Press) of 1996, p. 6, since the French translation, *Les Allemands*, was not published until 2017.

30 [Ed. note] Elias, *The Germans*, pp. 44–119.

31 [Ed. note] This colloquium was organized at Neuchâtel on 3 December 1999. Bourdieu's intervention was published under the title 'L'inconscient d'école' in *Actes de la recherche en sciences sociales* (135, 2000, pp. 3–5), as the introduc-tion to the issue collecting the other contributions. It is reproduced as Chapter 3.4 of the present volume.

32 [Ed. note] The educational syllabus of the primary school under the Third Republic was made up of titles by the naturalist writers. The Goncourt Academy, founded in 1903, would represent this movement, excluded from the Académie française.

33 'Workfare' is a governmental plan under which welfare recipients are required to accept public-service jobs or to participate in job training.

34 P. Casanova, *La République mondiale des lettres* (Paris: Seuil, 1999).

35 [Translator's note] See I. Kant, *Groundwork of the Metaphysics of Morals*, trans. M. Gregor and J. Timmermann (Cambridge: Cambridge University Press, 2012), p. 45.

36 [Ed. note] This refers to Ngũgĩ wa Thiong'o, a Kenyan writer who decided to renounce the literary use of English to return to his native language, Gikuyu. See Casanova, *La République mondiale des lettres*, pp. 374–5.

Notes to pp. 112–126 177

37 [Ed. note] L. Wacquant, *Les Prisons de la misère* (Paris: Raisons d'agir, 1999).
38 [Ed. note] An allusion to the book by Charle, *La Crise des sociétés impériales.*
39 [Ed. note] These preparatory notes for the seminar figure in the private archives of Raisons d'agir publishers, filed by Marie-Christine Rivière.
40 [Ed. note] In his essay *L'art comme procédé,* trans. R. Gayraud (Paris: Allia, 2008), the Russian Formalist Viktor Shklovsky explains that literature has the power to 'defamiliarize' or 'make strange' aspects of the world that habit and routine have rendered indistinct or automatic, such as hearing the sound of waves when you live close to the sea (*ostranenie* in Russian means 'estrangement' or 'making strange'). Shklovsky recommends resorting to poetic language to fight against the alienation implied by this process of ordinary routinization, in particular through everyday language.
41 [Ed. note] Pascale Casanova replied to this criticism in the preface to the later edition of *La République mondiale des lettres* (Paris: 'Points', 2008).
42 [Ed. note] According to Alexander Gerschenkron, professor of economic history at Harvard, the fact that capitalism in Russia did not enjoy the same development as in England, France or other countries was due to its later start. See his book *Economic Backwardness in Historical Perspective* (Cambridge, MA: Belknap Press, 1962).

3.4 The Scholarly Unconscious

1 [Ed. note] This article was initially published in *Actes de la recherche en sciences sociales*, 135, 2000, pp. 3–5.
2 [Ed. note] In his *Lectures on the Philosophy of History* (1832), Hegel distinguishes three main types of history: original history, a sort of immediate chronicle of the present times; reflective history, where the historian takes his distance from the past; and the philosophy of history as the perception of universal Reason in history.
3 [Ed. note] On the debate triggered at the end of the 1990s in the intellectual field by the publication of official recommendations for the modernization of spelling, see note 14 to Chapter 2.2. The writers to whom Bourdieu alludes here are d'Ormesson and Sollers, who were opposed to the suppression of the circumflex accent.
4 [Ed. note] Cf. the Neuchâtel colloquium, 3 December 1999.
5 [Ed. note] See note 40 in Chapter 3.3 on Viktor Shklovsky.
6 [Ed. note] É. Durkheim and M. Mauss, 'De quelques formes de classification. Contribution à l'étude des représentations collectives', *L'Année sociologique*, 6, 1901–2, pp. 1–72.
7 I attempted a first elaboration of this programme, which I revealed a little prematurely in an article entitled 'Systèmes d'enseignement et systèmes de pensée' (*Revue Internationale des sciences sociales*, 19/3, 1967, pp. 367–88), in a sort of experimental analysis of the classificatory schemas that French teachers practise in their operations of classification. Cf. P. Bourdieu and M. de Saint-Martin, 'Les catégories de l'entendement professoral', *Actes de la recherche en sciences sociales*, 3, 1975, pp. 68–93.
8 [Ed. note] In *La méthode instrumentale en psychologie* (1930), L. S. Vygotsky expounds a genetic method of apprenticeship based on the processes of appropriation of a child's social environment. This historico-cultural theory is cited

178 *Notes to pp. 127–135*

by P. Bourdieu and J.-C. Passeron in *Reproduction In Education, Society and Culture*, trans. R. Nice (London: Sage, 1977), p. 46.

9 See J. Goody, *The Logic of Writing and the Organisation of Society* (Cambridge: Cambridge University Press, 1986); *The Domestication of the Savage Mind* (Cambridge: Cambridge University Press, 1977).

10 [Ed. note] See G. Murdoch, *Atlas of World Cultures* (Pittsburgh: University of Pittsburgh Press, 1981).

11 [Ed. note] See C. Lévi-Strauss, *Structural Anthropology*, trans. C. Jakobson and B. Grundfest Schoepf (New York: Basic Books, 1974 [1958]).

12 [Ed. note] There are many references to these research perspectives in 'De la Maison du roi à la Maison de l'État: le champ bureaucratique', in P. Bourdieu, *Microcosmes* (Paris: Raisons d'agir, 2022), chapter 4.2, pp. 369–93.

13 [Ed. note] Here Bourdieu is citing M. Alvesson, *Cultural Perspectives on Organisations* (Cambridge: Cambridge University Press, 1993).

4.1 The Olympics: An Agenda for Analysis

1 This text is an abridged version of a talk given at the 1992 Annual Meeting of the Philosophical Society for the Study of Sport in Berlin, held in Berlin on October 2, 1992. It was subsequently published in the *Actes de la recherche en sciences sociales* 103, June 1994, pp. 102–3. The text was published in English in Bourdieu's *On Television* (New York: The New Press, 1998).

2 "Sponsors were offered a complete communication package based on product category exclusivity and continuity over a four-year period. The programme for each of seventy-five matches included stadium advertising, official supplier's titles, the use of mascots and emblems and franchise opportunities." For £7 million [$14 million, at the time of publication in 1996] each sponsor in 1986 had the possibility of a share of "the biggest single televised event in the world," with "unparalleled exposure, far in excess of other sports." Vyv Simson and Andrew Jennings, *The Lords of the Rings: Power, Money and Drugs in the Modern Olympics* (London: Simon & Schuster, 1992), p. 102.

3 The top competitive sports increasingly rely on an industrial technology that calls on various biological and psychological sciences to transform the human body into an efficient and inexhaustible machine. Competition between national teams and governments increasingly and ever more emphatically encourages the use of prohibited substances and dubious methods of training. See John M. Hoberman, *Mortal Engines: The Science of Performance and the Dehumanization of Sport* (New York: Free Press, 1992).

4 See Pierre Bourdieu, *The Rules of Art: Genesis and Structure of the Literary Field*, trans. Susan Emanuel (Cambridge: Polity, 1996 [1992]).

5 For a gross indicator of the real value of different actors in the Olympic "show business," the presents distributed by the Korean authorities to different important figures went from $1,100 for IOC members to $110 for the athletes. See Simson and Jennings, *The Lords of the Rings*, p. 153.

6 One could, for example, imagine an Olympic charter that would define the principles to be followed by everyone involved in the production of both shows (beginning, obviously, with the men who run the Olympic Committee, who are the first to benefit from transgressions of the financial disinterestedness they are supposed to enforce), or an Olympic oath that would bind the athletes

Notes to pp. 136–149 179

(prohibiting them, for example, from joining in patriotic demonstrations such as wrapping themselves in the national flag for a lap of honor) and those who produce and comment on the images of these exploits.

4.2 The Global Legal Field

1 [Ed. note] This text has been recomposed from Bourdieu's 'Foreword' to the book by Yves Dezalay and Bryant Garth, *Dealing in Virtue: International Commercial Arbitration and the Construction of a Transnational Legal Order* (Chicago: University of Chicago Press, 1996), pp. vii–viii, and his unpublished working notes on this book.
2 [Ed. note] The nickname given to a group of Chilean economists in the 1970s, followers of the doctrines of Milton Friedman and Arnold Harberger, whom they had discovered on the occasion of the cooperation agreement between the Catholic University, of which most of them were members, and the University of Chicago. It was in this spirit that the group contributed to the reform of the Chilean economy under the dictatorship of Pinochet. See Y. Dezalay and B. Garth, *The Internationalization of Palace Wars: Lawyers, Economists, and the Contest to Transform Latin American States* (Chicago: University of Chicago Press, 2002).

4.3 The Internationalization of the Economic Field

1 Public lecture delivered at Keisen University, Tokyo, Japan, October 3, 2000. This text was published in English as "Unite and Rule," in *Firing Back* (New York: The New Press, 2003).
2 Karl Polanyi, *The Great Transformation: The Political and Economic Origins of Our Time* (Boston: Beacon Press, 2001 [1947]).
3 Pierre Bourdieu, *Algeria 60: Economic Structures and Temporal Structures* (Cambridge: Cambridge University Press, 1977).
4 Claude Lévi-Strauss, *Race et histoire* (Paris: Gallimard, 1987 [1955]).
5 Oliver Williamson, *Markets and Hierarchies: Analysis and Antitrust Implications* (New York: The Free Press, 1975).
6 Cf. François Chesnais, *La Mondialisation du capital* (Paris: Syros, 1994), and M. Freitag and É. Pineault (eds.), *Le Monde enchaîné* (Montreal: Éditions Nota Bene, 1999).

Guide

1 'Traduction. Les échanges littéraires internationaux', *Actes de la recherche en sciences sociales*, 144, 2002, ed. J. Heilbron and G. Sapiro.
2 G. Sapiro (ed.), *Translatio. Le marché de la traduction en France à l'heure de la mondialisation* (Paris: CNRS Éditions, coll. 'Culture et Société', 2008); *Traduire la littérature et les sciences humaines* (Paris: DEPS-Ministère de la Culture, 2010); *Sciences humaines en traduction. Les livres français aux États-Unis, au Royaume-Uni et en Argentine* (Paris: Institut français-CESSP, 2014). This research was conducted in collaboration with Johan Heilbron, author of

180 *Notes to pp. 149–150*

an article of theoretical and methodological reference: 'Towards a Sociology of Translation: Book Translations as a Cultural World-System', *European Journal of Social Theory*, 2/4, pp. 429–44. For a theoretical and methodological summary, see J. Heilbron and G. Sapiro, 'Translation: Economic and Sociological Perspectives', in V. Ginsburgh and S. Weber, *Palgrave Handbook of Economics and Language* (London: Palgrave Macmillan, 2015), pp. 373–402.

3 Such as the pioneering study conducted by Ioana Popa, *Traduire sous contraintes. Littérature et communisme* (Paris: CNRS Éditions, coll. 'Culture et Société', 2010).

4 See Chapter 2.1 in this volume and the issue of *Actes de la recherche en sciences sociales* on 'La circulation des idées' (145, 2002).

5 For a theoretical reflection on the 'circulation pattern' which has proliferated in research and the different significations and approaches that it covers, see A. Vauchez, 'Le prisme circulatoire. Retour sur un leitmotiv académique', *Critique internationale*, 59/2, 2013, pp. 9–16. For a methodological reflection articulating comparison and transfers on three levels, macro, meso and micro, thanks to the concept of the field, see G. Sapiro, 'Comparaison et échanges culturels: le cas des traductions', in O. Remaud, J.-F. Schaub and I. Thireau (eds.), *Faire des sciences sociales*, vol. 2, *Comparer* (Éditions de l'EHESS, 2012), pp. 193–221; G. Sapiro and J. Pacouret, 'La circulation des biens culturels: entre marchés, États et champs', in J. Siméant (ed.), *Guide de l'enquête globale en sciences sociales* (Paris: CNRS Éditions, 2015), pp. 69–94.

6 See in particular the issue of *Actes de la recherche en sciences sociales*: 'La culture entre rationalisation et mondialisation' (206–207, 2015), edited by J. Pacouret, M. Picaud and G. Sapiro; D. Marchetti (ed.), *La Circulation des productions culturelles. Cinémas, informations et séries télévisées dans les mondes arabes et musulmans* (Istanbul: Centre Jacques Berque, 2017); and the theses published by J. Pacouret, *Les Droits des auteurs de cinéma. Sociologie historique du copyright et du droit d'auteur* (Paris: LGDJ, 2019); M. Picaud, *Mettre la ville en musique. Paris-Berlin* (Paris: Presses universitaires de Vincennes, 2021); D. Guijarro Arribas, *Du classement au reclassement. Sociologie historique de l'édition jeunesse en France et en Espagne* (Rennes: PUR, 2022); Q. Fondu, *La Scène et l'amphithéâtre. Sociologie et histoire de la discipline des études théâtrales en France et dans les deux Allemagnes (1945–2000)*, doctoral thesis, Paris, EHESS, 2021.

7 F. Matonti, 'L'anneau de Mœbius. La réception en France des formalistes russes', *Actes de la recherche en sciences sociales*, 176–177/1–2, 2009, pp. 52–67; M. Joly, *Devenir Norbert Elias* (Paris: Fayard, 2012); M. Hauchecorne, *La Gauche américaine en France. La réception de John Rawls et des théories de la justice* (Paris: CNRS Éditions, coll. 'Culture et Société', 2019). On the importation of gender studies into Eastern Europe, see I. Cîrstocea, *La Fin de la femme rouge? Fabriques transnationales du genre après la chute du Mur* (Rennes: PUR, 2019). See also F. Lebaron, 'Le "Nobel" d'économie', *Actes de la recherche en sciences sociales*, 141–142, 2002, pp. 62–5; and, in a comparatist perspective, M. Fourcade, *Economists and Societies: Discipline and Profession in the United States, Britain, and France, 1890s to 1990s* (Princeton: Princeton University Press, 2009).

8 The network was coordinated by Franz Schultheis, and the CSE was a member. See the collection synthesizing the reflections developed in this network:

Notes to p. 150 181

G. Sapiro (ed.), *L'Espace intellectuel en Europe. De la formation des États-nations à la mondialisation XIXe–XXIe siècles* (Paris: La Découverte, 2009). See too, among the publications of the network, G. Sapiro (ed.), *Les Contradictions de la globalisation éditoriale* (Paris: Nouveau Monde, 2009); and A. Boschetti (ed.), *L'Espace culturel transnational* (Paris: Nouveau Monde, 2010).

9 It was coordinated by Gisèle Sapiro and run by the Centre européen de sociologie et de science politique (born of the merger in 2010 of the Centre de sociologie européenne and the Centre de recherches politiques et sociales de la Sorbonne).

10 Among the publications produced by the project, see in particular: J. Heilbron, R. Timans and T. Boncourt (eds.), 'The Social Sciences in the European Research Area', *Serendipities. Journal for the Sociology and History of the Social Sciences*, 2, 2017; M. Santoro and G. Sapiro (eds.), 'Travelling Theories: The International Circulation of Key Thinkers and Their Works', special issue of *Sociologica*, 1, 2017; C. Fleck, V. Karady and M. Duller (eds.), *Shaping Human Science Disciplines: Institutional Developments in Europe and Beyond* (Basingstoke: Palgrave Macmillan, 2019); J. Heilbron, G. Sorá and T. Boncourt (eds.), *The Social and Human Sciences in Global Power Relations* (Basingstoke: Palgrave Macmillan, 2018); G. Sapiro, P. Baert and M. Santoro (eds.), *Ideas on the Move in the Social Sciences and Humanities: The International Circulation of Paradigms and Theorists* (Basingstoke: Palgrave Macmillan, 2020).

11 Translated into English by M. B. DeBevoise, published by Harvard University Press in 2004, and reissued in paperback in 2007. *La République mondiale des lettres* was originally published in French in 1999 by Seuil; reissued in Points, 2008, with a new Foreword. The Foreword was translated by D. Damrosch in *Journal of World Literature*, 5, 2020, pp. 169–73.

12 G. Sapiro, 'Le champ est-il national? La théorie de la différenciation sociale au prisme de l'histoire globale', *Actes de la recherche en sciences sociales*, 200, 2013, pp. 70–85; English trans. 'Field Theory from a Transnational Perspective', in T. Medvetz and J. Sallaz (eds.), *Oxford Handbook of Pierre Bourdieu* (Oxford: Oxford University Press, 2018), pp. 161–82; L. Buchholz, 'What is a Global Field? Theorizing Fields beyond the Nation-State', *Sociological Review*, 64/2, 2016, pp. 31–60; L. Buchholz, 'Rethinking the Center–Periphery Model: Dimensions and Temporalities of Macro-Structure in a Global Field of Cultural Production', *Poetics*, 71, 2018, pp. 18–32.

13 G. Sapiro, 'The Transnational Literary Field between (Inter)-nationalism and Cosmopolitanism', *Journal of World Literature*, 5/4, 2020, pp. 481–504; and G. Sapiro, *Qu'est-ce qu'un auteur mondial? Le champ littéraire transnational* (Paris: Gallimard/Seuil/EHESS, 2024; forthcoming in English with Polity Press).

14 See in particular Larissa Buchholz's thesis published under the title *The Global Rules of Arts* (Princeton: Princeton University Press, 2022). Without referring to the concept of field, Alain Quemin's research into galleries is also inspired by Bourdieu's reflection on cultural intermediaries, and he studies in particular the phenomenon of global galleries in *Le Monde des galeries* (Paris: CNRS Éditions, coll. 'Culture et Société', 2021).

15 J. Duval, 'Une république mondiale du film', *COnTEXTES*, 28, 2020.

16 'Champs intellectuels transnationaux', *Actes de la recherche en sciences sociales*, 224, 2018, coordinated by M. Brahimi, T. Leperlier and G. Sapiro.

182 — *Notes to pp. 150–151*

17 See, for example, the thesis by M. Bustamante, *L'UNESCO et la culture. Construction d'une catégorie d'intervention internationale, du 'développement culturel' à la 'diversité culturelle'* (Paris: EHESS, 2014), the thesis by L. Dugonjic-Rodwin, published under the title *Le Privilège d'une éducation transnationale. Sociologie historique du baccalauréat international* (Rennes: PUR, 2022), and the book by V. Gayon, *Épistémocratie. Enquête sur le gouvernement international du capitalisme* (Paris: Raisons d'agir, coll. 'Microcosmes', 2022).

18 See G. Sapiro, T. Leperlier and M. Brahimi, 'Qu'est-ce qu'un champ intellectuel transnational?', *Actes de la recherche en sciences sociales*, 224, 2018, pp. 4–11. See also, on internationalization, *Actes de la recherche en sciences sociales*, 246–247, 2023.

19 See C. Ducournau, *La Fabrique des classiques africains* (Paris: CNRS Éditions, coll. 'Culture et Société', 2012); T. Leperlier, *Algérie. Les écrivains de la décennie noire* (Paris: CNRS Éditions, coll. 'Culture et Société', 2021). See also the article by M. Bedecarré, 'Prizing Francophonie into Existence: The Usurpation of World Literature by the Prix des Cinq Continents', *Journal of World Literature*, 5/2, 2020, pp. 298–319 (extract of his thesis *La Francophonie à tout prix. Le rôle de la Francophonie institutionnelle dans l'accès à la reconnaissance des écrivains africains d'expression française* (Paris: EHESS, 2018).

20 'Constructions européennes. Concurrences nationales et stratégies internationales', *Actes de la recherche en sciences sociales*, 166–167, 2007, coordinated by A. Cohen, Y. Dezalay and D. Marchetti.

21 See D. Georgakakis (ed.), *Le Champ de l'eurocratie. Une sociologie politique du personnel de l'UE* (Paris: Economica, 2012); A. Vauchez, 'The Force of a Weak Field: Law and Lawyer in the Government of the European Union', *International Political Sociology*, 2, 2008, pp. 128–44.

22 See the two issues of *Actes de la recherche en sciences sociales* coordinated by S. Dezalay, J. Hagan and R. Lévi: 'Les crimes de guerre et l'ordre juridique international' (173, 2008) and 'La force du droit international et le marché de la paix' (174, 2008).

23 See P. Dixon and C. Tenove, 'International Criminal Justice as a Transnational Field: Rules, Authority and Victims', *International Journal of Transitional Justice*, 2013, pp. 1–20.

24 See D. Bigo and M. R. Madsen (eds.), 'A Different Reading of the International: Pierre Bourdieu and International Studies', *International Political Sociology*, 5/3, 2011, pp. 219–24; R. Adler-Nissen, 'Inter- and Transnational Field(s) of Power: On a Field Trip with Bourdieu', *International Political Sociology*, 5, 2011, pp. 327–45; R. Adler-Nissen (ed.), *Bourdieu in International Relations: Rethinking Key Concepts in IR* (New York: Routledge, 2013).

25 See Y. Dezalay and B. Garth, *The Internationalization of Palace Wars: Lawyers, Economists, and the Contest to Transform Latin American States* (Chicago: University of Chicago Press, 2002); and *Actes de la recherche en sciences sociales*, 151–152, 2004, edited by Y. Dezalay: 'Sociologie de la mondialisation. Héritiers, cosmopolites, mercenaires de l'impérialisme et missionnaires de l'universel'.

26 See the issue of *Culture et Conflits* (119–120, 2020): 'Quelle sociologie politique pour l'enquête globale?', and in particular the introduction by G. Daho and A. Vauchez, 'Le sociologue en globe-trotter. Réceptions, apports et difficultés de la sociologie de l'international d'Yves Dezalay'.

Notes to pp. 151–152 183

27 See A.-C. Wagner, *Les Nouvelles Élites de la mondialisation. Une immigration dorée en France* (Paris: PUF, 1998), and the issue of *Actes de la recherche en sciences sociales* edited by her on 'Le pouvoir économique. Classes sociales et modes de domination' (190, 2011).

28 See in particular F. Lebaron, 'Les élites européennes comme champ(s). Réflexions sur les usages de la prosopographie et de l'analyse géométrique des données à partir de trois expériences de recherche collective sur des objets transnationaux', *Cultures et Conflits*, 102/2, 2016, pp. 121–47.

29 See for example A. Garcia and L. Canêdo, 'Les boursiers brésiliens et l'accès aux formations d'excellence internationale', *Cahiers du Brésil contemporain*, 57/58–59/60, 2004–5, pp. 21–48; M. Börjesson, 'The Global Space of International Students in 2010', *Journal of Ethnic and Migration Studies*, 43/8, 2017, pp. 1256–75.

30 'Plages, territoires contestés' (*Actes de la recherche en sciences sociales*, 218, 2017), edited by J. Bidet and E. Devienne; 'Capital social en migration' (*Actes de la recherche en sciences sociales*, 225, 2018), edited by H. Bréan, S. Chauvin and A. Portilla.

31 See the issues of *Actes de la recherche en sciences sociales*: 'Politiques impérialistes. Genèse et structure de l'État colonial' (171–172, 2008), edited by G. Steinmetz and G. Sapiro; and 'Représenter la colonisation' (185, 2010), edited by G. Sapiro, G. Steinmetz and C. Ducournau.

32 See G. Steinmetz, 'The Colonial State as a Social Field: Ethnographic Capital and Native Policy in the German Overseas Empire before 1914', *American Sociological Review*, 73, 2008, pp. 589–612; G. Steinmetz (ed.), *Sociology and Empire: The Imperial Entanglements of a Discipline* (Durham, NC: Duke University Press, 2013); J. Go, 'Global Fields and Imperial Forms: Field Theory and the British and American Empires', *Sociological Theory*, 26/3, 2008, pp. 201–29.

33 J. Go, 'Field Theory and Global Transformations in the Long 20th Century', in M. Albert and T. Werron (eds.), *What in the World ? Understanding Global Change* (Bristol: Bristol University Press, 2021).

34 A. Vion and F.-X. Dudouet, 'Penser l'impérialisme à partir de la théorie des champs', *Cultures & Conflits*, 119–120, 2020.

35 See the special issue edited by Julian Go and Monika Krause, 'Fielding Transnationalism', *Sociological Review*, 64/2, 2016.

Index

academic publishing, internationalization of 40–42
accumulation of national symbolic capital 64–8
Algeria 3, 4, 7, 20, 22–3, 139
allodoxia 42, 56, 71, 82, 84
Anderson, P. and Nairn, T. 104, 117
anthropology 36, 57
aristocracy 105, 107, 118
artistic production and Olympics 135
avant-gardism 29

Bachelard, G. 8
Barthes, R. 83
Belgium
    delinquency, national comparative study 11–12, 94–5
    limits of literature field and political frontiers 76–8
    and Switzerland 15–16, 64
Bell, D. 89–10
Bender, T. 39
Benveniste, E. 100–11, 116
Bergson, H. 59, 114
Blackwell publishing house 40–11
book covers 54
bourgeoisie
    English 105, 117
    German 107
    new 137–8
    translation of term 12–13, 98

Brazil 36–8, 40, 41–42, 73, 75
Britishness, crisis of 103

capital and labor 142, 146
capitalism
    and political economy 105
    and 'precapitalist' societies 4
    utopian 142
Casanova, P. 112, 150
Cassirer, E. 3–4, 59
Centre for European Sociology (CSE) 5, 6, 7, 11, 94, 149
Centre for the Sociology of Education and Culture (CSEC) 5, 6, 7, 11
Chicago school/Chicago boys 30, 137–8
Chalmers, M. 72–3, 74
Charle, C. 101, 106
Chiva, I. and Jeggle, U. 57
Chomsky, N. 54
Civil Rights Movement, US 37, 41
civilization and culture, France and Germany 106–8
class
    concept of underclass 40–11, 42–4
    relations 88–9, 105, 107, 118
classification systems 57–8, 126
cognitive patterns/structures 123–7
collectivists and individualists 36
Colley, L. 13, 102
common places 33, 34
common sense *see* doxa

Index

communism and class 88–9
'communitarianism' and 'liberals' 35–6
comparatism
  against ethnocentrism and
    evolutionism 3–7, 87–8
  bibliography 119–22
  history of social science 57–8
  method 128–9
  structural 7–13
  see also national histories (comparative
    history of differences)
Comte, A. 64–5
context
  historical, neutralization of 33–4
  texts circulated without 50–11, 81
cultural capital 10, 11, 65–6
  and cultural practices 7–9
cultural imperialism 30, 31, 33
'Cultural Studies' 41, 98
cultural system as ideology 90
culture, universal 20–21
culture-civilization antithesis 106–8

delinquency, national comparative study
  9, 11–12, 94–5, 101–102, 117
democracy
  and lower classes 89
  myth of 29
Derrida, J. 81–82
descriptive phase of research 62
Dezalay, Y. 112–13, 151
  and Garth, B. 137
differentiation and undifferentiated
  societies 128–9
disciplinary divisions and hierarchies
  124
disciplinary unconscious and national
  unconscious 99
double domination 15–16, 63
double historicization 100, 116–17
double meaning of 'globalization' 140–44
doxa 123, 124
  allodoxia 42, 56, 71, 82, 84
  and endoxic discourse of global legal
    field 136–7
  US 39, 40

Duke University lecture, US 17, 81–86
Durkheim, E. 4, 5, 13, 58, 59, 93, 95, 108,
  117, 126, 128

East European countries 73–4
economic globalization *see* global
  economic field
education system 9–10
  and academic/disciplinary hierarchies
    124
  national differences 97–8, 99, 109
Elias, N. 13, 102, 106–8
empathy 91
Engels, F. 104–5
England
  and conditions for revolution 88–10,
    102, 104–6, 117–18
  national identity 13, 103
epistemology 99–10
ethnocentrism 105, 127
  and evolutionism, comparatism
    against 3–7, 87–8
  inverse viewpoint 104–5, 106–7
ethnology 128–9
  and anthropology 57–8
  and sociology 97, 98, 128
Europe/European Union (EU)
  new internationalism 21–22
  research 149–11
  research centres 5, 6, 7, 11, 94,
    149–10
  and US 34–6, 40–11, 42–6
  vocabulary of institutions 100–11, 113,
    116–17
  see also national histories (comparative
    history of differences); *specific*
    countries
Eurostat 95, 113
exclusion, concept of 43

field of production and field of reception
  51–52, 70–11
financial and economic advantages of
  globalization, US 142–3
financial regulation and financial
  concentration 145–6

186 *Index*

firms/companies
  and global economic field 145–8
  multinational corporations 134, 148
Flemish literature 77–8
foreign authors 52–4, 67–8
Foucault, M. 55, 81, 85
France
  and Belgium 76–8
  and England/Britain 13, 103
    see also French Revolution
  and Quebec 15–16, 64
France and Germany 13, 36
  comparative national histories 106–8
  international circulation of ideas 49–11, 53, 55–9, 61–62, 67, 69–10, 71
France and US 20–21, 27–32, 64
  academia: Duke University lecture 17, 81–86
  Quebec 15–16, 64
French Revolution 27–8, 88
  and England 102, 104–6, 117–18

Garcia, A. et al. 74
Garcia, M.-F. 75
Geertz, C. 90
German Democratic Republic (GDR) 10–11
Germany 7–8, 13, 14–15
  delinquency, national comparative study 11–12, 94–5
  see also France and Germany
'ghetto'/'ghettoization' 35, 44
global economic field 22–3, 139–48
global legal field 23–4, 136–8, 151
globalization 20–23
  bibliography 119
  double meaning of 140–44
  Olympics 134–5
  polysemic notion of 34–5
  and related terms 150
  and US 39–46, 141–44, 151
Goffman, E. 5

Greece 112
delinquency, national comparative study 11–12, 94–5, 101–102
Guilbaut, S. 30

Habermas, J. 55–6
Hanchard, M. 37
Hegel, G. W. F. 123
Heidegger, M. 7, 53, 56, 58, 59
hierarchies
  academic/disciplinary 124
  ethnic/immigrant groups, US 87–8
  see also class; classification systems
historical context, neutralization of 33–4
historical reflexivity 115–16
historical unconscious 12–13, 99–11, 116
  and socially constructed perception 110–11
history and explanation of present 93–108
'human rights' 40
Hungary 73
Husserl, E. 3–4

ideology, cultural system as 90
immigrants, US 87–8, 90–92
imperialist reason
  cunning of 33–46
  to international field 18–24
import/export
  agents 16, 66–7
  cultural 62
  intellectual 49
  juridico-economic strategies 137–8
individualists and collectivists 36
inequality 22–3, 141, 144
  see also 'race', US
initial traumatism, bibliography 121
Institute for Advanced Studies, Princeton, US 5
intellectuals 49–10, 105–6
inter-echoing effect 112–13
INTERCO-SSH 150
International Association of Sociology 5
international circulation of ideas and texts 14–18, 40–42, 49–60

Index 187

neutralization of historical context 33–4
research programme 61–75
guide to 149–52
international fields
imperialist reason to 18–24
national and 15–16, 63–4
strategies in 16–17, 67–9
International Monetary Fund (IMF) 144, 147–8
International Olympic Committee (IOC) 134
International Parliament of Writers 19, 20
internationalism
methodological 17, 69
and nationalism 69–11
new 21–22
scientific 19, 50, 82
internationalization
of social sciences 18–19
see also global economic field; global legal field; globalization
inverse ethnocentric viewpoint 104–5, 106–7
see also outsider/foreigner viewpoint

Japan 8–9, 104
journalism/sociologist-journalists 43–5, 111
Jünger, E. 50
Jurt, J. 15, 61–62

Kant, I. 28
Karady, V. 5, 7
Keynes, J. M. 147

labor
capital and 142, 146
trade unions 22, 106, 118, 147
vocabulary and problems of comparison 111–12
language 68–10
of European institutions 100–11, 113, 116–17

problems of comparison 111–12
see also linguistic; literature
Latin America *see* Brazil
Lazarsfeld, P. 5, 6, 90, 98
Le Seuil publishing house 54
Lebaron, F. 109, 111–12
legal field *see* global legal field
Lenoir, R. 11
Lerner, D. 90–92
Lévi-Strauss, C. 4, 54, 64–5, 84, 128
lexical fallacy 13, 100
'liberals' and 'communitarianism' 35–6
linguistic capital and foreign languages 68–9
linguistics/philology 74–5
Lipset, S. M. 88–9
literature
arts and 65–6
concept of literary field 85
limits of field and political frontiers 76–8
national language and 69–10
The World Republic of Letters (Casanova) 112, 150
Lyotard, J.-F. 81, 82

Marx/Marxism 27–8, 50–11, 53, 81, 104–5, 106
Communism and class 88–9
Mauger, G. 109–10
Mauss, M. 4, 5, 54, 58, 126
media
and modernity 90–92
representation of Olympics 133–5
methodological internationalism 17, 69
methodological nationalism 7
Mingione, E. 40–11
modernization/modernity
and globalization 141, 142
and traditional societies 4, 90–92, 128–9
'multiculturalism' 34
Multilateral Agreement on Investment (MAI) 148
multinational corporations 134, 148

Index

multiple cultural traditions 31–32
Myrdal, G. 44

national histories (comparative history of differences) 11–13, 93–108
  crisis of Britishness 103
  final discussion 109–13
  preparatory notes 114–22
national identity construction 13
national and international fields 15–16, 63–4
national symbolic capital 16
  accumulation of 64–8
national unconscious
  and disciplinary unconscious 99
  and literature 70
nationalism 31
  and internationalism 69–11
  methodological 7
neoliberalism 35
Nietzsche, F. 55, 87

objectification 125–7
Olympics: agenda for analysis 133–5
outsider/foreigner viewpoint 99, 115–16
  see also inverse ethnocentric viewpoint

Panayotopolos, N. 101
Panofsky, E. 3–4
Parsons, T. 5, 87, 88
Pascal, B. 51, 52
Passeron, J.-C. 5
Peterson, P. 42
philanthropic foundations 6, 40
philology 74–5
Polanyi, K. 139
political capital 10–11
'political correctness' 35
political creation, 'global market' as 140–11
political interventions 19–20, 21–22
Pollak, M. 6
postmodernism 17, 35, 84
prefaces 53–4
protectionism 143, 147

Quebec 15–16, 64

'race', US 39–10
  and Brazil 36–8, 40, 41–42
  and Europe 34, 43–4
  immigrants 87–8, 90–92
radical chic 29
reflexivity 31
  historical 115–16
Renyi, A. 73
resentment, and cultural habitus of Germans 107–8
resistance to new forms of imperialism 30–11
revolution, conditions for 27–8, 88–10, 102, 104–6, 117–18
Ricoeur, P. 54
Ringer, F. 33, 58
Rockefeller Foundation 40
Routledge publishing house 41

Sartre, J.-P. 53, 84
scholarly unconscious 13, 109, 123–7
  comparative method 128–9
Schultheis, F. 11
scientific internationalism 19, 50, 82
scientific rationality 30
  and autonomy 19, 86
  and historicist approach 55–6, 57
  and theology 106
  as 'war of intellectual liberation' 6
selection of texts for international publication 51–54, 66–7
self-thematization 107
Smith, A. 105
social structures and structures of perception 87–92
specialist critics of foreign books 63
Spinoza, B. 126
statistics 62, 98, 114, 115
  Eurostat 95, 113
strategies in international field 16–17, 67–9
structural comparison 7–13
structural misunderstanding 71

Index

structuralism
  Benveniste and 101
  confronting 84
  symbolic 85
  'subjectless structuralism' 54
structure of academic field 82–3
Switzerland and Belgium 15–16, 64
symbolic advantages of globalization, US 143
symbolic capital 53–4
  see also national symbolic capital
symbolic interactionism 5
symbolic power relations 64, 65–6

television *see* media
texts *see* international circulation of ideas and texts; literature
third world, domination by East European countries 73–4
Thompson, E. P. 13, 81, 104–6, 117–18
Tocqueville, A. de 29, 46, 120
trade unions 22, 106, 118, 147
traditional and modern societies 4, 90–92, 128–9
translations/translators 52–3, 62–3, 67, 74–5, 149
  culture and theory 7–9
  untranslatable texts 60
transnational intellectual fields 150

unconscious *see* historical unconscious; national unconscious; scholarly unconscious
underclass, concept of 40–11, 42–4
universalism/unification 20–22, 33–4
  two imperialisms of 27–32
  see also global; globalization
university, role of 68
US 35, 36
  American exceptionalism 46, 119–21
  and Europe 34–6, 40–11, 42–6
  and globalization 39–46, 141–44, 151
  immigrants 87–8, 90–92
  sociology 5–6, 7–8, 87–8, 90
  see also France and US; 'race', US
utopian capitalism 142

Valéry, P. 29, 30, 69
vocabulary *see* language
Vygotsky, L. 126

Wacquant, L. 8, 20, 112
Wagley, C. 37
Weber, M. 3–4, 5, 128
Williamson, O. 146
World Bank 144
The World Republic of Letters (Casanova) 112, 150
World Trade Organization (WTO) 141, 144, 147–8